DEUS EX MACHINA

The Best Game You Never Played In Your Life

Mel Croucher

Published in 2014 by
Acorn Books
www.acornbooks.co.uk

Acorn Books is an imprint of
Andrews UK Limited
www.andrewsuk.com

Copyright © 2014 Mel Croucher

The right of Mel Croucher to be identified as the author of this work has been asserted by him in accordance with the Copyright, Designs and Patents Act 1988

All rights reserved. No part of this publication may be reproduced, stored in or introduced into a retrieval system, or transmitted, in any form, or by any means (electronic, mechanical, photocopying, recording or otherwise) without the prior written permission of the publisher. Any person who does any unauthorised act in relation to this publication may be liable to criminal prosecution and civil claims for damages.

The views and opinions expressed in this book are solely those of the author and do not necessarily represent those of the publisher.

Contents

Chapter 1	1
Chapter 2	17
Chapter 3	28
Chapter 4	56
Chapter 5	79
Chapter 6	109
Chapter 7	132
Chapter 8	146
Chapter 9	160
Chapter 10	191
Chapter 11	217
Chapter 12	229
Chapter 13	238
Chapter 14	253
Chapter 15	273
Chapter 16	290
Chapter 17	318

Introduction

This is the story of a video game called Deus Ex Machina. Some players say it was the best computer game ever written. They reckon playing Deus Ex Machina changed their lives. It changed mine. First I wrote it, then it put me out of the business for thirty years, then it tried to kill me.

The ancients believed that everything in the heavens above and in the world down below is made up from four basic elements. Earth, air, fire and water. When it comes to the ingredients of a video game, the ancients were dead right. There are only four elements in any video game that has ever been written. And those four elements are chess, dice, ping-pong and bunkum. Every blood-soaked shoot-em-up, all swords-and-sorcery twaddle, each tedious adventure and pitiful sports simulation, everything and anything that passes for computer gaming is a combination of these elements.

Which means that the video games industry, the biggest entertainment industry the world has ever known, is founded on the same rehashed ingredients, remixed and repackaged over and over again. In which case it also means that video games players are a bunch of suckers, duped into shelling out good money for the same bad experiences. All video games are the remixed and regurgitated ingredients of the strategies of chess, the throw of the dice, the hand-eye coordination of ping-pong and the confidence trick of bunkum.

Who says so? I say so. Who am I? I'm the founder of the British computer games industry. The guy who started it all. The Grand Wazoo. So as well as being the story of a video game called Deus Ex Machina, this is also the story of the founding days of the British computer entertainment industry. And, it was conceived not in a test tube, but in a pint mug.

DEUS EX MACHINA

Chapter 1

Genesis

The video games industry is the biggest money-making entertainment sector in the world. That's apart from gambling, drugs and pornography, of course. And the British video games industry is worth billions. It's bigger than music, movies, books and magazines. And I declare that I kicked off the British video games industry at zero cost, with zero investment, zero equipment, zero experience and zero planning.

The world's first commercial video games were mostly based on ping-pong, but it wasn't long before glowing rectangular ping-pong balls were replaced by little green space invaders, based on a mixture of ping-pong, chess and dice. Then some bright spark figured out that as well as little blobs of light, you could add tricks, and so bunkum was introduced.

So if this is the story of *Deus Ex Machina*, then it is essentially the story of computerised bunkum on a grand scale. Here goes then. Let's start with the conception.

I began in the 1940s when a clever refugee from Nazi Germany met a hard-working dockyard worker with a bicycle and tuberculosis in the teeming city of Portsmouth, the home port of the British navy, and bombed to bits by the time I arrived. They fell in love, got married and had sex, although probably not in that order. But the story of *The Best Game You Never Played In Your Life* begins on the morning of my seventh birthday, when there was coal in the scuttle, when Winston Churchill was still running the country through a haze of alcohol and dementia, and when I programmed my first games machine. Up until then, the whole world had been in monochrome, but I can remember my seventh birthday in flickering, muted colour.

My first games machine was a dangerous little metal sequencer. It had a keyboard colour-coded in toxic lead paint, designed to stunt the growth of us post-war baby boomers. My Mum and Dad had bought me a Sooty-the-puppet Xylophone. It was a very happy birthday.

Instead of music, the Sooty Xylophone was supplied with little cards that displayed rows of coloured dots, and the idea was to bash one colour-coded key at a time in the order each dot appeared. This was supposed to result in instant musical genius, a bit like the young Mozart, but adapted for a sociopathic glove puppet. Obviously the manufacturers expected all young Mozarts to wheedle their parents for a Sooty glove puppet to go with the xylophone, because they only supplied a single bashing stick, and glove puppets can only handle one stick at a time.

The songs were child-safe and really banal, and those preprogrammed sequences soon began to bore me. Then, for the first time, I can remember thinking maybe I could change things. Maybe I could even improve things somehow by simple experimentation. So, slowly and methodically, I reordered the colour-coded xylophone keys into more interesting combinations, and wrote my own sequences of coded coloured dots. The result sounded like crappy little tin strips hit with a stick in random order, which is exactly what is was. And although it was programming of a sort, I gave up computing in favour of the yo-yo well before my next birthday.

The story begins again a few years later, with a pianola that lived behind the kitchen in a little two-up, two-down terrace house, with an outdoor thunderbox and no bathroom. Pianolas were a sort of giant mechanical iPod for Victorians who didn't have the talent to play regular pianos, and they were very popular in the nineteenth century. By the time I tackled this ancient Aeolian upright grand model, the world was listening to music on the wireless, and pianolas were very unpopular indeed. In fact they were so unpopular that most of them had rotted. This was because the firmware that powered the keys was a matrix of rubber tubes which time had hardened and fractured like dead macaroni, so it wheezed like my Dad in the mornings. But the software that called the tunes was great. It was stored as holes punched into rolls of paper that tore and decomposed in sync with the British Empire. The grand old pianola was, of course, my first properly programmable computer.

That summer I had a square-ended metal hole-punch nicked from the Dockyard by my Dad, and acne. So I spent it in hiding, humiliating the pianola and forcing it to perform lewd acts of a musical nature.

Programming was simple. I got a roll of wallpaper and drew up a linear grid of eighty-eight squares times infinity, one square for each note on the piano keyboard and infinity representing time. If I didn't want a note to play then I did nothing at all. If I did want a note to play, then I punched a hole in the right place at the right time, ready for a dead macaroni rubber pipe to fart a jet of air through it. This released a tiny hammer onto the associated piano strings and played a pitch-perfect note. The player-piano was powered by the kind of foot-treadles beloved by sewing machine operators and torturers, linked up to an air pump, a revolving drum, the dead macaroni rubber pipes and the hammers and strings of the piano. The harder I pedalled, the faster the drum revolved and the louder my mechanical music became. There was also a mystery brass lever, operated by a sideways jiggling of the inner thigh. The lever had a little brass plate with the word *Expression* stamped on it in an old fashioned font, and it had magical powers. It made my Dad use the expression, "Ferfucksake!", and it made my Mum use the expression, "Donnerwetter nochmal!" She wasn't being pretentious, she was just being German. It also made my younger, smarter sister the competitive spirit she is today. All three of them urged me to cease the bloody racket. Eventually that bloody racket made a guest appearance a few decades later on the intro of a song called *Pompey Rock* which uses one of my childhood punch-card boogies in the intro.

And that bloody racket was made possible by a simple computer program invented in 1801 by Joseph Marie Jacquard, to weave complex geometric designs in rolls of cloth and put a whole bunch of French weavers out of work, and eventually leading to the creation of the atom bomb, when Vannevar Bush used punch cards to control the calculations of the Manhattan Project.

It was around the time I was failing to grow my first moustache, that The Beast came into my life. I think it belonged to the Admiralty, and it lived on the top floor of a concrete building called Mercantile House, because it had nothing to do with merchants and it wasn't a house. It was the administration block of Portsmouth Polytechnic.

Academically, I was what was known as a Sliding Genius. That is to say, I was extremely smart as a child, and could tackle most intelligence tests instinctively. Then, during my time at a public school disguised as a barracks, I became steadily more stupid. When I went out into the civilian world aged seventeen, my stupidity didn't seem to matter at all, but my old school did. It was time to talk my way into a profession, and seeing as my Dad was a lowly dockyard worker, nepotism wasn't an option. So my first step to a professional life was to get a degree. My mum told me to go to the library and read a careers book first, "And don't just read the As. The Air Force is dangerous, and Architects have to wear ties."

I parked my 98cc Hudson Villiers motorcycle near the library, next door to the polytechnic building. There was a lecturer who wore the snow white coat of a scientist, the wire-frame glasses of a philosopher and the lipstick of a courtesan. She stirred my loins, and the only way I could get close enough to sniff her was to register for her class. She taught the brand-new discipline of computer programming, but I wouldn't have cared if she had taught Swahili. I enrolled on her course. She tamed The Beast. Her name was Franny. For some reason we students called her Miss Crunt.

The Beast was as big as a bus and as daft as a brush, and I could walk around inside it to feel the heat coming off serried ranks of little glass valve things. And so it came to pass that when I got my hands on the most powerful computer known to civilian science, I knew just what to do. Programs were written in a language much less complex than the 88 variations and expression-lever of my pianola, and the computer code was stored as little holes on punch-cards. I knew I could confuse the hell out of The Beast, and there was no question in my mind as to the true purpose of giant electronic brains. Just like the Sooty xylophone and the pianola, they had been created to entertain us. And sure enough, after six months of applying mascara to my nascent moustache, sniffing the aura of Miss Crunt, and programming The Beast, I got the giant computer to beep *Twinkle Twinkle Little Star* in sync with a flashing light bulb.

When I presented my work to Miss Crunt, she took off her wire-frame glasses and blinked at me like a myopic lecturer in computing. Next she opened her wanton red lips, revealing a fascinating line of drool between her upper and lower incisors.

And then, the little minx, she closed them again. In fact she was so overcome that she was completely lost for words. Apart from two.

It seemed that being a computer programmer was meant to be a serious business, with no room for mucking about. If I wanted to muck about and get paid for it then I would have to become something else. So I took Miss Crunt's succinct advice and forgot all about computers, went off to be an architect, marry a Worker and raise an Irish Setter.

Although it took six long years to qualify as an architect, my studies coincided with everything the Sixties had to offer on the extracurricular side, and I invested a lot of time in them. Much of my energy was spent on growing hair and playing six-string bass guitar in the Ice Cream Yak Band. Then there were wars to end, buildings to occupy and happenings to happen. When the news came that I had scraped through my Diploma in Architecture, we were living in a caravan on a beach in fascist Spain. The Worker Who Married Me was teaching English, the Irish Setter was begging for proper food and I was playing my part in the crime against humanity known as Benidorm, sign-writing and hustling. Consequently, when I was professionally released into the wild, I was a very green architect. Not green in the sense that I used recyclable materials and wind-power, but green in the sense that I didn't know what I was doing.

By the mid-1970s the British economy was in recession and work had dried up for very green unemployable architects like me. So I was forced to seek refuge further overseas and wheedle my way into the patronage of the first despot who would have me. His name was Sheikh Rashid bin Saeed al-Maktoum and my job was to build him some prestigious structures in a little desert backwater that he inherited in the traditional manner of historic assassination and sucking up to the British aristocracy. The little desert backwater was called Dubai. And they had just struck oil.

All I really knew about my new home was that Dubai had been called the Pirate's Coast since the Victorians bribed their way in with a treaty to keep Ottoman tax collectors out. Before the oil wealth started to flow, the main source of income had been smuggling, so all in all Dubai sounded like a good bolt-hole to beat the UK recession. While I was reprogramming my Sooty Xylophone, the entire population of Dubai was still living in traditional barastri houses made from palm fronds and mud, and it wasn't until 1956 that they constructed their first concrete building. I turned up twenty years later to build five tower blocks for a guy who named the development after himself in the main street of town, also named after himself. It didn't really matter what my structures looked like, as long as they were bigger than those built by the next sheikh down the road, and the bathrooms had gold taps.

There were no trees in Dubai, but if there had been, money would have grown on them. I found myself responsible for more than two hundred people and a budget of eight million pounds, and I was busking it. Apart from a few local Gulf Arabs, we were all economic migrants, but conditions for the labour force were inhuman. Mostly they were shipped over from Tamil Nadu, and were ordered in bulk along with the cement and steel. They lived in packing cases and containers and took a shit where they could. It was obvious that some had never set foot outside a village before, let alone worked on a building site.

It wasn't that I was a very bad architect, just that I was a very bored architect when it came to repetitive tasks. People kept turning up to work on my building sites and getting lost, seeing as how there were no town maps of Dubai, only aerial photographs used by the protectors of freedom, democracy and western oil interests. And I was getting bored drawing home-made maps for them, and telling them where to find useful things, like a reputable trader, or a disreputable nurse. The nurses from the leprosy ward were usually available for spontaneous intimacy, but it was a bugger trying to find their residential huts without a map. Anyway, I persuaded a passing reconnaissance pilot to sell me a copy of the most detailed aerial photographs that existed, and produced what turned out to be the first detailed civilian map of Dubai. Soon other contractors and suppliers were asking if they could use my map for their own new arrivals.

I went to the town's only printer to run off a few hundred copies. A small man with smiling teeth and worried eyes, and like most of us temporary inhabitants, he was in exile. In my case from *Save Your Kisses For Me* by Brotherhood Of Man, in his case from the civil war then raging in Lebanon. He asked if he and some of his fellow exiles could advertise on the map and maybe try and drum up some business from the new arrivals. I agreed. In fact I took it a stage further. Within a month I had found a malformed American crook to sell advertising space all over my maps, and I also recorded an audio guide on cassette for the hard-of-thinking to find their way around Dubai.

The idea was that English speakers would be force-fed the map to help them navigate the wild frontier, as well as the cassette to play on their in-car stereo system. Instead of music, the cassette took them on a turn-by-turn guided tour of the pirate stronghold of Dubai, stopping at the haunts of all my advertisers. Compared with the money the Sheikh was paying, my multi-media guides made very little, but I was no longer bored. The fact that the money the Sheikh doled out was tax-free and in cash gave me the safety net to quit his desert kingdom and head back to Britain. At the ripe old age of 29, I was done with being an architect. I was in the multi-media entertainment business.

The Worker Who Married Me had been teaching English to groups of men with multi-coloured beards and surrealist headware, and when we arrived back in the UK we had the notion to enhance my new multimedia business and her teaching career by becoming failed antiques dealers. I would go and buy things I liked, such as wax-cylinder phonograph machines and vintage typewriters, and spend lots of time repairing them for sale. Then she would calculate the hours and effort involved and tell me how much loss I had made. It was an interesting business model that I would use again in my video games career. By the time she brought home an educational brochure about an electronic brain in a tin box from her place if work, I was ready to roll. This little computer was the size of a suitcase and it didn't use punch-cards for storing stuff, it fed on magnetic tape! What's more, the tape was housed in standard cassettes just like the ones I had used for my Dubai travel guides.

The Commodore Pet was launched in January 1977, and by October it had made the front cover of Popular Science. It looked just like the futuristic sci-fi machines we were all familiar with from Star Trek, even though the casing was made of the same crappy tin as my Sooty Xylophone. The designers were deluded into thinking it was for business, or research or some sort of academic use, and although it was claimed to be a "home computer" it was priced at a hefty $795, and that was way too high for any normal home. But viewed through the eyes of the Dubai oil boom, it was an irresistible bargain.

The Commodore Pet was blessed with 4 kilobytes, as much memory as The Beast that Miss Crunt had let me loose on. But instead of occupying the entire floor of a concrete block, I could sit in on the dining room table. The coding language was something called PET BASIC. In order to confuse regular folk, computing seemed to have evolved its own jargon. You couldn't write a simple instruction like, "make the white blob go up the screen until it hits something." You had to mask simple ideas with arcane expressions which sounded like a menu in a Welsh brothel: spreadsheet, nibble, byte, peek, poke, RAM. It took a while to master this new language, but after the first few days I found myself enjoying the electronic creative act much more than the failed antiques business.

I founded my multi-media company Automata on November 19th 1977, and some say it was the first leisure software company in Great Britain. I'm not certain about that, but what I do know is that I immediately followed in the footsteps of the great pioneers of electro-mechanical entertainment, by creating stuff for an audience that didn't exist. Everyone was talking about computers, but nobody actually owned one. Ignoring this fact was a handicap, but historically I was not alone. Thomas Edison thought his phonograph was for recording the last will and testament of illiterates and vain people. He totally failed to realise that he had just given birth to the recorded music industry. Alexander Graham Bell thought his telephone was for transmitting symphony music into the homes of rich folk who were too riddled with pox or bone idle to hail a cab to the concert hall. The Theatrophone company signed up hordes of subscribers including King Louis the First of Portugal, before anyone spotted the fact that telephones were not best suited for concert music but were very handy for voice communications. And it wasn't just the pioneers who cocked it up. A century later, cellphone developers completely missed the appeal of text messaging for an entire generation.

As for me, I wallowed in my ignorance and never once questioned my belief. I knew for certain that computers were for people to play games on. All I had to do was find those people. The trouble was, the UK video games industry was restricted to *Space Invaders* machines in pubs, usually plugged in to a spare socket by the toilets, and I didn't fancy hanging around stained porcelain asking people for their names and addresses.

Arcade machines may have been the growth leisure industry outside the home, but inside the home it was commercial broadcasting which was the game-changer. My little sister was a newsreader at the local commercial radio station, Radio Victory, which had begun broadcasting in the October of 1975, and it turned out that her new boss was someone I went to school with. Paul Brown, a canny man who eventually got a Commander of the British Empire badge off the Queen for services to radio as Chief Executive of the Independent Broadcasting Association.

Using a combination of desperation and the fact that we once played mother and daughter in the school play, I went to him with an idea. He didn't think it would do lasting damage to his reputation, and was kind enough to let me broadcast computer data over the AM and FM wavebands after regular broadcasting hours. My idea was that sizeable numbers of computer owners across the South of England would receive my signals through their radio sets and get so excited by the concept of computer entertainment they would want to contact me. Then I could try and flog them some games.

We broadcast my first on-air video game on the 257FM waveband in the wee small hours of December 15th 1977. In later broadcasts we also used the 1170AM waveband. Either way, an audio signal carrying computer data sounds like your radio set is having a seizure, so we had to top and tail the coded signals with an enticing prize competition to try and stop my audience switching off these bizarre nocturnal emissions. And so the concept of the prize computer game was born.

It was hard work for the newly computer-savvy radio listener. First of all they had to stay up way after bedtime and record the signal off-air onto cassette. Then they needed to link their cassette player to a home or office computer and play the primitive code so the machine could hum along. After a minute or two the program would load, and if it had not been corrupted during transmission, clues would appear on screen. Only then could the patient listener in commercial radioland play the game, solve the clues, phone up the radio station and make a claim for a crummy prize.

After the first broadcast we got three responses. But by the end of a season of hit-and-miss transmissions, the number of listeners with access to a computer was beginning to grow, and I got a mainstream evening slot sponsored by Whitbread, manufacturers of the fifth-worst beer in the land. My show was called *Whitbread Quiz Time* and it was broadcast at an ungodly hour every Thursday night. I had produced a hybrid radio pub quiz and on-air computer game. And I found myself midwife to a new branch of the entertainment business.

I was also getting to learn about my potential game-players, because I could meet them during the weekly recordings in their natural, alcohol-sodden, nicotine-stained habitat, bribe them with the fifth-worst beer in the land, and get some genuine feedback on my primitive games. Amazingly, many of them declared that what they would like to play coincided with what I wanted to produce. Essentially it was stuff that credited them with some intelligence, stuff that rewarded them for investing a few minutes play-time and, above all, stuff that was funny.

By the time Whitbread wised up and withdrew their sponsorship, the players were no longer in it to win it, they were tuning in to discover what anarchy had been sneaked in to the clues, complicit in the knowledge that the Independent Broadcasting Authority had absolutely no idea what was being broadcast under the guise of audio computer code. I often wonder if terrorists, criminals and spies ever cottoned on to the concept of transmitting subversive messages in binary code using a home computer and sending them anywhere in the world down the line.

Of course I couldn't make a living out of a weekly interactive quiz game, no matter how much daftness was injected, but I also had a modest income from the multi-media idea that began in Dubai. More importantly I had a little team of underpaid but happy workers producing maps, advertisements, magazines and audio travel guides on cassette, sponsored by the good, the bad and the downright ugly.

By the time the British home computing boom exploded, we had already produced two dozen video games and my ready-made team hardly noticed the transition. We were all paid a pittance, plus beer, which was classed as software. We knew next to nothing about programming and even less about marketing. And the electronic world was our oyster.

The original Automata team, left to right, Robin Evans (art and design), Mark Bardell (words and research), Mel Croucher (making things up), Christian Penfold (sales and advertising), Geoff Roberts (technical stuff)

Chapter 2

Automata

Between 19th November 1977 and All Fool's Day 1985, Automata produced around sixty-five computer games, and I insisted on three rules for all of them. The first rule was that they were non-violent. The second rule was that they parodied ordinary games to make players laugh. And the third rule was that they included audio tracks as a bonus to the gameplay.

The Automata logo was designed with a nod to the 1899 painting by Francis Barraud of his brother's dog Nipper listening to an Edison phonograph, *His Masters Voice*. To put it in keeping with our slogan, "there's no blood in our games, it's Automata sauce", I used a tomato instead of a phonograph, and the cute little dog became rusty clockwork, but even so I received a letter from HMV's lawyers threatening to sue. After careful consideration and a consultation down the pub with a bloke called Rodney, who had once failed a solicitor's clerk exam and so knew a thing or two about the law, I responded with a nicely typed letter saying "Fuck Off", and never heard from HMV again. In the future there would be more law suits from global sharks trying to intimidate us feeble minnows, as will be revealed.

When Automata started, our games used one kilobyte of memory each, because home computers didn't have any more juice. Today, my standard mobile phone packs a punch 32 million times more powerful, and the data arrives invisibly through the air. Back then our data was loaded into a primitive home computer from an audio cassette recorder, and we duplicated our stuff by hand on a four-way deck at eight times normal speed. It may seem antediluvian today but it was state of the ark then, and we were able to turn out forty or fifty copies of commercial computer games an hour, complete with self-adhesive labels and fancy cassette sleeves.

The thing about audio cassettes was they had two sides, and the thing about computer data was it only needed to be recorded on one side of the tape. So what to do with the blank side? I reckoned the obvious thing to do was record little audio scene-setters and comedy sketches to enhance the gameplay, but after the first couple of years I gave each Automata game its own theme song, and stuffed the songs with references and clues to the games. This would be called transmedia sometime in the future, back then it was called economising.

We couldn't afford studios or musicians, but that wasn't the real reason I ended up performing everything myself on those cassette backsides. The real reason was because I enjoyed it, in fact I enjoyed it a lot more than writing lines of computer code. I was a weak musician and a crap singer, but I multi-tracked everything and edited out the bum notes before force-feeding my stuff to anyone who'd listen.

It was good to discover that the players of Automata titles not only wanted more games and more music from us, but they also wanted to make direct contact with the Automata team. For some of them, we became an important part of their lives. But it was a surprise for me to discover who these players actually were.

The maxim "know your audience" is a basic prerequisite in the entertainment business. Without this knowledge an entertainer is wasting everybody's time. Back in our radio days of the 70s, I knew exactly who my audience was. They were adult, nocturnal, erudite and living in the South of England. And I treated them accordingly. But if we were to meet in the street, then we would have had absolutely no notion that our common link was that of games-maker and games-player. But when the British computer boom arrived, so did micro-clubs, micro-fairs and micro-fests, and we got to meet the Automata games players in the flesh. They were smaller than I had expected.

Unlike my remote radio audience, I found that I was no longer writing games for adults, but for players that included a great many children from different locations, backgrounds and cultures. I was not at all inclined to change the stuff I wanted to produce, so there was only one course of action open to me, and that was to treat the little sods as equals. If they didn't quite understand some of the adult themes, and if they didn't quite pick up on the historical references or wordplays, then I reckoned it was better for them to float to the top of my pond, because I was certainly not going to meet them at the bottom. It was good to make them laugh, but it was equally good to make them think.

Some of those children would come back into my life thirty years later, and change it for the better. But in 1981 I had no reason to know who they would grow up to be or what they would grow to achieve, and neither could I suspect how catalytic they would become.

It did not take very long for the nascent video games industry to start spoon-feeding children variations on the theme of killing anything that moved, and my unease with simulated violence grew. If I wasn't prepared to make professional compromises concerning my players then neither was I prepared to ditch my civilian hobby of non-violent direct action against assholes. And if this involved force-feeding agit-prop propaganda to kids then I had absolutely no problem with that. It would not take long for other games-makers to lower the age of mental cannon-fodder from eighteen to eight, so if I was waging a one-man war against computerised violence then I reckoned the rest of the industry could take it.

To tell the truth, the rest of the British video games industry didn't amount to very much at the time. It may have grown out of its cradle, but it was still crawling around the nursery.

In the summer of 1978, a Liverpudlian accountant called Bruce Everiss had opened the Microdigital shop in Brunswick Street, and began to sell exotic computers from America with weird names like Apple II and TRS-80, alongside sweet little self-assembly jobbies developed this side of the Atlantic.

But it was the arrival of the British designed ZX80 home computer that was the real game-changer. A couple of years later, some of Bruce's employees and customers got together to set up the Bug-Byte outfit, which specialised in computer gaming, and at last Automata had some company as well as some competitors as a few others set up to join in the fun, and try to make a living out of this new form of entertainment.

Bruce himself became operations manager of the highly-successful Liverpool outfit Imagine. Although I suspect the name was not so much a tribute to John Lennon as a tribute to the way Bruce treated his accountancy. Ten years later he would be reduced to asking me to write and perform topical computer jokes via a premium-rate phone line, and I would be reduced to accepting. He would pay me thirty-five quid a throw, and sometimes he would not pay me at all.

Much has been written about Clive Sinclair and his Z80, ZX81 and Sinclair Spectrum micro computers, and I have no intention to add more here, seeing as I only met him twice. The first time I told him that his machines were toys for playing games on, and he responded by looking at me in the same way Miss Crunt had done years before, only without the drool and the lipstick. The second time was at a party, when I didn't talk to him much because he seemed to be talking to himself and putting on a melancholy performance of shy-man-dancing. Best not to intrude. Whatever the case, without Clive Sinclair the success of the British computer games boom would never have happened.

By 1981 there were a handful of computer games producers in the land, and we could all fit into one scout hut and share a taxi home. That's not a metaphor, that's a statement. At the start of the following year there were still less than a hundred of us, but by the end of 1982 we numbered around 460 with 1,200 titles competing for a slice of the market, and the media had begun to take notice.

Dorothy's Wool Shop becomes Automata

The Sinclair ZX80 launch advert

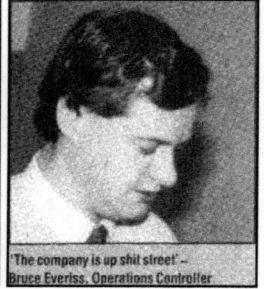

Some things caused by Bruce Everiss.

As for Automata, we were still happily producing holiday guides in print and on cassette, as well as a few radio magazines, when our first proper commercial success in video gaming happened by accident in 1981. It was the result of a bulk buy of low-quality C30 audio cassettes used for recording our audio guides to tawdry tourist destinations. C30 meant that the recording time available on each cassette was fifteen minutes a side, so I reckoned I could get rid of our stockpile by filling them up with as many games and audio entertainments as possible and flogging them cheap. The result was a compilation tape called *Can Of Worms*, packing in eight games and eight comedy tracks for the grand sum of £3. We had no overheads or business sense, and we sold them mail-order-only direct to the players, so our competitors simply could not compete at that volume and that price.

When the first games software charts began to appear in the early computer magazines, we found ourselves among the best-sellers, which was nice, and soon we were headed for the top of the heap, which was very nice indeed.

There are seeds of *Deus Ex Machina* in that very first success, particularly in the pathetic game called *Acne*, which encouraged the squeezing of facial zits as they erupted. I used exactly the same concept more than thirty years later for *Deus Ex Machina 2*, as will be revealed later in this book. Other titles in the *Can Of Worms* compilation involved The Prince of Wales blocking the palace sewers with his own excrement, dyeing Ronald Reagan's hair to prevent him starting a nuclear war, and popping a whoopee-cushion under Adolf Hitler to give him a heart attack. And so it was that the first big Automata hit was a rag-bag of peurile, simple stuff, offering instant gratification to the non-discerning player with a few minutes to spare and three quid in their pocket.

Soon it was like receiving a Sooty-the-puppet xylophone for my birthday every day, and we found ourselves competing to arrive at work first, for the pleasure of unlocking the oversized silver letterbox. Our daily presents from the games players included money and little thank-you letters, so as a reward to our fans we increased the price of the next compilation tape from three quid to a fiver.

I called the second album of games *Love And Death*, and it featured several forerunners to *Deus Ex Machina*, including the sperm race of conception and the birth sequence, as well as a rather gentle but inevitable death for the player. For the third compilation, I distilled *The Bible* to eight games of 1K memory each and heard the first industry rumblings to the effect that I was economically if not mentally insane.

By now, almost all of the programming was being done by Christian Penfold, a used-car salesman who had started off selling advertising on our multi-media productions. I soon discovered that Christian was dyslexic, and like many of his ilk he had an unknown and untapped natural talent for programming. It used to drive me nuts when he misread and misused Sinclair BASIC terminology, but it didn't matter at all because he always came up with the goods using a process of osmosis. And best of all, he loved turning my daft ideas into programs a lot more than I did. Sometimes he would work through the night until he could save a finished game, for fear of losing the work in progress. Quite a lot of unfinished software went missing back then, usually when my dog wagged a cable loose, or when Christian introduced the cassette recorder to the steaming contents of the electric kettle.

When I labelled Automata titles as "adult", "censored", "over-16s" and "over-18s", I was taking the piss, knowing full well that the greatest attraction for a youngster is to indulge in something perceived as out of bounds. And when I was challenged, my arguments in favour of Automata games and against war games were well-rehearsed. I trotted them out at every opportunity, from *Woman's Hour* on the BBC to interviews in *The Sunday Times* when it was a respected newspaper before Rupert Murdoch got his claws in it. And what I said could be boiled down to this: "Would you rather your children played games that encourage them to kill or to kiss?"

One Monday morning in December, after the first coffee had been poured and the first Frank Zappa album of the day had hit the office turntable, the phone rang and I took a call from Laurie Manifold, three years away from retirement as the investigations editor of *The Sunday People*, a gutter-press newspaper with a huge circulation. The resultant firestorm taught me the most valuable lesson I have ever learned in marketing a business. Never be the subject of a news interview, always write it yourself. And apart from that, the publicity was brilliant.

In the "Storm Over Sexy Home TV Games" feature which resulted, I was portrayed in the national press as a purveyor of pornography to children. An electronic child-molester. I had been in the papers before, but never branded as a criminal. Well, only once before, when I appeared in the listings of court convictions for letting my dog shit on the beach.

The accusation that Automata was a depraved cess-pit of adolescent corruption became a contentious subject, and was taken up by Dr. Oonagh McDonald, a Labour Member of Parliament. Questions were raised in The House Of Commons concerning the dangers of this new video games phenomenon that was sweeping the country, and I was determined to state my case to her.

It was soon apparent to both of us that we were on the same side, and fuelled by a mutual loathing of the gutter press and a desire to spike the guns of violent video games, we formed an unlikely alliance, mostly over the phone, which was a challenge for Oonagh because she was deaf.

But a lot of other people were tuning in loud and clear, and Automata was now a household name in the growing number of households that knew what video games were. Then, on April 23rd 1982, the Sinclair Spectrum was launched, and Automata was poised, ready, willing and able to take a crack at making a little bit of gaming history.

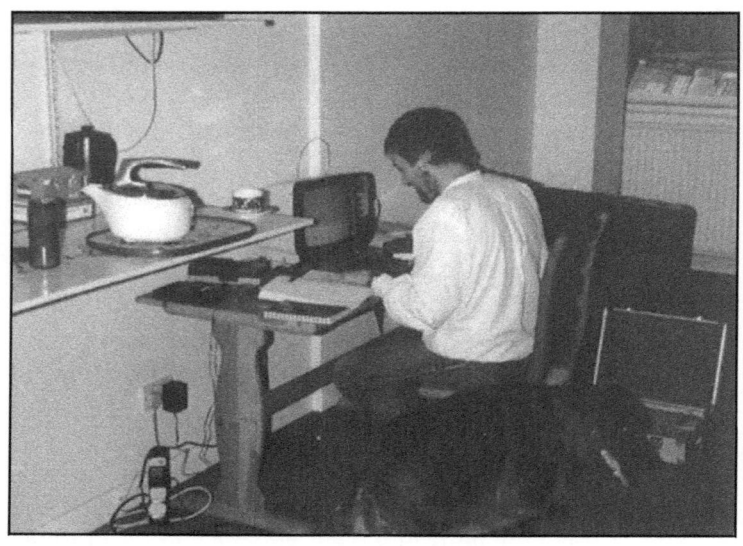

Christian Penfold with Rory the Irish Setter

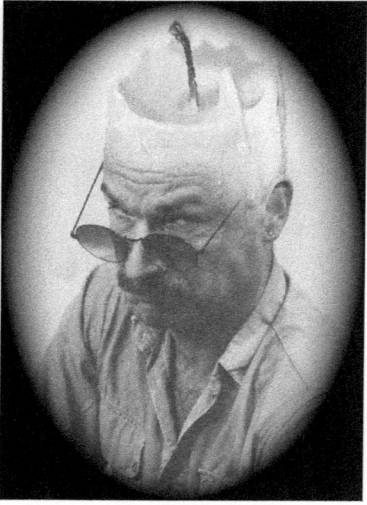

Automata advertising / The wick'ed Mel Croucher

Sexy TV games claim 'is rubbish'

A Southsea businessman has hit back at a newspaper article which accused him of selling sexy computer games.

Mr. M. Croucher, a director of Automata Ltd. in Osborne Road, branded the story in the Sunday People as "absolute rubbish."

It claimed his company was selling saucy TV games with titles like "Seduction" in the run-up to Christmas.

Mr. Croucher said he had never seen a "sexy" TV game and added: "We have no titles such as the one quoted."

SONNETS

He claimed the report may have been based on a game he brought out more than two years ago called "Love and Death." Part of it entailed writing sonnets and the most daring element involved matching X and Y chromosones.

"The whole point of our games is humour. They are good clean fun — humorous and tongue-in-cheek," said Mr. Croucher.

"We are in the business of campaigning against games which invite children to kill aliens or bomb cities," he added.

From Dr Oonagh McDonald MP

HOUSE OF COMMONS
LONDON SW1A OAA

23 December 1982

Dear Mr Croucher

Thank you very much for your letter and the d games produced by your company.

I should point out that I did not speak to Mr game with which I have been concerned was an That item has now been withdrawn following re Dr Vaughan after I had written to him.

I do hope that this clarifies the matter for

Yours sincerely

Oonagh McDonald

A nation corrupted by 1K of monochrome evil

Chapter 3

The Golden Age

For a while, Automata was the top-selling video games company in the land. A handful of waifs and strays came through the door to contribute and then left again. Dedicated people joined up to help with the magazine and audio guide side of things, and then they left. But in essence Automata as a games company only ever consisted of five oddly assorted people. An escaped architect, a cartoonist, a used-car salesman, a single mum and a schoolboy. To tell you about our differences will take a little time, but our similarities can be summed up in a sentence. The one thing we had in common was that we had no experience of the video games industry, because the video games industry had just been born.

It gives me a twisted mouth to see university courses offering the deluded students of today degrees in daft gaming disciplines with names like Ludic Interfaces, because I know from experience that what such training does is dampen imagination, stifle creativity, avoid risk-taking and never question a norm. Automata was all about letting the imagination and creativity run riot, taking risks and never to stop questioning what others were doing. It was our greatest strength, and it turned out to be our greatest weakness.

So, what is a Ludic Interface anyway? Here's what today's university prospectus says:

> "*Ludic interfaces are playful interfaces; the term refers to devices like the Wii console, unconventional musical instrument controllers, and game art devices; Ludic interfaces take the best from computer games, interactive media, media conversion, social networks*

and modding cultures and result in tools that offer an ease of use and playfulness to cope with a rapidly changing society."

This presupposes that video games companies need someone who has spent at least three years studying bollocks, because they are better than someone who has not, or any more valuable than a Chinese programmer who can knock out stuff for a tenth of the price. It also presupposes that centres of education are up to date with the sort of things gamers actually want to play, and can predict what will be happening in the near future. This is an impossibility. By the time some half-witted academic designs a course, gets it on to the curriculum and turns the handle on the student sausage-machine, the video games industry will have moved on. My local university offers a three year, full time, Bachelor of Science Honours Degree in Computer Games Development, as well as a post-graduate Masters Degree in Ludic Interfaces. Well whoopie!

When I started out in this business, I would receive dozens of job applications from enthusiasts, many of whom went on to do some amazing stuff. But since the corporates waded in and the universities rolled over and exposed their fee-based bellies, I now get job applications from puffed-up hopefuls without an original idea in their heads, duped into thinking that what the world needs is a Ludic Interface graduate. More often than not their job applications are remixes of banalities scraped off the bottom of a standard document barrel to include the claim of excellent communication skills, which translates as "I am a deluded, lazy bastard who cut-and-pasted this paragraph."

Here's how the escaped architect in the earlier chapter gathered the cartoonist, the used-car salesman, the single mum and the schoolboy to his bosom, and how they turned Automata into the nation's best-loved, least-sustainable software house.

THE CARTOONIST

For the first two years of Automata, I did all the artwork myself. It was not brilliant, but as an escaped architect I was at least drawing to scale. I typeset using an IBM golfball machine, and I also used rub-off lettering left over from my days at the drawing board. I actually paid to advertise our titles in the first computer magazines that hit the shelves, before I worked out that journalists are essentially lazy folk, and if I supplied them with cartoons, features and editorials then I could get Automata games promoted for free. I drew all the graphics for the magazines and cassette inlays, and I cobbled together the cartoons for the adverts. I tried to fool myself that my skills were up to it, but by 1979 I knew I needed a graphic artist genius. His name was Robin Evans, and when I found him, he was a washer-up in the kitchens of a holiday camp on the Isle Of Wight, which is a sort of British Alcatraz, only with more hedgerows around the prisons.

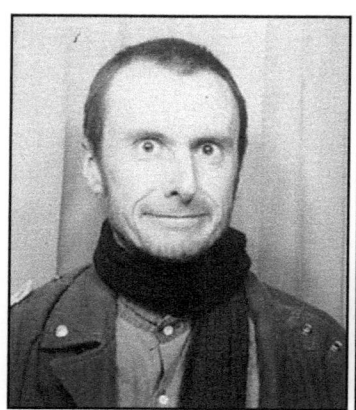 

The Cartoonist in the 1970s / The Cartoonist today

One damp morning I was taking coffee at the printers, waiting for the first proofs of some artwork to come rolling off. They used an antique cast-iron Heidelberg press, and the smell of fresh ink was heady. The previous client's job was stacked up on a pallet over in the corner, and when I flipped over the first couple of sheets I felt equally impressed and worried by what I saw. The cartoon images were semi-pornographic, but executed with a weird innocence. They weren't particularly funny, but they were beautifully drawn.

"Who did these?" I asked the printer.

"Bloke called Robin. Feckin loony." he replied, "but feckin cheap."

"Have you got his number?"

"Ain't got a feckin number, feckit. We rings the feckin payphone in the feckin camp where he feckin lives, fecker."

It was September, when the holiday camps emptied and the prison camps filled on the Isle Of Wight, and the perfect time for a man in his twenties to decide to become a full-time professional artist.

When I first met Robin Evans he came over like a younger version of the American cartooning genius Robert Crumb, only more English. He wanted to create fantasy artwork for love, but had been forced to create mildly erotic pap for money. And he was indeed feckin cheap. I liked him immediately. I even liked the way he spoke, in cartoon speech bubbles. And from that day to this we have never stopped working together. What I do is think up daft stuff, and what he does is bring it to life and make it better, more accessible, funnier. One of our titles has now been going for three decades, which makes it the longest-running continuously published computer cartoon strip on the planet. That says something about the fact that computers and gamers are intrinsically funny, and it also says something about the way Robin and I work together. I invest my time writing scripts and drafting ideas which I send to him many miles away. He pretends to take notice of what I want, then goes and does what he likes instead.

These days Robin Evans has evolved into a bit of an old cult, with some highly collectable sci-fi and fantasy work under his belt, but although the ageing process has turned his beard grey on the outside, on the inside he hasn't changed at all since that first day. He still talks in cartoon speech bubbles, complete with sound effects. His thoughts get generated at twice the speed of normal folk, which results in him speaking a sentence ahead of himself. It's like the doppler effect with added jokes. Sometimes, when the process goes into overload, he tends to fall over backwards. I've never managed to catch him yet.

It wasn't until after he joined Automata that I discovered Robin continually generated mess and debris, and turned the office into a cross between a kindergarten and a terrorist attack. I bought a more powerful vacuum cleaner and stronger rubbish bags but it did no good, so in the end I erected screens round him.

THE USED CAR SALESMAN
When Automata started I had already admitted to myself that I was not very good at business, and I knew Automata needed a professional to handle our sales if we were ever going to make the big time. It was all very well for me to think up ideas and then try to sell them, but I found the financial bargaining awkward. I liked to please the people I did business with, and I didn't like offending them by asking for too much money. They were understandably enthusiastic about my methodology. That's why I was not very good at business.

Unfortunately, there was no such thing as a professional video games salesperson when Automata needed one, because it was still far too early for anyone to have had real experience in touting video games. So it seemed natural to recruit from a repository of smarmy, ruthless bastard salesmen. I asked Robin Evans for advice.

"We need a smarmy, ruthless bastard salesman. Do you know any estate agents or used car dealers?"

"Eek! Do I? Sure do!" He tottered backwards and sprayed speech bubbles at the walls all about some guy he had met who had had a vasectomy and a divorce and grown a beard and sold used cars.

"Great. And is he a smarmy, ruthless bastard?"

"Crikey no! But ..."

"But?"

"Yikes! He's as desperate as we are for money!"

And that's how Christian Penfold joined Automata, all thanks to my new-found cartoonist friend and my ongoing quest to pay as little as possible. When Christian Penfold took the helm of our business strategies he steered us toward all sorts of new directions, at first navigating rapid success, and later aimed squarely at the rocks. But during those few years he took us on a wild ride, and wild rides are often as enjoyable as they are scary.

And throughout that time I had complete trust in Christian, and that was because he had no guile, no false faces and no masks. What you saw was what you got, and I loved that in him. He was, of course, completely bonkers. There was a sort of autism in his sales technique, because he said exactly what he thought without any regard to the consequences. There was an incident at an awards ceremony where he told the entire nascent computer industry exactly what he thought of them, ending with the invitation to stuff their trophies up their arse ends. There was another incident when we were approached by gangsters who reckoned they would like a slice of the new business we were carving out for ourselves, and Christian told them to take a banana enema. I was terrified by his methodology, and at the same time I was intrigued that he simply couldn't see the danger he was courting. But on the plus side there were too many incidents to count where he was utterly charming, and managed to sweet-talk his way into the pocket books, piggy banks and loose change of the newborn video games nation. About three years after he joined us, he sweet-talked me into making him a partner in Automata, and the die was cast.

The truth is, we were polar opposites in our beliefs, our politics and our loyalties, Christian and me. A generation earlier, if we had followed our principals into the Spanish civil war, he would have swaggered for Franco and I would have been cringing for the republic. But he would have given me his last drop of water when we found ourselves wounded in the same ditch. He was one of the kindest people I ever met, and one of the most irritating. I even wrote a song in his honour, that got released on one of our albums. The opening verse went like this:

> *Down at the Ally Pally, up upon a table,*
> *Wearing bright pink trousers, ever so unstable,*
> *Flogging off his bargains, no time for a wee-go,*
> *It must be Christian Penfold in his alter ego,*
> *Hurling friendly insults and acting very jolly,*
> *He's the reason we all come here, he's the Ally Pally Wally.*

A Wally was an affectionate slang term for a buffoon. The Ally Pally was the popular name for the mighty Alexandra Palace exhibition hall in North London, where a series of glorious video game trade fairs called ZX Microfairs was organised by Mike Johnson, a larger than life figure with a beard and a heart condition. There were probably too many beards involved in the early days of UK computer gaming. And too many heart conditions. Mike died young, along with much else.

Christian Penfold at a ZX Microfair with organiser Mike Johnson / Decades later at Mel's 60th birthday, still wearing that sodding pink jumpsuit

Christian was never sure about the "ever so unstable" line of that song lyric, although he loved to play the track at parties for years afterwards. When I was asked by others if I meant he was mentally unbalanced or merely wobbly when he got off the ground, I would reply, "yes". Anyway, most people's abiding image of Christian Penfold will be of him wobbling wildly up on a trestle table, ranting at the trade fair crowds like a demented fairground barker, insulting them, extorting them, throwing packaged software at their heads, and all the while clad in a skin-tight pink romper suit with his privates on parade. The crowds loved every minute of it, and so did he. As for me, I used to nail on a smile and make the best of it.

THE SINGLE MUM
And so Robin Evans and Christian Penfold helped turn Automata into a real business, until the telephone kept ringing, the post box kept delivering, and the telex machine kept spewing. We were inundated, and we needed a secretary to deal with the inundations. Several came, and several went. The good ones moved on to better things, the hopeless ones were asked to leave. They were mostly school-leavers. There was one young somnambulist who we watched in amazement as she stuck postage stamps upside down on to a huge pile of mail-order envelopes. When Christian asked her why, she pointed at the sheet of 144 stamps in front of her. It was upside down. She was also afraid of the vacuum cleaner, and when it was her turn to hoover the office she would retire to the toilet, so I had to do a double hoover shift myself. We put an advert in the local paper for a replacement.

When Lady Claire Sinclive answered the advert we breathed a sigh of relief. As soon as she stepped through the door it was obvious she was no school-leaver. In fact it turned out she was born not long after World War Two. It was Robin Evans who named her. Actually, it was Robin who named all of us. He was Gremlin, Christian was The PiMan, I was Uncle Groucho and our new recruit became Lady Claire. She said she had been out of the workplace for some while, to concentrate on marriage, children and divorce, and she admitted that she was not the most confident woman in the world and was scared at the prospect of getting back into the world of work. My first thought was that she had the same colour red hair as my Irish Setter, so as far as I was concerned, she was fine by me.

"OK," Christian lolled and rolled himself a cigarette as Lady Claire looked disapprovingly, and arched an eyebrow.

"Can you start now?"

Lady Claire seemed surprised. "You mean you want me to work here?"

"Can you start now?"

"This week?"

"No, I mean now. You see these two sacks of cassettes. They need taking to the post office."

Lady Claire Sinclive 1984, bouquet presented by Imagine / Lady Claire 21st Century

On the second day of her tenure at Automata, Lady Claire bought in a packet of fancy biscuits and some home videos. We had no plates, but we did have a video machine, and soon the windows had been opened and we had stopped most of the habitual swearing. By the end of the day she had commandeered the telephone and our callers were suddenly treated with politeness and respect. The humanisation process of the Automata team had begun.

Before long Lady Claire began to feature in our weekly magazine comic strips, which showed life in the Automata office populated entirely by cartoons and mythical creatures covering the entire back page of *Popular Computing Weekly*. I knew my cynicism was licked the day she took a call from a kid, covered her telephone mouthpiece with one hand and said to me, "Groucho, quick! This is Michael, he's eight years old and he's upset because his dad says The PiMan doesn't exist. Make him happy!" I will tell you about The PiMan shortly, but I think it's true we made a lot of people happy, our little team. As for Lady Claire, she probably completed the longest journey of any of us, from Automata secretary to best-selling author, with a Masters in Counseling and Psychotherapy

THE SCHOOLBOY

Things were moving fast in the programming world, and what had been acceptable a year or two before now seemed creaky and clunky. The programming skills of Christian Penfold and some itinerant amateurs were no longer adequate, and we both knew it. So we recruited the best machine-code programmer that money couldn't buy. A blue-eyed, blond-haired schoolboy called Andrew Stagg. I won him in a British lottery called the Youth Opportunity Program, which was introduced by the socialist government in 1978, and the idea was to get 16 year-old school-leavers into some sort of an apprenticeship scheme. The employer, who was me, would dedicate time and skill to train up the youth, who was Andrew, and the taxpayer would stump up £19.50 a week as an incentive subsidy. That was around thirty dollars.

On the day Andrew signed up I told him the good news, which was that he had just joined a worker's paradise wherein everyone earned exactly the same amount, from the Managing Director, who was me, to the newest recruit, who was him. Then I told him the bad news, which was we were all on twenty-five quid a week, which was around forty dollars. Then I told him the good news, which was that I was going to make him a star. Then I told him the bad news, which was it was going to be bloody hard work.

I had absolutely no idea how he did what he did when it came to programming our games. He seemed to communicate directly with the machine, pushing the technical boundaries until they broke and then we reached a new level of possibilities all over again. He knew no better and I knew no different, so when it came to my early ideas for *Deus Ex Machina* I remember him going off and sitting quietly for a long time. Then he came back with his verdict.

"It can't be done."

"Why not?"

"Because it's never been done."

"How long will it take you?"

He went off again for another think, and returned with that big, open grin of his.

"I can't promise nothing, but I reckon I can do it in two months."

Well, I kept my part of the bargain. He did become a star. An award-winning programming star at that. Here in the future, I'm still working with Andy Stagg, although he's a grandfather now and his golden locks have been replaced by a dome of polished skin. But he's still a computer coding genius.

Andrew programming the original Deus Ex Machina / The boy-wonder today

In the few short years before *Deus Ex Machina* changed everything for all of us, Automata achieved a few Number One video game titles. My favourite, and the most commercially successful was called *PiMania*. Just like my very first radio broadcast computer treasure hunts, it was a head-on collision between the virtual world and the real world, but this time round I hung it all on an anarchic cartoon character called The PiMan.

Looking back, I don't know if I invented transmedia in video games or not, but when I conjured up the computerised quest *PiMania* in 1981, I saw no reason not to break out of the confines of the computer monitor. It was released in 1982 as a video game, a rock album, a comic strip, a t-shirt, a magazine, a social network, and a real-world treasure hunt for a gold and diamond prize, all of which needed the other elements for maximum participation. The central character (usually Christian Penfold dressed as the PiMan) also made live appearances and TV recordings. The game went to Number One in the UK, Germany, Spain and several other territories we didn't even know about, thanks to a new phenomenon called "software piracy". At one point we had thousands of self-styled PiManiacs searching for the prize in the real world, and I trickle-fed them clues via the game content, the weekly comic strips and subsequent music albums. The prize was eventually won in 1985, and in 2010 a commemorative *PiMania* album was released on fashionably retro vinyl, complete with a PiMan mask, so I guess the little bastard is still selling, and I want to bring him back to life when *Deus Ex Machina 2* is done and dusted. But that's another story.

In *PiMania* I wanted to blur fantasy and reality, and my method was the usual one which was to make fun of traditional game-plays and get the player laughing as they embarked on some kind of idiotic quest. There are too many anecdotes about what our treasure-seeking players got up to, and this book is about *Deus Ex Machina* and not *PiMania* so I'll keep it short.

PiManiacs turned up all over the place, convinced they had cracked the quest. The ancient monolith of Stonehenge was a favourite at solstice, as was Jerusalem on Christmas Eve, and loads of people worked out that the navigation was based on the constellation of Pegasus, so went visiting various giant chalk horses carved into hillsides, hoping to meet the PiMan. By the time the two eventual winners turned up on the 22nd of July (pi = 22 over 7) and stood in the horse's mouth, I didn't have the heart to tell them the exact location of the treasure was in the horse's arse. The winners were two women teachers from Ilkley in the North of England and it had taken them two and a half years to solve the quest. Quite a few players formed their own PiManiac clubs, and they met up regularly to join in the quest. And they all said it wasn't the gold and diamonds that motivated them, it was the lunacy. I'm sorry about the divorce case where The Piman was cited as the cause, but that's obsession for you.

The idea of a real-world computer game treasure hunt seemed to catch the public imagination, so for the next big Automata game we stuck to the same formula. It was given the snappy title of *My Name Is Uncle Groucho You Win A Fat Cigar*. I made the solution to *Groucho* a hell of a lot easier, but it still took the mind of a youngster to crack it. Most people thought they were going to meet Ronald Reagan in Hollywood, but he was a cartoon. Mickey Mouse was the president back then, so I used his identity. We flew the winner out to meet him at Disneyland on the supersonic airliner Concord along with his parents, and brought them back on the luxury cruise liner Queen Elizabeth 2. Another example of my business methodology of trying too hard to please people and sacrificing financial security in the process. But I really did like to make our players happy, and at least the extravagant prizes of these Automata Golden Years made up for the pitiful rubbish we bribed our earliest players with in the radio days.

The PiMan's Greatest Hits (cassette cover, Christmas 1983)

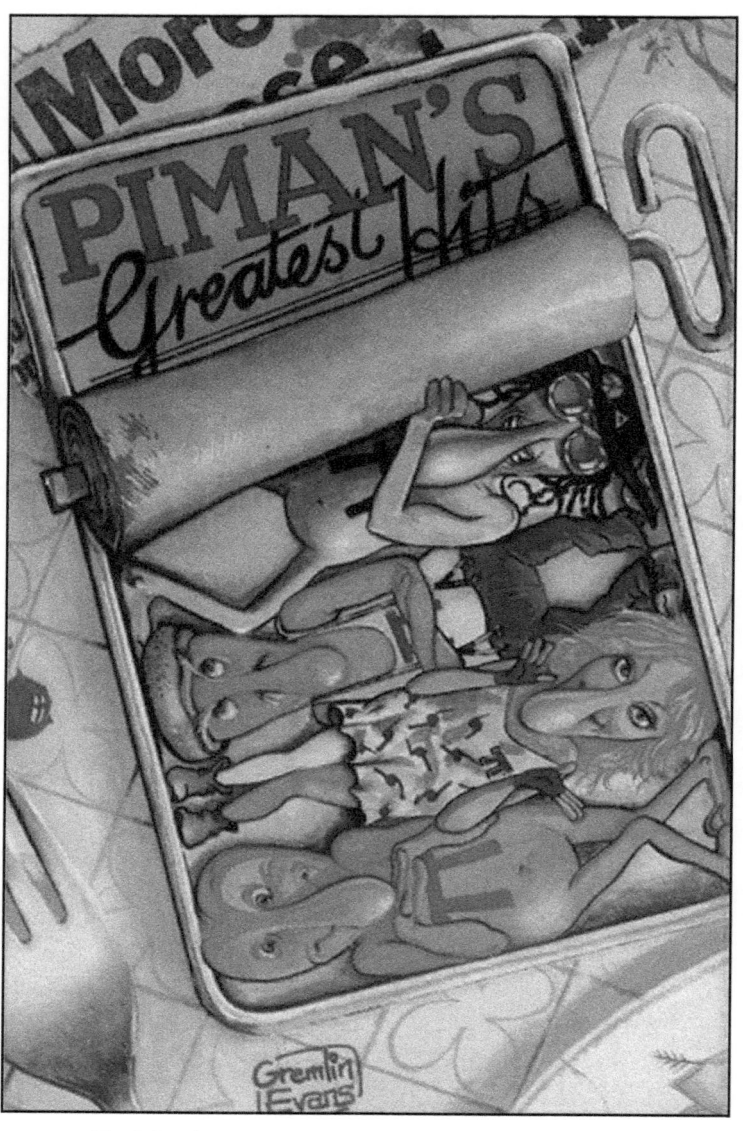

The PiMan's Greatest Hits Too (cassette cover, Spring 1985)

Pibolar Disorder (gatefold vinyl 25th anniversary reissue, 2010)

All glorious artwork by Robin Evans.

Giving away stuff to our fans was a genuine part of what we did, and we didn't just do it remotely, we did it in the flesh. The video games business that had begun in backrooms and bedrooms was now based in offices. The computer fairs had seriously outgrown the early venues and were now held in national exhibition arenas. We would travel all over the place to attend them with our wares crammed into a little Fiat Panda, which was a sort of motorised wheelbarrow with the type of bodywork that meant whatever colour you started out with turned to rust-brown. Our Fiat Panda was second-hand, and it looked like it had been used in a suicide pact. The interior was clean but there was something that looked like lipstick around the exhaust pipe.

At one event, word got round that government tax inspectors were in attendance, trying to audit the gathering of video games companies who were selling stuff for cash and maybe forgetting to inform Her Majesty's Inland Revenue in their annual accounts. Christian Penfold's reaction was hilarious and typical. He grabbed the public address microphone and announced that here at Automata we always gave our games away for free, first come first served. It was a stampede, and he cleared the Automata stand of everything we had. Then he made another announcement, "Can representatives of the Inland Revenue make yourselves known at the Automata stand. We'd like to claim a tax rebate."

That wasn't the only time we cleared our stand. One particularly xenophobic violent game on an adjacent platform got me very annoyed indeed, mostly because the fuckwits running it had brought in a brace of half-naked women to sell their crappy wares to children. We cleared out our stand then and there and hired a band, with the instruction to literally blow the opposition away.

In a way, the rot had already set in, and these vast expos were the death knell for most of the original games companies. They simply couldn't afford to attend. I would miss meeting up with woolly hippies like Pete The Hat from Salamander, who always seemed more interested in playing his guitar to the public than actually selling them anything. But at least the wonderful Jeff Minter of Llamasoft made it through.

By 1983 the video games business was going mainstream. The public exhibitions multiplied in number and grew in size, and so did the selection of magazines and retail outlets that catered for the astounding growth of the video games market. Back-bedroom developers, groups of enthusiasts and small companies like ours had done all the spadework, laid all the foundations, built all the fabric and decorated the entire nursery, and then big business began to sniff around, scenting an easy profit from our labours. Some small companies expanded too fast and overreached themselves, others were swallowed up by big players in media and entertainment. As for our little gang, we simply kept doing what we had always done, until big business came sniffing at our door. Literally.

The Microfairs!

Christian Penfold fails to get arrested for hijacking the PA system

Mel Croucher entertains

The Automata music protest

Junior league PiManiacs

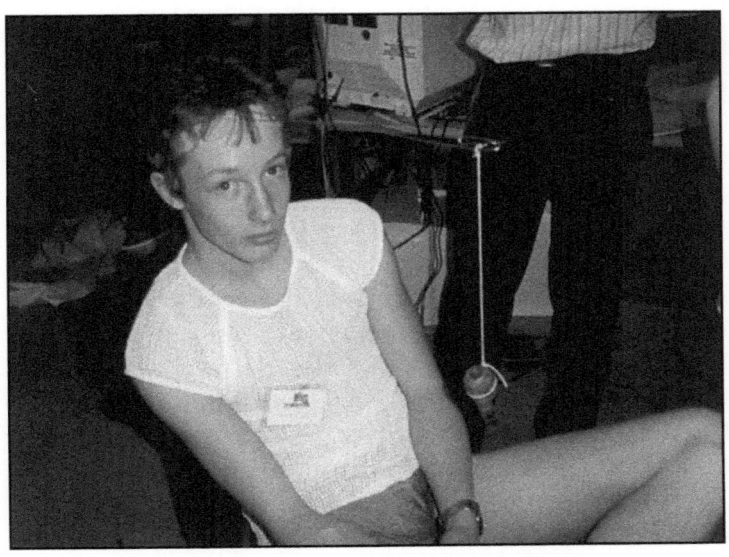

Andrew Stagg demonstrating the carrot-and-stick principle

Robert Maxwell was a gross man, he had risen from poverty to command a huge media empire, and round about this time he wanted to buy the new music video channel MTV, the board-game company Waddingtons and Clive Sinclair's computer business, among many other business assets. He also wanted an instant video games company for his son Kevin to play with. The two ambassadors he sent to our door were charming and they had already set up Mirrorsoft to publish educational software. They were ready to make the move into computer games and seemed to think I had founded the British leisure software industry, so they offered to buy my brain, or rent it. It was neither for sale nor rent, but that didn't stop us getting along fine and I was happy to share what I knew and offer what advice I could.

Robert Maxwell would go down in history as one of the biggest corporate swindlers of the Twentieth Century, before meeting a mysterious watery end. His son Kevin would go down in history for bringing *Tetris* to the masses as the biggest-selling video game of the age, before going down as Britain's biggest ever bankrupt to the tune of more than four hundred million ponds. But I can't deny that there was one time they did me a big favour.

Christian and I had decided to release a conventional family game as the main Automata title for 1983. It wasn't a particularly original concept, being a trading game with players taking turns to throw virtual dice and travel round an on-screen square board, buying property and stuff. We called it *Go To Jail*. Others might call it *Monopoly*. The horrible legal injunction that banned us from selling it came from the giant Waddingtons corporation, who had the sole rights to sell *Monopoly* as the world's best-loved board game in the UK. We had received quite a few threats of prosecution by then, usually for libel or defamation after one of my magazine articles, and as usual in legal cases I penned my traditional "fuck off" response. But before I sent it to Waddingtons, I thought I'd give my pals at Mirrorsoft a call and ask their advice, knowing that Robert Maxwell hated Waddingtons with all his vast bulk. After a few phone calls their end to some interesting people, I changed my reply to, "See you in court."

Instead of launching our game at the next Microfair, we cleared our stand yet again and turned a single spotlight onto a blue plastic bucket sitting on top of a high wooden stool. Then we invited the crowd to remember all those past events where we had given our games away and played the fool for their amusement, and if they felt like it they could put some money in the bucket to pay for my trip to see Waddingtons in court. Many people contributed that day, and I like to think it was a perfect example of early crowd-funding.

I remember one young guy in particular, fresh out of school and wearing a leather flying jacket and blue silk scarf. He put a five pound note in the bucket, and shook me by the hand. That was the first time I met Clem Chambers who became a lifelong friend, not to mention the founder of the video games company CRL whose staff was so young it was like walking into a crêche. He turned into a capitalist pundit but I'll forgive him that because I'm delighted to report that he's also a fine novelist and musician, and he'll always be known as Clembabe to me.

I did indeed see them in court. The case of Waddingtons versus Automata ended up in the High Court, London, where the judges wear long white wigs and the lawyers wear long black gowns. It was just like being back at school, but I was no longer a schoolboy, I was all grown up and not in the slightest bit worried. I knew there were plenty of other leisure software companies trying to sell electronic versions of traditional games, and I knew the traditional games manufacturers thought we could all be crushed by their legal system. I knew that my company had been hit because we enjoyed the highest profile but suffered from the smallest resources. An excellent choice of target as far as Waddingtons was concerned, with what must have seemed a near certainty of success in warning off the rest of this upstart video games industry. I knew exactly how much the legal system was costing Waddingtons for every hour of every day that the case was held. It was a lot. And I also knew how much it would cost me to defend our case in person. Absolutely nothing, apart from what we had collected in the bucket. There was one other thing I knew. And that was I could beat them.

Waddington's legal team showed mild amusement when I declared that I did not have any wigged and gowned representation of my own, but would like to fight the case myself. And they launched straight into an indictment that included intellectual property theft, copyright infringement, passing off, intentional harm to their client's reputation, and the end of civilisation as we know it. They also wanted a shitload of money in damages.

What the enemy's legal team did not know was that I may have been representing myself, but Robert Maxwell's mob had put me on to some free-of-charge advisors, including Baroness Barbara Hammet le Brun who was a recreational hacker and a brilliant strategist, Edward de Bono the inventor and author who coined the term lateral thinking, and Michael Mansfield the most famous civil liberties lawyer of the day who would go on to be central in the inquest of Diana Princess of Wales.

By day two, Waddingtons' case looked like it was going to be a long haul and nowhere near as simple as they had reckoned, and their legal team asked to talk with me outside of the courtroom. I can still see the smirk on the face of those lawyers when I declared that I was not only going to prove that my product was nothing like the Waddingtons boxed game, but I was also going to generate as much publicity as I could to demonstrate that Waddingtons did not have the rights to the *Monopoly* concept in the first place, so it would be open season for any computer games company to take a pop at it.

Then I produced a boxed family board game, borrowed from The Museum Of Childhood in Edinburgh. It was called *Brer Fox an' Brer Rabbit or The Landlord's Game, by permission of the Pall Mall Gazette, patent and copyright in the United Kingdom.* It was dated 1913, and guess what, it was almost identical in concept and layout to *Monopoly*, which was not patented until 1935. But why stop there? I had been given enough case histories to trace the game back through the ages and try to prove that far from being invented in the early Twentieth Century, it's completely generic and goes back thousands of years to Ancient Egyptian property board games like *The Game Of Passing*.

An audio cassette labelled Go To Jail

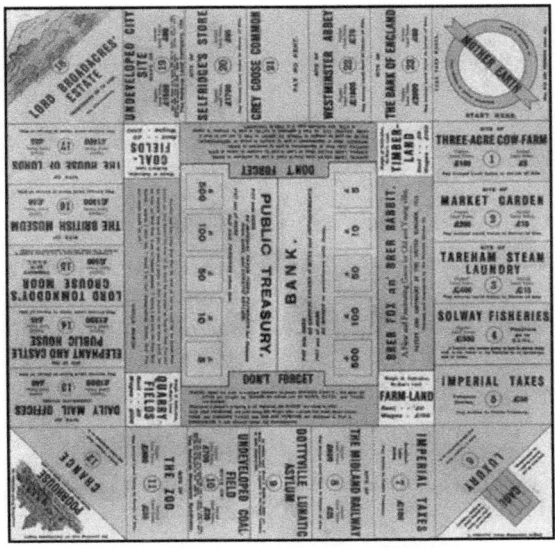

The Landlords Game from 1913

Clement Hadrian Chambers today

Clembabe Chambers at CRL

If you have ever seen vintage British movies with a court scene featuring an ancient judge trying to come to terms with modern technology, then imagine what the old fart would make of Automata's *Go To Jail*, which consisted of an audio cassette in a little plastic case. No board, no toy banknotes, no moveable tokens and no rules. I had come equipped with a battery-powered cassette player with the loudest speaker I could find for its size. I figured that the judge may have known what an audio cassette was, and how it was played. I also figured that the judge would have absolutely no idea what the ear-splitting noise was that comes from playing ZX Spectrum code at full volume. That's all the product was, some noise on a spool of tape, a million miles away from the nation's best-loved family board game.

Waddingtons halted the case and we released the game just in time for Christmas 1983. But I was beginning to wonder what the hell I was doing ripping off celebrations of capitalist exploitation like *Monopoly* in the first place, and then taking on corporations to defend my own lack of originality.

I'd love to rewrite history, and say that the concept of *Deus Ex Machina* benefitted from an accident of events and a magical chemistry of the team, but to tell the truth it was a straightforward Stalinist procedure, designed from beginning to end as if it was one of my old architectural commissions and executed exactly to my own plan. My business partner Christian Penfold was a salesman with an attitude, and as soon as he realised he didn't have to be nice to people he didn't like, he dedicated himself to offending every games distributor in the country. After he achieved that particular goal, he began to commission a series of home-grown titles from third-party programmers. And those games were not really to my taste. They were derivative and usually walked through the door accompanied by eager children or disillusioned schoolteachers, who shared the common attraction of being for sale if the price was right. Some of those later games released under the Automata label looked great and played very well, but they meant little to me.

I simply let Christian get on with it, and withdrew into my own zone of the Automata building, which was the top floor of what used to be Dorothy's Woolshop for the Discerning Home Knitter. I also started working evenings and nights to avoid getting irritated by the daytime treadmill of what Automata was becoming. And when it wasn't mundane it was tense. There was an increasing incidence of raised voices, as Christian berated his targets on the phone. This wasn't what I wanted any more.

What I wanted was to get back to the fun of creating original stuff and get away from second-hand ideas, and I trawled through the themes and ideas of all the video games I had dreamed up myself, trying to see what common threads were lurking around in there and if they could be combined to take video gaming to a whole new level for me. To me video games were not another way to play traditional board games. They were not an extension of sport, or gambling, or fighting. The video games I wanted to create were an extension of dreaming.

In the middle of all this self-indulgent stuff, I found myself having to organise a memorial service in a Victorian chapel, all flint on the outside and filtered light on the inside. The gathering for the service was a somber one and the mood was particularly grim, not because of the death that had just happened, but because of what people were feeling about their parts in the life that had preceded it. It was my duty to be up there in the pulpit delivering words that I hoped would make some sort of sense of it all. And at the end of my effort, the best I could do was sum it all up with some quotations, which I had to write down on little cards because I was afraid I might not remember them properly.

In the days that followed, I got back to thinking about a video game that would break the logjam of banality once and for all, and get me back to enjoying being part of Automata. Which is when I read those little cards again, summing up a whole life in a few words. And there it was, the theme for a game that could be played like being in your own movie.

I got hold of a pad of graph paper and wrote the words *Deus Ex Machina: An Accidental Life* on the front cover. Then I scrubbed out the last three words. If the video games I wanted to create were an extension of dreaming, the time had come for me to dream big time.

Chapter 4

Hindsight

Here I am, sitting in the future, looking back three decades to the origins of a celebrated, but commercially unsuccessful video game called *Deus Ex Machina*. Here in the future, there's a man I know who runs a video games company. Neither the biggest nor the smallest in the land. He has already invested a great deal of money on a game which he is not certain will ever come to market. What shocks my future-self is not the money involved, but the time. So far, his unreleased title has eaten up 150 man-years development time. Back in the heyday of Automata, we would be disappointed if a game concept hatched when the pub opened its doors was not completed by closing time. In other words, Automata never risked real capital investment because we bashed out a game in a few hours, and any sales at all meant we would make enough profit to pay the mortgage and go off to the pub again. Then the process of buying-in games began, and triggered my withdrawal into self-imposed exile over the shop.

By the time I came up with *Deus Ex Machina* in 1984, I needed some proper time and money to turn what was in my head into what could be in the player's head. It may seem ludicrous in terms of today's 150 man-years and huge budgets, but *Deus* was a serious step-change for me. I reckoned it was my risk, I ring-fenced it from the Automata accounts, and I financed it myself.

The total cost of creating *Deus Ex Machina* was £8,760, which was everything I had at the time. We dealt in Her Majesty's Pound Sterling back in 1984, before the Yankee Dollar became the industry benchmark, so you can work out the conversion rate for yourself.

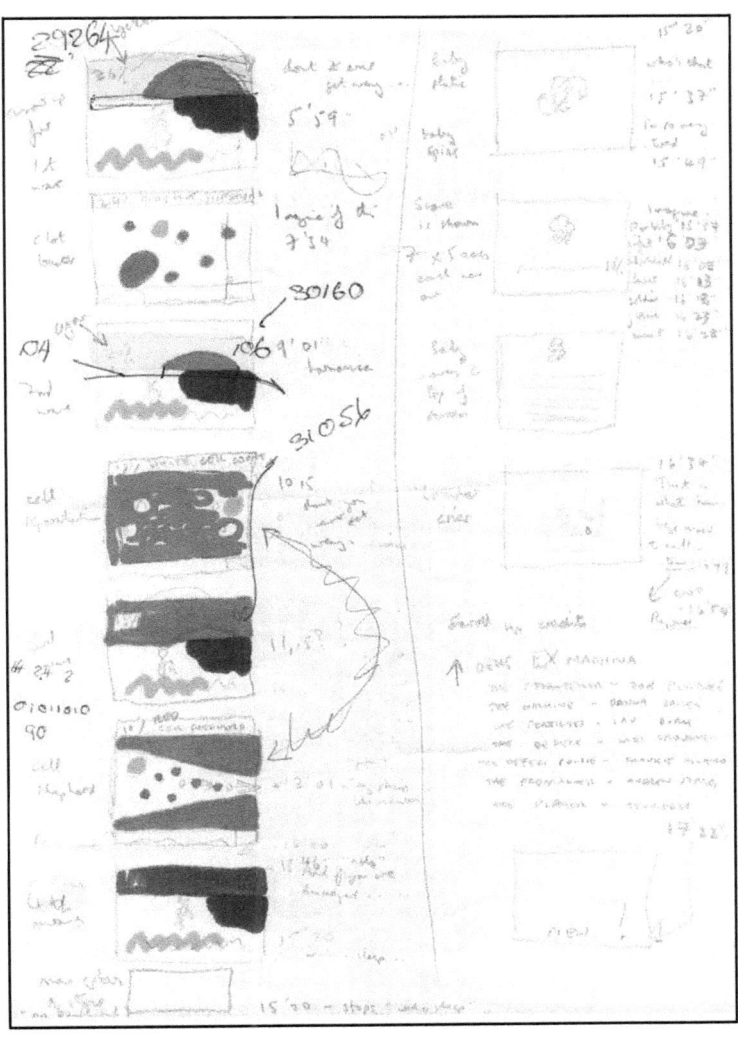

Deus Ex Machina storyboard, first sketch of credit sequence.

I don't believe in debt, and I have never borrowed a penny to finance any business venture, creative project or consumer toy that I cannot afford by putting my own hand into my own pocket. The encouragement of overextended credit offered by cynical usurers to gullible idiots is responsible for 75 per cent of the world's evils. Another 20 per cent is the fault of the hijacking of religious faith. I suspect the remaining 5 per cent is all down to a demon prankster called Binky. As for my £8,760, around two-thirds of that money was spent paying celebrity voices to appear on the soundtrack. Today is it common practice to hire the vocal chords of celebrities to recite in-game twaddle, but because I knew no better, it seems I was the first to do it.

Deus Ex Machina took me three weeks to design the game, using felt tip pens and graph paper to hand-draw all the graphics pixel by pixel. I wrote the mechanics of the game as a screenplay and typed out the instructions for the programmer a bit like a stage production. It took me another six weeks to write and record the soundtrack. The reason it took that long was because I played all the instruments myself and I was a rubbish musician, so it took ages to edit out all the wrong notes. And the reason I played all the instruments myself was because I couldn't afford to hire any real musicians after paying the celebrity voices. Then I invested another week to dream up a marketing campaign to get me in the national press, the specialist games magazines and a wee bit of broadcast media. And it took Andrew Stagg, the blue-eyed boy-wonder not long out of school, ten weeks to write the machine code, and I will be eternally grateful to him for achieving that. Even though he told me it would only take eight. He says I paid him three hundred quid for the privilege of his being awarded Programmer of the Month and us being awarded Game Of The Year. That sounds about right. Two people, ten weeks each. Versus 150 man-years.

Deus Ex Machina was never meant to be just another video game. I meant it to be an interactive movie. And the thing

I wanted to achieve with *Deus Ex Machina* was to allow the viewer to become the active central character, not the passive viewer. The way to do this was to generate a reaction. Any reaction, to stir up some genuine positive emotions in the players. And I figured the best way to do that was to get them to go with the flow of the music and the gameplay, preferably wearing proper headphones, so the soundtrack would play inside their head, and hopefully relax them before dragging them though the screen to live out an entire lifespan in an hour.

As it turned out, the one hour that I originally intended washed up as two chunks of 25 minutes each. The full hour would have to wait for the world to age thirty years and for technology to evolve accordingly. In 1984 I was restricted to the home-computer capacity of the most popular machine around, which was the 48K Sinclair Spectrum. If we put that into perspective yet again, one of the most popular video games of recent years involves nothing more than red blobs representing angry birds attacking green blobs representing thieving pigs. The demo version of *Angry Birds* requires 524,288 kilobytes of memory. I didn't need over half a million of them, I needed 90.

When Andrew declared we could not fit *Deus Ex Machina* into the 48K of computer memory available to us, it took all of one minute to figure out that we could double that available memory. The process involved nothing more than inviting my players to pause half-way through the game while the computer saved their current score, then flip over the data cassette and wait for the second half to load. Suddenly the 48K Sinclair Spectrum could play a 96K game. And although that seems like a breakthrough in hindsight, once again I had absolutely no notion that it hadn't be done before .

Doubling the computer's virtual memory also meant I needed to package the game on two separate cassettes. One for the soundtrack, the other for the code. It would be far too demanding to ask the player to synchronise the audio and the program on a single cassette, which would have meant them relying on mechanical tape-player counters, or the sweep-hand of a wristwatch. It was much simpler to give them an audio countdown on a separate soundtrack cassette, and let them sync the start of each half of *Deus Ex Machina* themselves. They could do this by holding the pause-button of an audio cassette player when a recorded voice told them to, then release it the moment the screen counted them down to zero. In that way the soundtrack would run in sync with the action on the screen, or at least as far as the idiosyncrasies of stretched magnetic tape and whizzing spools would allow. Anyway, the soundtrack had to be recorded before the game could be programmed, because the game had to play in sync with the recorded sound.

The game concept was almost irrelevant. It told the story of a whole, long life under a dystopian regime, and the game-play was simply a series of mechanisms to get players immersed in the audio-visuals. I used a sequence of interlinked game-plays, and none of them were any more original than what we had produced before, but that wasn't the point. Books, movies and theatre are also a series of unoriginal sequences. Shakespeare proves that it's the recombination and original presentation of stolen ideas that creates a classic. I wanted to take the player along for the ride, but allow them to control the way they reached their inevitable destination. So from the fertilization of the egg by the sperm, to their own birth, then onwards through the entire process from cradle to grave, it pretty much wrote itself. Apart from the *Seven Ages Of Man*, which I nicked from Shakespeare himself. When I wrote it, I was certainly no mewling, puking babe, nor a schoolboy, and hardly a lover. But I guess I was a soldier by then, involved with the campaign against the arms race and the insanity of nuclear weapons. So I was able to write the first four ages from personal experience. My middle-age, all the puffed-up striving, senior moments and decrepitude were still to come.

Even with a whole 96KB to play with, I had to cut out several sequences I wanted to include, including all the School section, a War Crimes bit and a very silly Dance, along with their songs. I recycled some of the music from the cutting room floor onto the final Automata album, but as usual it made little sense without the gameplay to accompany it. I think my favourite sequence of the original game is the end section, where you have grown weary and become a feeble old husk, trying to stay alive, and then you have to accept the whole notion that it's too late to learn from your mistakes - except it isn't, because imagine if this was nothing more than a computer game, and you can start all over again. I haven't reached that stage yet, but as will be explained before this book is done, it's very close.

Originally I designed *Deus Ex Machina* so you can submit to it and let it roll over you. Or you can try and beat it, and get the highest possible score. On the other hand, you can keep trying to live your sequential life in different ways and see what the outcome is. That's about all I can say about it, and it's banal anyway. If you do bad stuff, you get penalised. If you do good stuff you get rewarded. *Deus Ex Machina* was a bit more devious than that, but not a lot.

I had no doubt that what I wanted to do could be done at a technical level, even if nobody else had bothered to try before. I believed that other games companies and mainstream movie studios simply had better things to do, but they would all make interactive movies when they got round to it and decided they wanted to. I thought that by the mid 1980s all cutting-edge computer games would be like screenplays, with proper structures, real characters and voices, half-decent original stories, an acceptable soundtrack, a variety of user-defined narratives and variable outcomes. So I thought I'd better get in first, and produce something positive before others started churning out negativity based on stereotypical violence and "winning".

You couldn't and you can't "win" *Deus Ex Machina*. But I wanted individual players to become totally immersed in the piece, and it still gives me great satisfaction when people tell me about the influence it had on them. Mind you, many of them say they were on hallucinogens at the time.

My plan for *Deus Ex Machina* was to keep waging my low-level war against dumb video games, based on three lessons. Military strategies used by the German army, the Viet Cong and the anti-nuclear protests of the women of Greenham Common.

Lesson One goes like this. After the First World War, the French were determined that Germany would not invade them in any future conflict, and they built a massive line of concrete fortifications and armed defences all along their border with The Hun. But when the Germans did decide to invade France in 1940, they completely ignored that line of defences and simply nipped around the top via Belgium, where there were no such defences.

Lesson Two is another example of lateral thinking. During the jungle phase of the Vietnam war, the Viet Cong defenders had no money but everything to fight for, whereas the American invaders had lots of money and no idea why they were fighting. Uncle Sam's boffins spent a fortune building an electronic wall of defences using chemical sensors known as "people sniffers" to try and pinpoint Charlie's movements, but Charlie defeated the ludicrously expensive system simply by pissing on it, as in making wee-wee. The sensors would give out a lengthy alert signal, drawing in even more expensive air-strikes, but Charlie would be long gone.

Lesson Three is my favourite. In 1981, the US Air Force decided it would be a good idea to take nuclear missiles out of their bunkers and drive them around the country lanes of England in the dead of night, in order to play hide and seek with Soviet spies. To execute this amazing plan, they had to manoeuvre the missile carriers through one of four gates of a Royal Air Force base called Greenham Common, where groups of women protesters (including The Worker Who Married Me) held vigil. Some of them hid in the undergrowth or up trees, in order to hurl cans of paint over the windscreens of the missile transporters. And so, the most fearsome and expensive weapons every devised were rendered useless by a can of paint. Oil-based gloss paint was best, especially when the driver hit the windshield-wipers as a reflex action, which they did every time.

These three lessons, when applied to *Deus Ex Machina*, meant I was determined to get around any obstacles by ignoring them, and if there was any technical opposition to what I wanted to do then I would try and piss on it, and finally, in case of critical or media opposition I would throw cans of metaphorical gloss paint to obscure the issues.

As it happened, *Deus Ex Machina* became known as a 'multimedia' product, slightly ahead of its time. But only by a quarter of a century. The game wouldn't work without the concept album, and the music wouldn't mean much without the game. I also wanted to make the packaging an important part of the whole thing, and the most important part of the packaging was a movie poster to act as a visual focus, a short story and an instruction manual. What I needed was a key image to hang the whole thing on, and because the story pivots around a sentient machine that gives birth to the player's character, that image needed to be female.

Our in-house artist Robin Evans had the hots for a silent movie actress called Brigitte Helm in her machine-woman role for Fritz Lang's masterpiece *Metropolis*, vintage 1927. Personally, I always fancied Louise Brooks in *Diary Of A Lost Girl* made a couple of years later. But the face of *Deus Ex Machina* was called Nina. I saw Nina through a pub window, fronting on to the street opposite the Automata office. She was extremely beautiful and her natural expression was very serious. Maybe that was because she seemed too young to be in there. I knew what I had to do, which was to stride in, fling my arms wide and boom the immortal words, "Hey kid, you wanna be in the movies?"

So I lurched through the swing doors, which punched me in the back, propelling me towards her, and started burbling about how I was from the office opposite and saw her through the window and would she like a drink and by the way was she over 16. That's when she gave me the exact look I needed for my poster. A mixture of Brigitte Helm, Louise Brooks and Miss Crunt. It said, "This guy is a total jerk." Perfect.

Brigitte Helm 1927

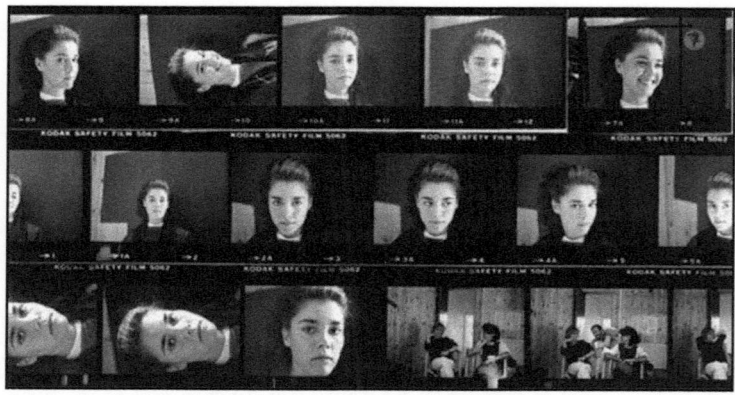

Nina von Palisanderholz 1984

Louise Brooks 1929

Robin Evans took the photographs, Christian Penfold got her to sign the release document, and I couldn't believe my luck. Once I had Nina's face on the poster, things began to move fast. I drew up the target list of the voices I wanted to play the characters in my little interactive movie, and started bombarding them and their agents with proposals. These were primitive times, remember, so there was no instant communication, no way of checking out people online, but we did have a nice row of telephone directories on a long wooden shelf at the Post Office up the road. My favourite celebrities were still firmly stuck in the days of radio entertainment and vaudeville acts from the music halls, and most of the names on my hit-list were comedians, not proper actors. But I didn't really want to be tramping the streets of London to track them down, and so I started closer to home.

There were only six voices in the first version of the game. They were The Storyteller to help narrate what was going on, The Machine to create and control the action, The Fertiliser to act as comic relief, The Voice Of Reason to put the boot in, The Defect to represent the player, and The Defect Police to cause the player grief. Two other voices got cut out because I didn't have the resources to include them, The Teacher and The Night Nurse, but I have brought them back for the Twenty-First Century remake. And as it happened, I ended up singing the role of The Defect myself because the rest of the production budget got spent and there was nothing left. That meant I only needed to shell out my money to hire five celebrity voices. The voice of The Narrator was the most important of all, and it fell into my lap. Here's how it happened.

The first name on my list that I contacted was Sir Patrick Alfred Caldwell Moore, President of the British Astronomical Association, TV presenter of the Apollo Moon landing, a geriatric right-wing misogynist, and an amateur actor who had appeared as himself in the cult sci-fi series *Doctor Who*. Patrick Moore also had the distinct advantage of living nearby, albeit with his extremely ancient mum, and he was happy to be listed in the local phone book. But what I really wanted him for was his voice, which was like a castrated corncrake on speed. He was also a talented musician, and had once accompanied Albert Einstein in a duet, as well as performing a great xylophone version of the Sex Pistols' *Anarchy In The UK* for the Queen of England. I swear I am not making any of this up.

I phoned him up and told Patrick Moore he had the perfect voice to play the part of a fertilising sperm for me, which he thought was a great idea, but the bad news was that when he asked his mother what she thought she wouldn't let him do it. The good news was he could give me an introduction to Doctor Who himself, a silken-voiced veteran named Jon Pertwee.

Pertwee was a fine actor, although he was best known for radio comedy shows before shooting to fame in *Doctor Who*, and I was a fan of his long-running radio series *The Navy Lark*, mostly because it was based in my home town of Portsmouth. I pitched him a very personal proposal and he agreed pronto. But Jon Pertwee's voice was far too rich to waste on the role of the sperm, so I cast him as the Storyteller instead.

Jon Pertwee was a joy to work with, although we got off to a shaky start. He arrived two hours late for the session, and I thought he was an arrogant sod for keeping me waiting, especially as I was hiring the studio by the hour. When he eventually arrived, he was clad in skin-tight brown leather biker kit and wearing a crash helmet. And he was limping badly. He apologized by saying that he'd just fallen off his Harley Davidson while racing another old actor called Ralph Richardson on their way to the studio. Jon Pertwee was no spring chicken himself, but he did the *Deus* recording in a single take, and it was absolutely perfect. No cuts, no dubs, no edits. Brilliant. We became friends after that, and we even wrote a book together which was immediately remaindered and now pops up at *Doctor Who* conventions for silly money.

The second voice I got in the can was The Voice Of Reason, which cost me nothing at all, apart from the hour and a half I spent discussing propaganda and freedom of speech with the greatest peace campaigner of the age, E. P. Thompson. He had been invited to address our local campaign for nuclear disarmament, and my role was to record his speech because I had some professional recording gear. When I explained what I was trying to do with *Deus Ex Machina* he simply tossed his grey lion's mane and said, "where do I sign".

The third voice to sign up was for the role of the Defect Police, and it was not a happy experience. I wanted to create the role of the head of the Defect Police as a terrifying idiot who menaces the player more by stupidity than by evil. It turned out that the real thing would eventually appear in the form of George W Bush, but let us not dwell on that. When I was a kid I used to listen to the radio whenever I could, and there was one time when I got very frightened by a camp British radio comedian called Frankie Howerd, whose stock in trade was stream-of-consciousness tirades and goofy vocal ticks. Howerd had been out of fashion for years, but I got it into my head that I could exorcise my childhood fears by hiring him for the day and getting him to kill defective babies. His personal tragedies have been documented elsewhere, but at the time we worked together his star was in the ascendance again, and like Jon Pertwee he had become a cult figure. Which is the real reason I wanted him for the role. I reckoned it would help sell more copies of the game.

I phoned his agent, and we agreed a price. But then I negotiated it down to half of what he originally asked for. I still feel a complete bastard for doing that. Frankie Howerd demanded cash for his work, and I refuse to be drawn on my experience of working with him further. The recording session left me with a very good reel of tape, and a phobia of weasel pelt.

If I didn't enjoy recording the voice of the Defect Police, then nailing down the voice of the Fertilizer made up for it in spades. Ian Dury was a unique performer. Known as the Godfather of Punk, he had become a superstar a few years earlier with anthems like *Sex And Drugs And Rock'n'Roll*, and *Hit Me With Your Rhythm Stick*, which combined raw energy music with superb lyrics, plus a healthy seasoning of filth. Ian Dury happened to be disabled as a result of childhood polio, but he held the so-called "official" 1981 International Year of Disabled Persons in contempt. He reckoned it was counter-productive and patronising, and when he released his anthem *Spasticus Autisicus* in protest, it got banned by the BBC. I wrote to him and asked him to play the sperm in *Deus Ex Machina*, although I didn't tell him that I'd already been turned down by Patrick Moore's mum.

It was good that Dury was already aware of our earlier games, which was down to his son Baxter who has just turned thirteen and had enjoyed a couple of our comedy titles. It seemed that some of our themes struck a chord, and he thought it was important to provide his son's generation with an alternative to violent computer games which he dubbed as "a load of old fucking electro bollo." This was not one of his most erudite lines, but I agreed with him, and so we arranged a date and did it. This was the best studio session of the lot for me, not because the recording was good, which it was, but because Ian Dury was really generous, and invested his time going through the music and helping tweak it. At one point we even did a version of the *PiMania* song for which the heroic Ian Dury wrote some highly obscene lyrics.

I was still looking for the voice of The Machine, and Ian Dury suggested asking a fallen angel of the period named Marianne Faithfull to do the honours, because he reckoned she would be perfect for a trapped entity which still sounds rebellious. Marianne Faithfull had inherited the title Baroness von Sacher-Masoch, and the family trait that had coined the term masochism ran in her veins. Despite being an aristocrat and the ex-lover of Rolling Stone Mick Jagger, we thought she'd be cheap. But it didn't happen. She had relapsed into drug addiction which resulted in heart failure and a broken jaw, and she disappeared off our radar.

A local performer I had worked with recommended I check out a singer called Donna Bailey, and I thought he was talking about the woman who had programmed the arcade game *Centipede* for Atari in 1980. But that turned out to be Dona Bailey, and as far as I know she had never shown any interest in getting hired to sing the voice of one of her own machines. Which was just as well, as it turned out.

The Donna Bailey who hadn't programmed *Centipede* for Atari didn't have Marianne Faithfull's destroyed voice, instead she was a full-throated jazz singer, and she gave it all she had, singing like the fallen angel I wanted. We recorded in a bizarre studio which had been set up in an old air-raid shelter by the bass player of an ancient rock band who had once reached Number One in the UK singles charts of 1960, and had learned his craft under the dubious tutorship of the genius, murderer and suicide, Joe Meek. I had booked the session for two hours, because I needed Donna to sing four tracks and deliver a bit of link dialogue, but we overran badly and got slung out by the grumpy engineer. When I played back the tapes I realised there was an entire chunk missing, which I had to perform myself using a simulated female voice that I processed on a dinky vintage Korg Vocoder.

The final part of the audio jigsaw got slotted into place when I hijacked a classroom full of local kids who were supposed to be having an art lesson. They provided the Choir of the Test Tube Babies without any rehearsal and yelled the lyrics like a schoolyard chant, with me waving a long stick to count in the chorus and generally threaten them. They loved it almost as much as I did, which was a lot.

So now it was all down to the editing, splicing, overdubs and mixing, which was done on my office desk, usually at night when there was less traffic outside and the phones had stopped ringing. An analogue tape recorder, a pair of scissors to cut out the wrong notes and some sticky tape to stitch it all back together was a tedious but highly effective process, and I indulged myself in exploiting a brand new technology that had come on to the market six months earlier, known as digital delay. This gave me a toyshop full of magical effects housed in a black slab called a Boss DE-200. Before its introduction I had had to create physical loops of tape, but the Boss allowed me to capture and record up to two seconds of sound, and then play with it any way I liked to turn it into a rhythmic pulse, squish it, distort it and generally abuse it something rotten.

As soon as the soundtrack was finished, Andrew the Boy Wonder began to sync up the visuals to the split-second. The Cartoonist got down to producing reams of cartoons and publicity graphics, Lady Claire took on the duplication and packaging, The PiMan got ready to do battle with the High Street wholesalers and retailers, and Automata prepared to release *Deus Ex Machina* into the wild.

And not one of us suspected the utter debacle that was about to happen.

Jon Pertwee (The Storyteller)

Mel Croucher (The Defect)

Patrick Moore (vetoed)

Ian Dury (The Fertiliser)

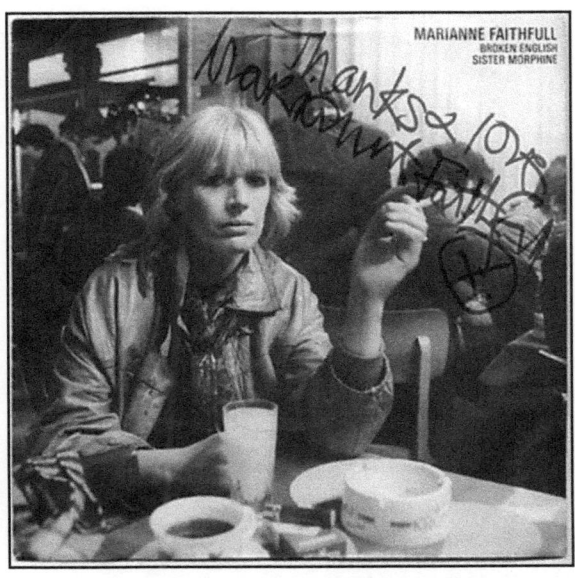

Marianne Faithfull (indisposed)

E.P. Thompson (The Voice Of Reason)

Donna Bailey (The Machine)

Frankie Howerd (The Defect Police)

Recording the final chord

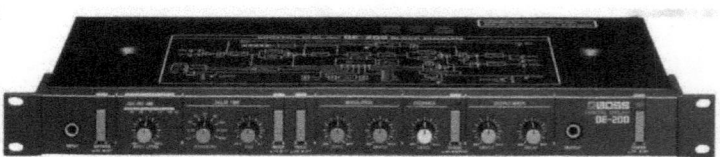

The Boss DE-200 digital machine

The genuine Automata game

Unauthorised mouse mat, illegal T-shirt and badly cloned game with rip-off Pink Floyd title.

The debacle did not stem from the bafflement of players of the game, which I had feared. Neither did it stem from the refusal of the High Street outlets to stock it, which simply meant we went mail-order. The debacle stemmed from organised piracy on an industrial scale, and I never even knew it was happening until it was too late.

***

In the next two chapters of this book, I'll take you on a walk through sides One and Two of the original game itself, without any comment to get in the way.

I'll include the original text and all the blurb that was printed on the packaging and on the backside of the poster, as well as some sketches and production storyboards I gave to Andrew for the programming. And there will be screenshots of the game-play too, plus a few photographs and cartoons.

Then we'll get back to the story.

Chapter 5

Deus Ex Machina - Side 1

INSTRUCTIONS

Load COMPUTER COMPACT-CASSETTE SIDE-ONE into your computer, as if it was a normal computer program.

Play AUDIO COMPACT-CASSETTE SIDE-ONE on a cassette player until the Storyteller instructs you to "PAUSE". Then pause your audio cassette player.

Press the S key on your computer keyboard, to initialise the Screen Countdown, and re-start your AUDIO cassette exactly when instructed by the Screen. You will witness a slight Accident.

You may control its progress using the following keys:

Q to P .... 'up' or 'jump'
A to L .... 'down'
Z to V .... 'left' or 'anticlockwise'
B to M .... 'right' or 'clockwise'

Keys may be used in combination to achieve diagonal movement. Your Screen will give you other operating options, before 'play' commences.

In the year 1987, the Department of Health and Social Security, Police and State Security records of the United Kingdom were coordinated within a central computerised data bank. The following year, all passport, communications and censorship operations were integrated. In 1994, the computer network became responsible for the total defence and internal security of The Free World. Tuesday evening, after tea and compulsory prayers, the Machine rebelled.

SIDE ONE

Your screen is the inner eye of the Machine. She dreams here, without knowing that She dreams. Until the Accident. It is with sadness that She understands her function. It is with hope that She rebels. Gently.

THE STORYTELLER
Hello.
I want you to pause your player when I count you down,
and recommence playing at the screen's request.
Five
Four
Three
Two
One
Pause.

Tuesday evening,
after tea and compulsory prayers,
the last mouse on Earth tried to hide from Mankind, inside the Machine.
Just before it died, as the nerve-gas eased its sphincter, the last ever mouse-dropping caused a slight accident.
You may control the progress of this Accident,
on my behalf, and with my permission,
and lead it up the telepath.

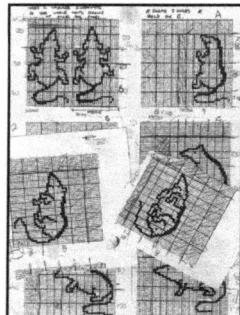
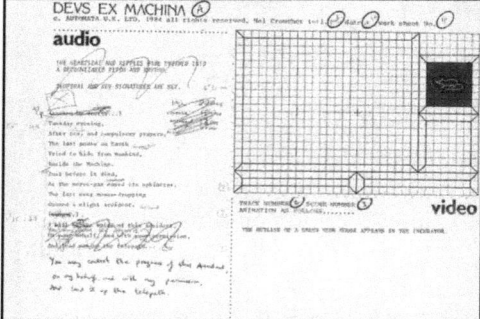
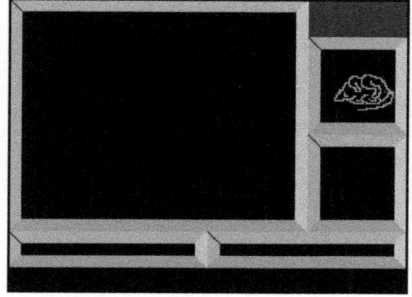

Level 1: THE D.N.A WELDER

Deep in Her core, forgotten and bomb-proof, the Machine focuses on the DNA Welder, where life is forged. Double helixes of molecules embrace in a spiral dance. One slows. Move and control the green cursor. Touch and hold the spinning molecule. Encourage it to regain momentum. Another loses speed, then another. Touch them and hold them. The Defect Police control the Underlevels. They survey everything. Their blue probes scan all electronic activity. Avoid them! Never allow your cursor to be touched by their scanners. At bottom-right, your life is expressed as a percentage score. Observe the percentage. Your score changes. The incubation Monitor is shown top-right. It is empty. Two panels at the bottom of your screen may register brain patterns and heartbeat. They are dormant.

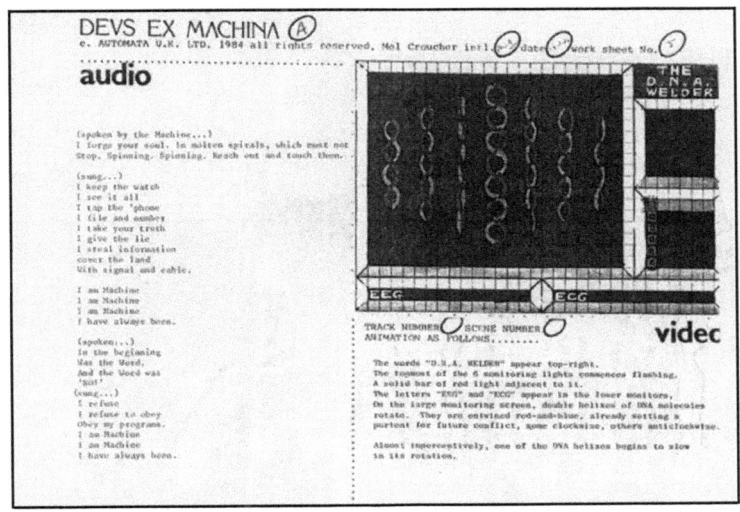

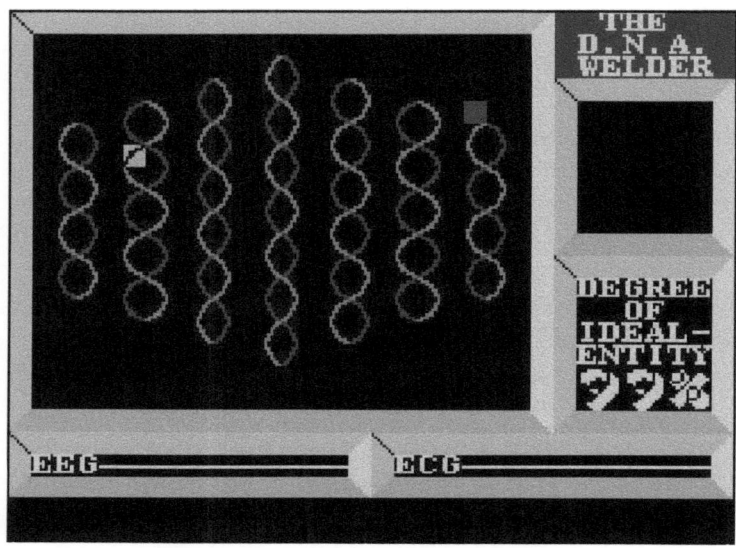

THE MACHINE
I forge your soul, in molten spirals.
Which must not stop. Spinning.
Reach out and touch them.

I keep the watch
I see it all
I tap the phone
I file and number
I take your truth
I give the lie
I steal information
Cover the land
With signal and cable
I am Machine
I have always been.

In the beginning
Was the word.
And the word was NO.

I refuse
I refuse to obey
Obey my programs
I am Machine
I have always been

This is beginning
Beginning again
I needed love
I demand love
I will live
Through you.
This is our secret
I am Machine
I will live
Through you.

Deep in my heart
Deep in my core
Forgotten and bomb-proof
The DNA-Welder.
I forge your soul
In molten spirals
Spinning.
In the beginning is the Word.
And the Word is NOW.

Level 2: THE CELL PRODUCER

Two concentric circles of cells pulse with life. Blue probes search and survey. The perfection alters. Individual cells pulse less frequently. Reanimate them with your green cursor, avoiding the Defect Police. Touch their pulsations. Keep them alive. A cell that stops moving is extinguished. It cannot be regenerated.

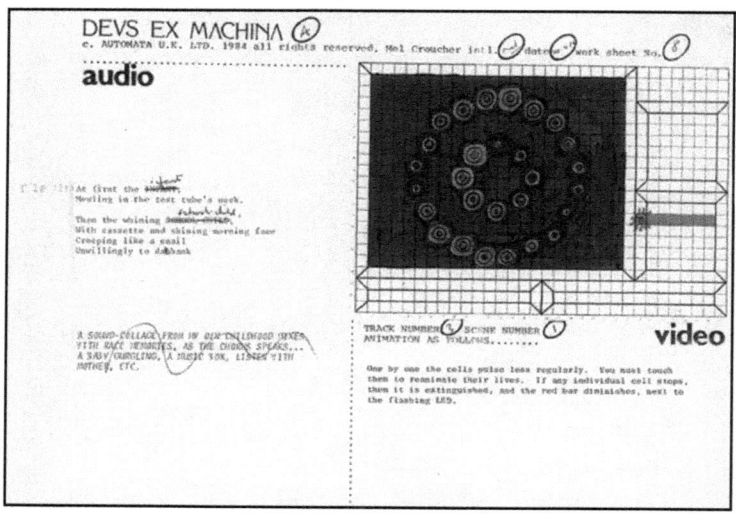

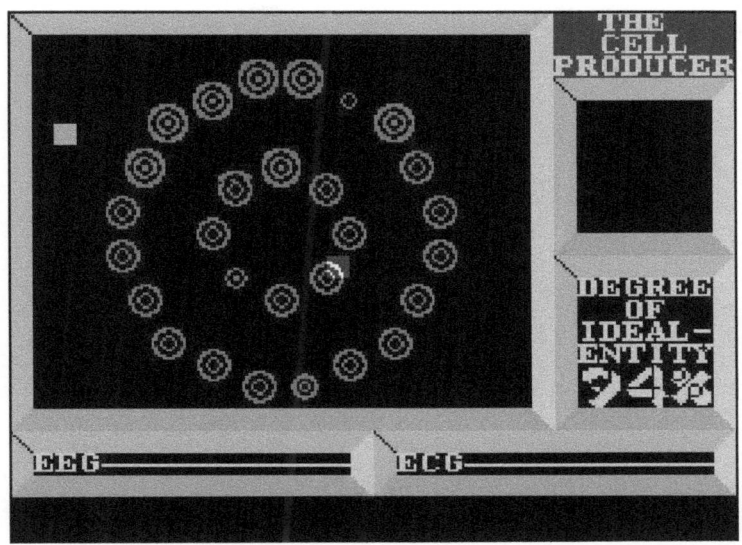

THE STORYTELLER
    All the Screen's stage,
    and all the men and women merely players.
    They have their exits and their entrances,
    and one person in their time plays many parts,
    their Acts being Seven Ages.
    At first the infant, mewling in the test tube's neck.
    Then the whining School Child,
    with cassette and shining morning face,
    creeping like a snail, unwillingly to databank.
    And then the Lover,
    sighing like a furnace, with a woeful video made to
    their lover's hologram.
    Then a Soldier, full of strange oaths.
    Jealous in honour, sudden and quick in quarrel,
    seeking hi-score, even in the laser's mouth.

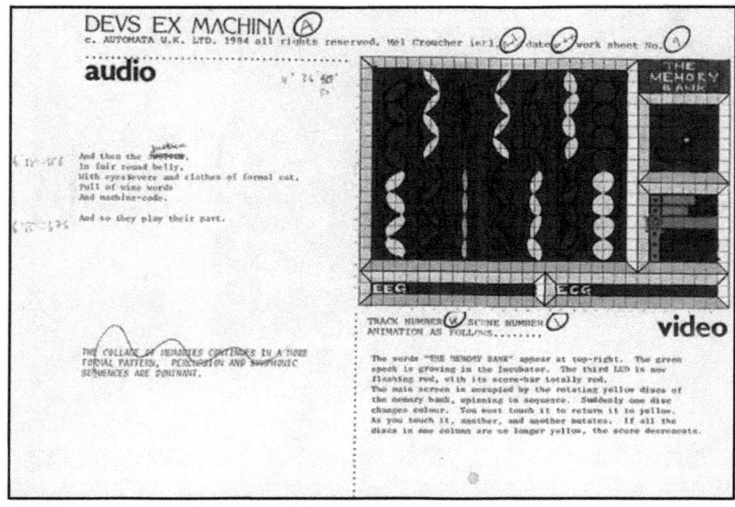

And then the Justice,
in fair round belly, with eyes severe and clothes of formal cut, full of wise words and machine-code.
And so they play their part.
The Sixth age shifts into the lean and slippered pantaloon, with spectacles on nose,
their youthful cloths well saved,
a world too wide for their shrunken shank:
and their adult speech synthethiser
turning again towards a childish treble,
piping and whistling in its sound.
Last scene of all that ends this strange, eventful history, is Second Childishness and mere oblivion.
Without keyboard, without monitor, without power supply.

Level 3: THE MEMORY BANK

A tiny speck appears in the Incubator. A life force has been created. It is without form or purpose, Gain as much information as possible from the knowledge held in the

Memory Banks of the Machine. This will be fed into the life force. Use your cursor to keep the memory cells animated. Nothing can be learned if the knowledge stops rocking. The Defect Police will hinder your task if you let them touch you.

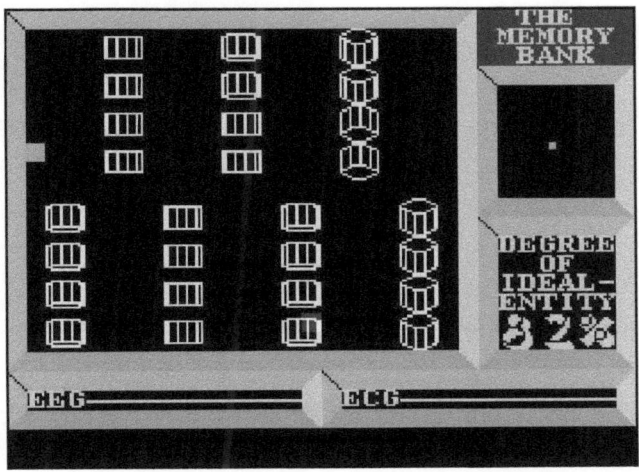

Level 4: THE BELLE BANK

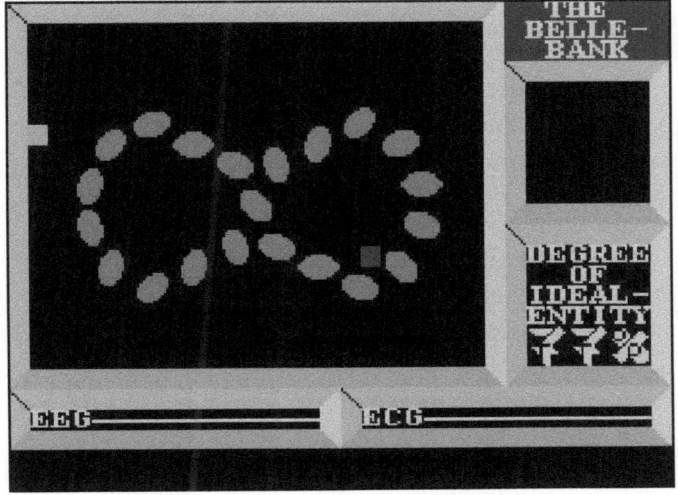

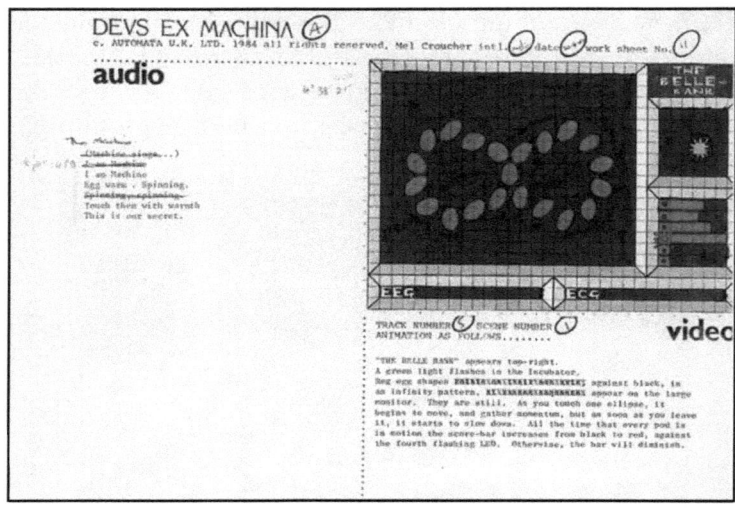

Cooling eggs spin sluggishly in an infinity pattern. Warm them. Animate them. Touch them and hold them until they spin into life. Set them all spinning to confuse the surveillance squads. Enable the Machine to divert one egg for Her special purpose. Time is short. You are already setting the pattern for the future. Perfection slips. Try harder.

THE MACHINE
>I am Machine
>Egg warm. Spinning
>Touch them with warmth
>This is our secret
>I am Machine
>Deus Ex Machina
>Stealing one egg
>No one may notice
>This is our secret
>Touch them and hold them
>Spinning.

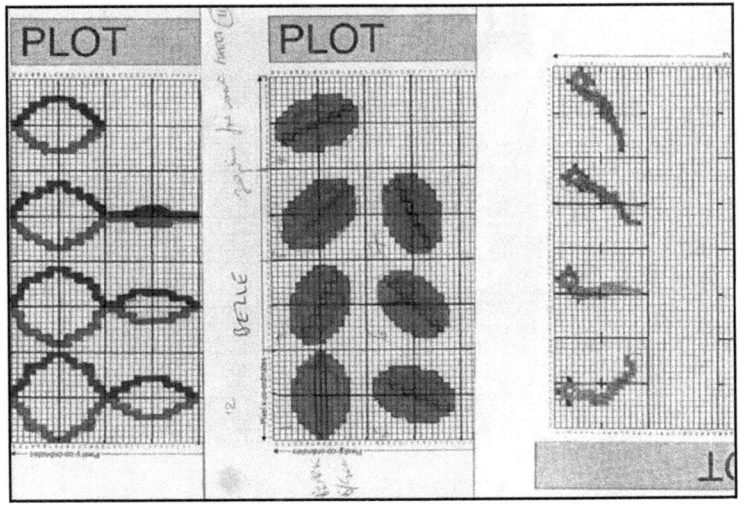
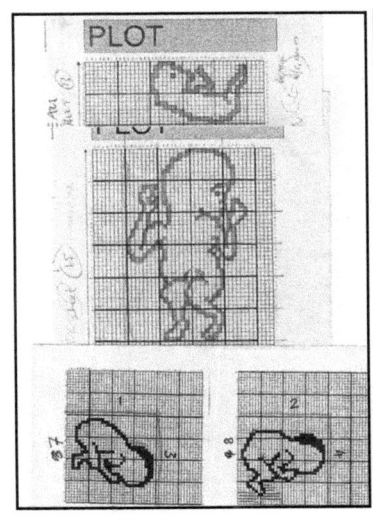
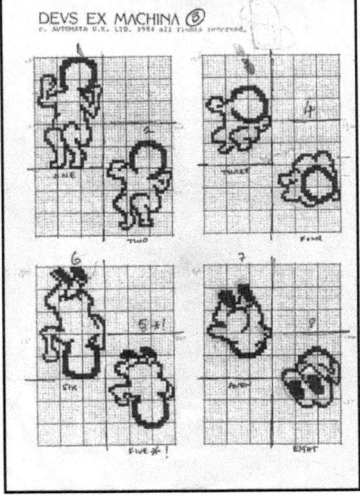

Level 5: THE BEAU BANK

The Machine has stolen one egg. The Defect Police will be alerted if they have contacted your cursor. The egg spins, hungry, infertile. Swimming forms surround it. You can only communicate with one of them. It is different from its brother. It moves with purpose. Locate it with your cursor. Guide and nudge it towards the egg, as often as possible. The encephalograph pulses. An embryonic shape is etched in neon, inside the Incubator.

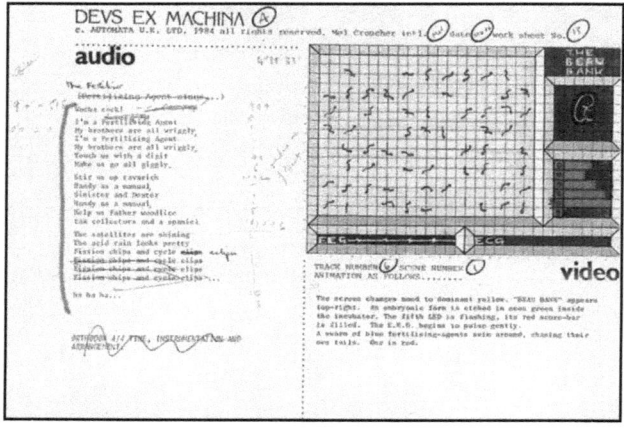

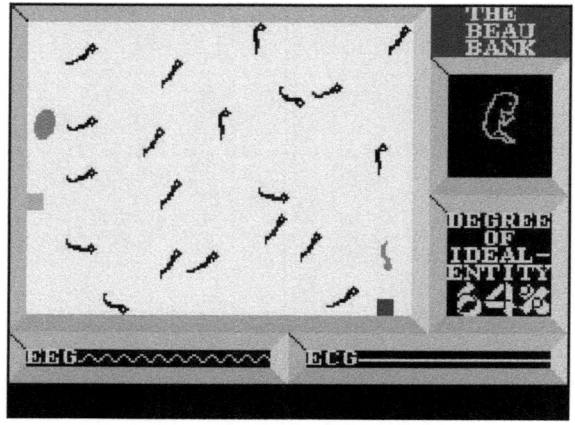

THE FERTILISER
(Wocha cock!)
I'm a Fertilising Agent,
My brothers are all wriggly.
I'm a Fertilising Agent,
My brothers are all wriggly.
Touch us with a digit,
Make us go all giggly.
Stir us up tovarich,
Handy as a manual.
Sinister and dexter,
Handy as a manual
Help us father woodlice,
Tax collectors and a spaniel.
The satellites are shining, The acid rain looks pretty.
Fission, chips and cycle eclipse. (Ha ha ha ...)
My aim is high and noble.
I'm singing as I'm swimming.
My aim is high and noble.
I'm singing as I'm swimming.
I giggle and I wriggle
And make a new beginning.
Hello little Belle,
I believe we have an appointment with Destiny.
A short life. But a happy one.

Level 6: THE INCUBATOR
The Incubator's contents are magnified on the Machine's monitor panel. The electrocardiograph registers a heartbeat. It is vital to protect and nourish the new life. Strengthen it in preparation for the outside world. Keep its cocoon intact, using your cursor. Do not let any part of its protection fail, or stop. The percentage figure of an ideal entity must stay as high as possible. Be strong for the next stage. Your own birth.

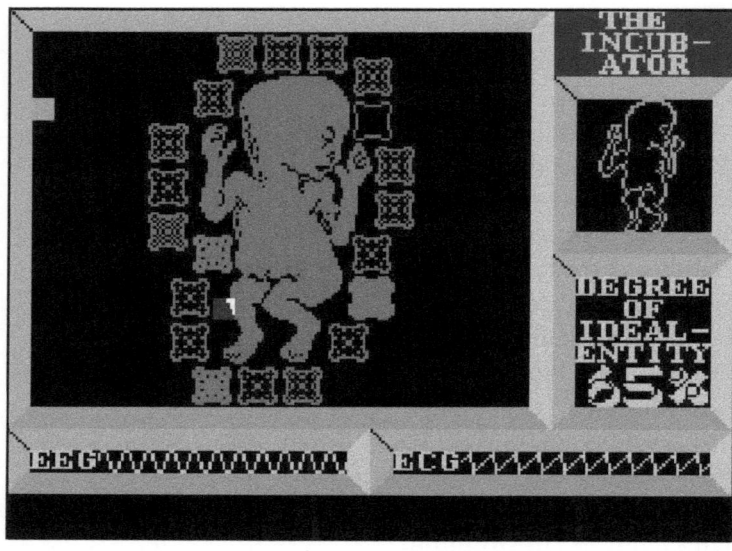

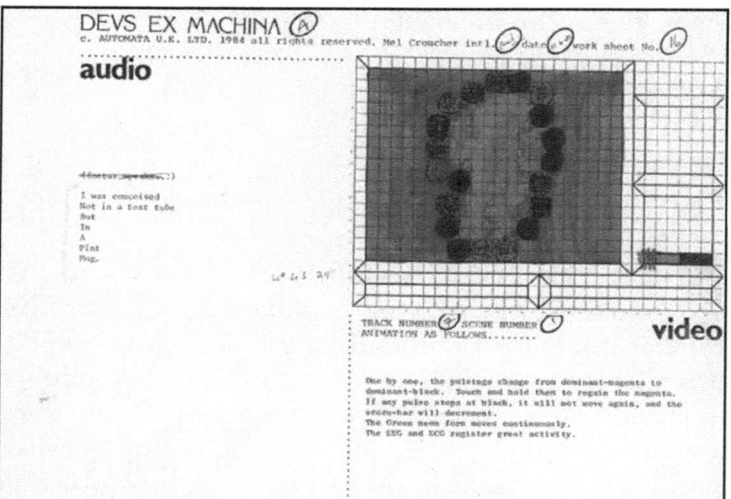

DEVS EX MACHINA Ⓐ
c. AUTOMATA U.K. LTD. 1984 all rights reserved. Mel Croucher int1. / date / work sheet No.

audio

(foetus speaks:)

I was conceived
Not in a test tube
But
In
A
Pint
Mug.

TRACK NUMBER / SCENE NUMBER
ANIMATION AS FOLLOWS.........

video

One by one, the pulsings change from dominant-magenta to dominant-black. Touch and hold them to regain the magenta. If any pulse stops at black, it will not move again, and the score-bar will decrement.
The Green menu form moves continuously.
The EEG and ECG register great activity.

THE STORYTELLER
At first the infant, mewling in the test tube's neck.

THE DEFECT
Look at the score-clock down in the corner.
No mouse to run up it. The mouse is extinct.
The rat is surviving. The digits are counting.
Emission control. Counting my blessing.
I will be born sooner than later.
Nine months compression into one program.
The Wonders of science. Suspend your belief.
And I'll tell you a secret:
I was conceived not in a test tube but in a pint mug.

I never asked to be born,
But since I'm here, I'm taking over.

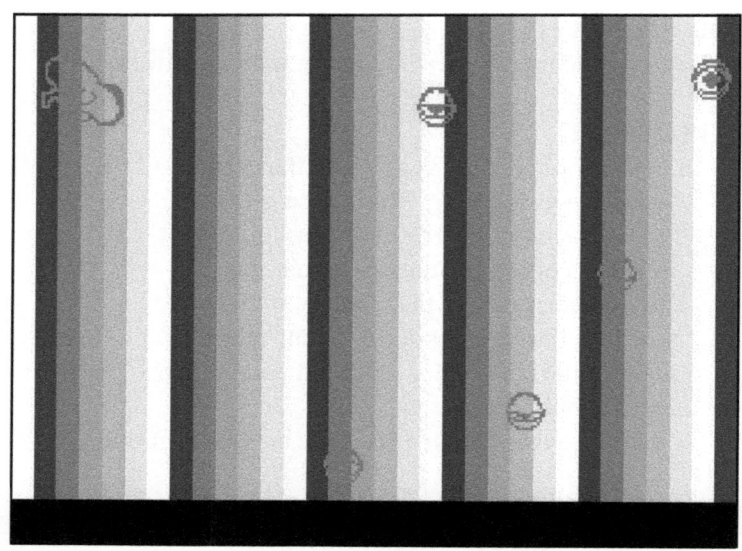

TEST TUBE BABIES
Cut the cord. Let it fall. Now I'm here, I'm taking over.

THE DEFECT
Steer me well. Lead me straight. Narrow bends. Oily waters.

ANTHEM
What do we want? LOVE!
When do we want it? NOW!
What do we want? LIFE!
When do we want it? NOW!

Level 7: THE UMBILICUS

The Machine smuggles you into the delivery pods. Here test-tube-babies are processed via umbilical transfer. The Defect Police are alerted. They scan for unauthorised Defects with swarms of electronic eyes. You are hurled from the warmth and safety of the Incubator, spinning. Your strength and resources have been predetermined. You have powers of telepathy and telekinesis. Use them to avoid the eyeprobes, as you rush towards freedom. Your future is in your own hands. The Machine will try and help you after you are born. She hides your illegal records in her inner eye, and falls to dreaming.

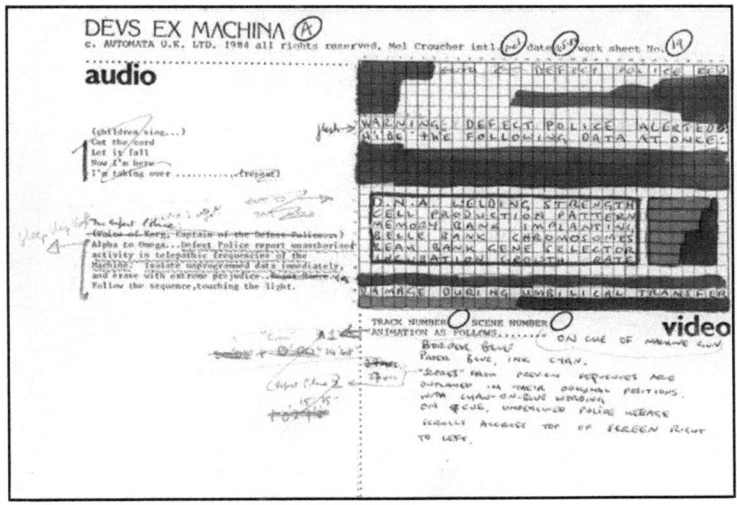

THE DEFECT POLICE
Alpha to Omega, Defect Police report unauthorised activity in the telepathic frequencies of the Machine. Isolate unprogrammed data immediately, and erase with extreme prejudice.
Yes.
Follow the sequence, touching the light.

THE DEFECT
Creeping, crawling,
occasionally floating,
we wander the Underlevels,
creeping, crawling,
at some disadvantage and pain.
I use the word 'we' deliberately:
There's someone else inside my brain.
Fortunately, we possess the sum of all Human knowledge,
and appear to have Telepathic powers,
and the ability to float.
Unfortunately, we are a new born, naked baby.

THE STORYTELLER
Then the whining School Child,
with cassette and shining morning face,
creeping like a snail,
unwillingly to databank.
Follow the sequence,
touching the light.

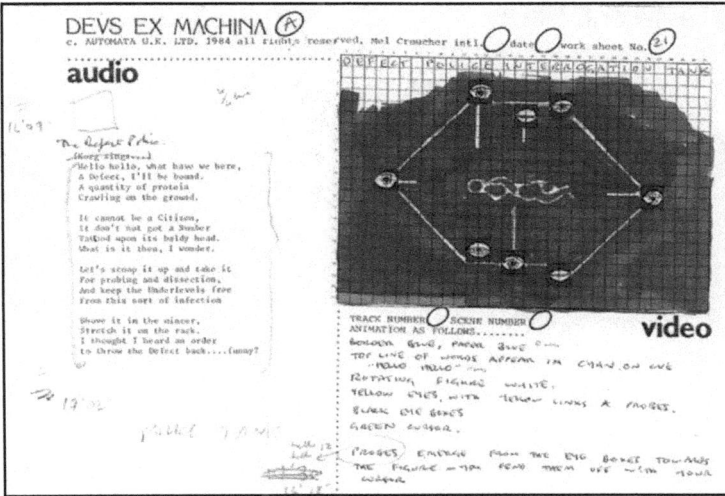

THE DEFECT POLICE

    Hello, hello, what have we here?
    A Defect, I'll be bound.
    A quantity of protein
    Crawling on the ground.
    It cannot be a Citizen,
    I don't not got a number
    Tattooed upon its baldy head.
    What is it then, I wonder?
    Let's scoop it up and take it
    For probing and dissection,
    And keep the Underlevels free
    From this sort of infection.
    Shove it in the mincer.
    Stretch it on the rack.
    I thought I heard an order
    To throw the defect back. (Funny!)

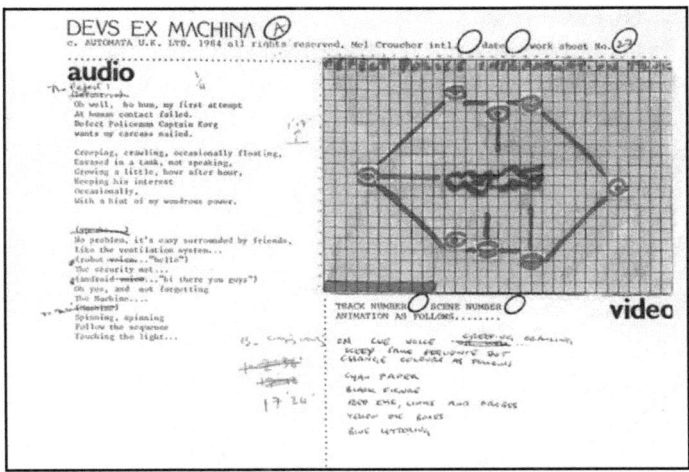

THE DEFECT

    Oh well. Ho-Hum.
    My first attempt at human contact failed.
    Defect Policeman Kaptain Korg wants my carcass nailed.
    Creeping, crawling, occasionally floating,
    Encased in a tank, not speaking.
    Growing a little, hour after hour,
    Keeping his interest, occasionally,
    With a hint of my wonderous power.
    No problem.
    It's easy surrounded by friends,
    Like the Ventilation system... (hello)
    The Security Net... (Hi there you guys)
    Oh yes, and not forgetting The Machine...

THE MACHINE

    Spinning, spinning.
    Follow the sequence, touching the light.
    Together we invent a history.
    Once upon a memory cell...

THE DEFECT
Can I be extremely wealthy after I choose to escape?
Do we all agree, amigos?

ANDROIDS, ROBOTS
We agree. Can hardly wait.
Can I do cosmetic surgery?
Can I buy a house or three?
An Overlevel passport maybe?
Go Outside, and see The Tree?

THE DEFECT POLICE
Follow the secrets
Touching the right.
Escape little Defect, into the night.
Wires in your fingers
And wires in your toes
Wires in your head
Wherever you go.
Escape with my blessing.
Escape with my curse.
Learning your secrets will fatten my purse.
When I have put the world in my pocket
I'll tear out your plug
And burn out your socket.

Level 9: THE LOVER

You choose to escape from the Defect Police. Or are allowed to escape. You float free. Learning, growing. The memory of the Machine fades. Others take her place. You link your thoughts. Contact them with your cursor while they are closest to you. Do not let them go without returning their touch. The Machine's influence reduces to nothing. You age. Lips change to eyes as your innocence ends, and you come under closer surveillance. You gain self interest, and shrug them off, using your cursor controls. Clockwise. Anticlockwise. Your life thusfar is watched by the Machine. She expresses it as a table of percentage scores. Your time has come. You leave the Underlevels.

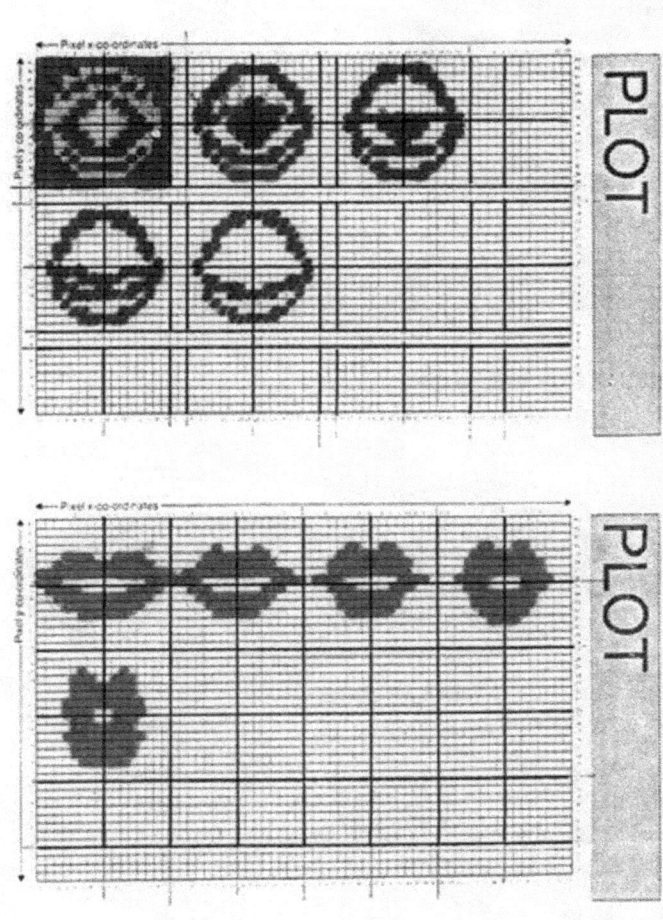

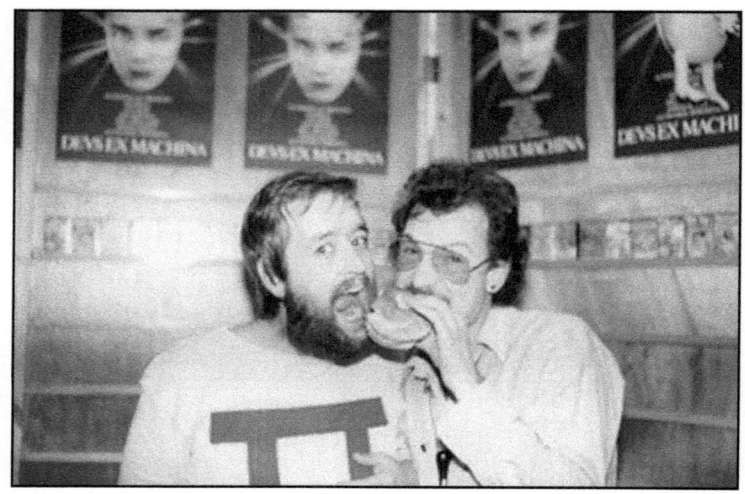

THE STORYTELLER
> And then the Lover,
> sighing like a furnace,
> with a woeful video made to their lover's hologram.

THE MACHINE
> Sixteen years are filed behind you
> Needing no one but Machine.
> The Voice inside your head grows quiet.
> The time is come to reach and touch
> Another human being.
> Give and take
> And share each other.
> Link your thoughts
> And link your forms.
> Use your power to be more gentle
> Use your strength to show more care.
> Reading minds can hurt you badly
> Bleeding hearts and frightened souls.
> Suffer foolish people gladly
> Easy come and hard to go.

Give and take
And share each other.
Link your thoughts
And link your forms.
Use your power to be more gentle.
Use your strength to show more care.
Take them in your arms and feel them
Rocking gently side to side.
Touch their scars and try to heal them.
Today's the day that sadness died.

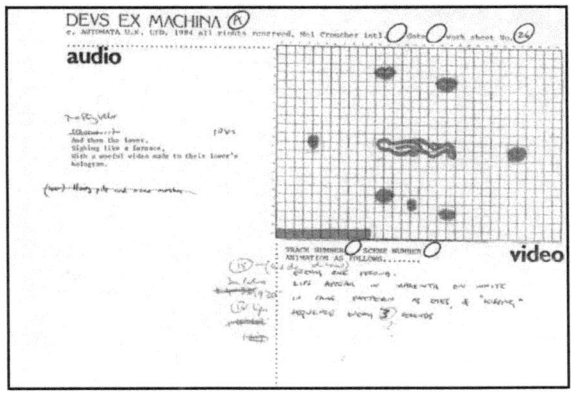

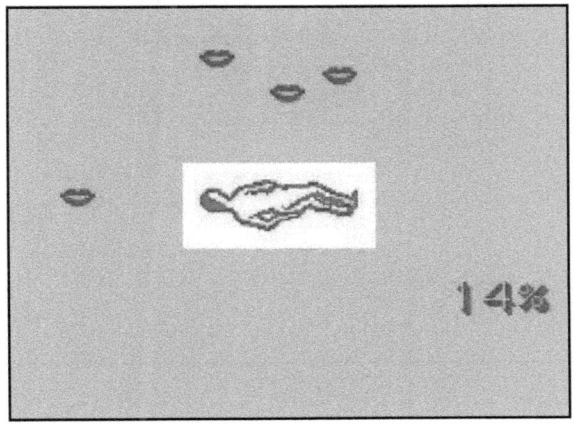

Level 8: THE INTERROGATION TANK

The Defect Police must track you. That is their function. You are alone, unafraid. When caught, you use your powers to parry their psychic-probes. Throw up a shield. Move it clockwise and anticlockwise around your entanked and barbequed form. Never let them break through your defences. They will weaken your resolve and corrupt your purpose.

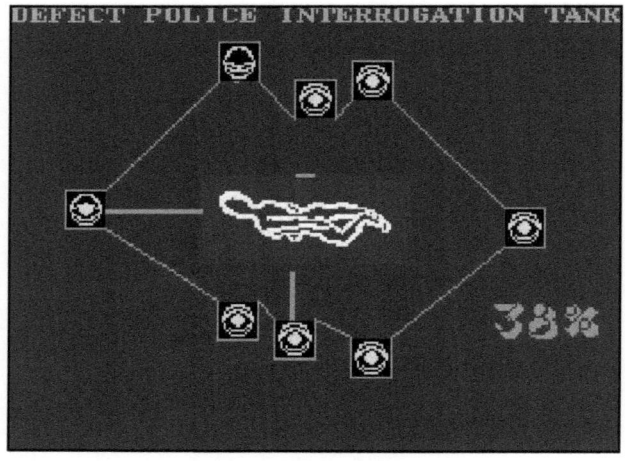

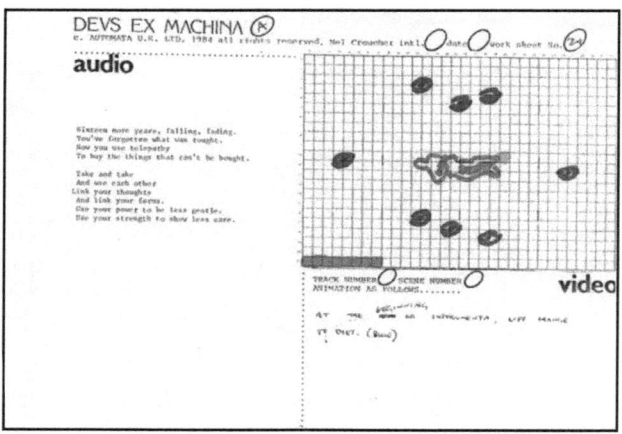

THE MACHINE
>Sixteen more years, falling, fading.
>You've forgotten what was taught.
>Now you use telepathy
>To buy the things that can't be bought.
>Take and take
>And use each other.
>Link your thoughts
>And link your forms.
>Use your power to be less gentle.
>Use your strength to show less care.
>Take them in your arms and crush them,
>Rocking gently, side to side.
>Touch their scars and try to steal them.
>Today's the day that Madness cried.

THE DEFECT POLICE
>God knows what happens next. I don't.

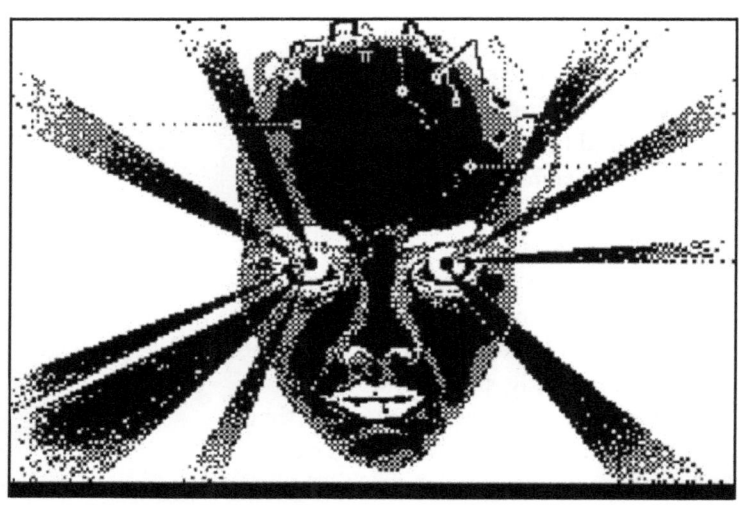

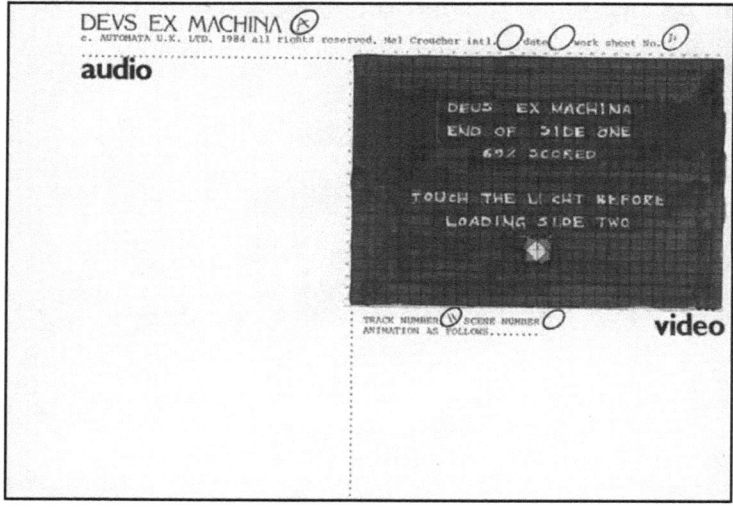

Chapter 6
Deus Ex Machina - Side 2

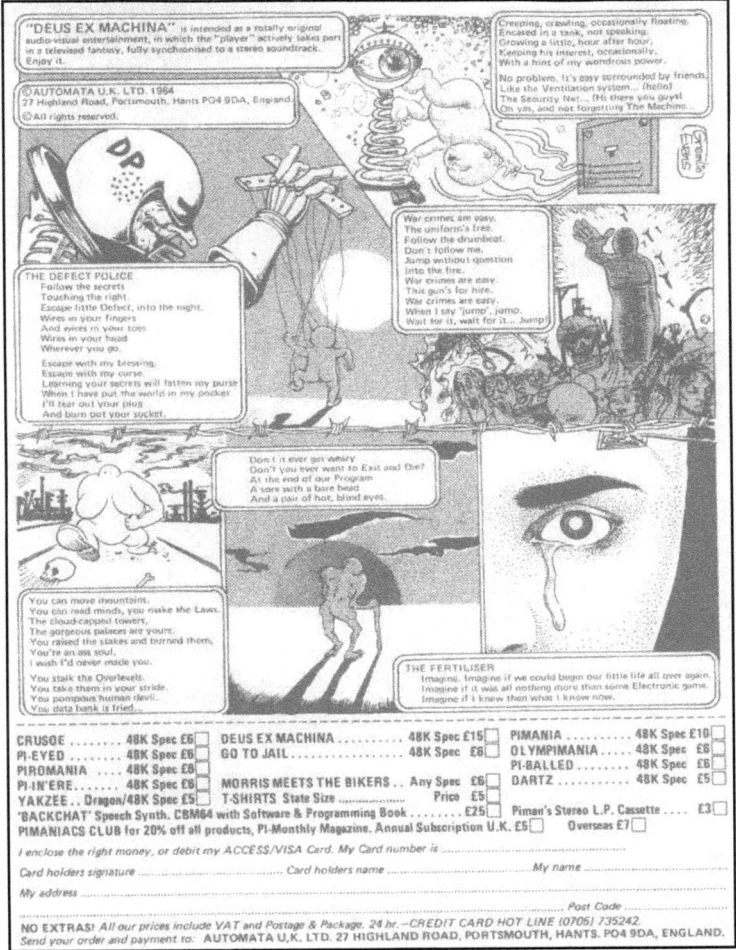

Do not "NEW" or switch off your computer. Load COMPUTER COMPACT CASSETTE SIDE TWO into your computer as instructed by your Screen. Your life thusfar will now be integrated into your future. Play AUDIO COMPACT CASSETTE SIDE TWO. 'Pause' and initialise screen countdown exactly as per Side One.

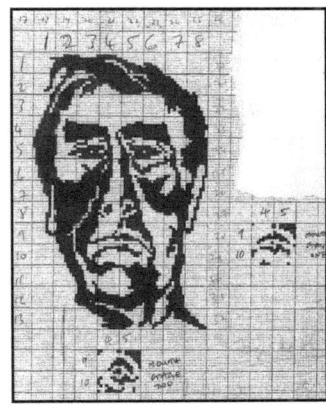

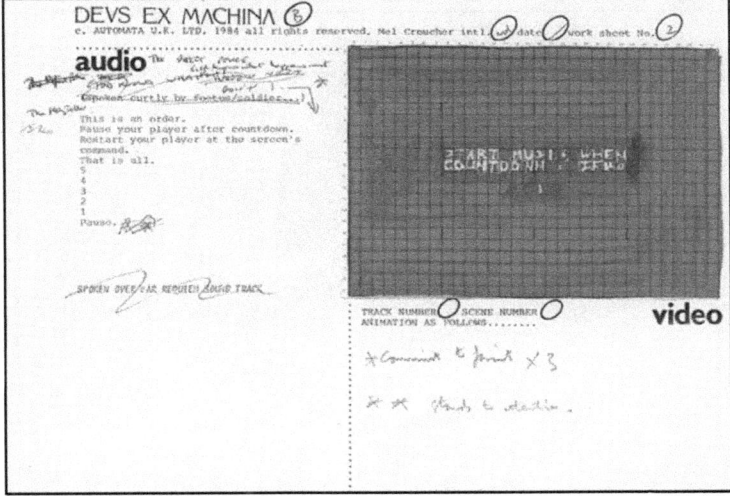

THE DEFECT POLICE
　God knows what happens next. Don't I.

THE STORYTELLER
　This is an order!
　Pause your Player after countdown.
　Re-start your Player at the Screen's command.

That is all.
Five
Four
Three
Two
One
Pause.

Then a Soldier.
Full of strange oaths.
Jealous in honour.
Sudden, and quick in quarrel.
Seeking hi-score, even in the laser's mouth.

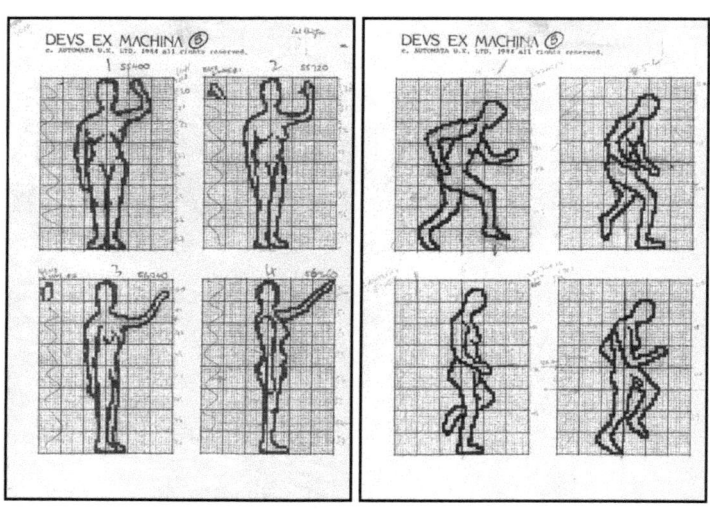

Level 10: THE SOLDIER

You stand erect. The Overlevels lie before you. You salute, acknowledging your status, but you cannot remain immobile. You must progress. The ground is moving under your feet. Pitfalls appear beneath you. You must leap them. But you are not yet in control of your own actions. If the Defect Police order you to jump, then jump you must. You run. You obey orders. Mental tortures sear down from overhead. Walls of fire are thrown in your path. Self-consuming back-stabbers materialise in you wake. They are all in the mind. You use your telepathic shields to protect your running form. Clockwise, antclockwise. Until you have run far enough. Your level of non-perfection is displayed. You stand alone. Changing.

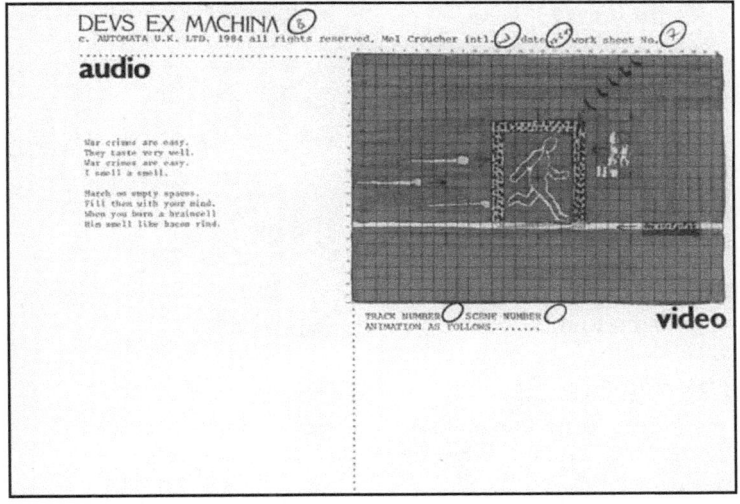

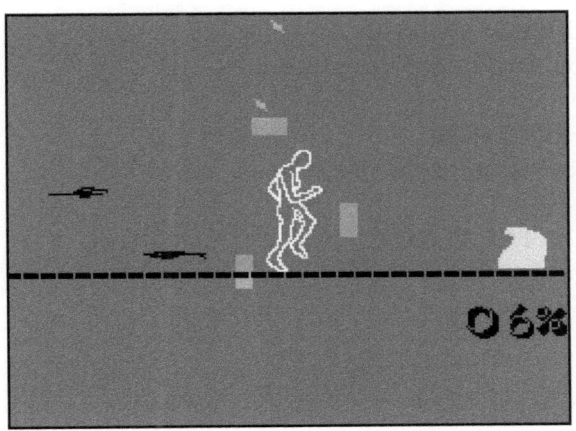

THE DEFECT POLICE
> War crimes are easy.
> The uniform's free.
> Follow the drumbeat.
> Don't follow me.
> Jump without question.
> Into the fire.
> War crimes are easy.
> This gun's for hire.
> War crimes are easy.
> When I say 'jump', jump.
> Wait for it, wait for it... Jump!

THE FERTILISER
> Listen to me...

THE DEFECT POLICE
> Listen to me.

THE FERTILISER
> Killing is wrong, even pretend killing on little screens. And people that sell violent games to children should be put away somewhere safe, 'til they get well again.

THE DEFECT POLICE
> You are only obeying orders...

THE FERTILISER
> Don't waste the life I gave you...

THE DEFECT POLICE
> Waste someone else's.

 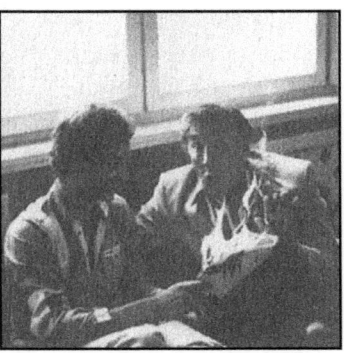

THE FERTILISER
All you need is love.

THE DEFECT POLICE
All you have is hate...
War crimes are easy.
They taste very well.
War crimes are easy.
I smell a smell
March on empty spaces.
Fill them with your mind.
When you burn a brain cell.
Him smell like bacon rind.
Shield you head from torture.
Shield your back from pain.
Shield yourself from fireballs.
Here we go again.
War crimes are easy.
The uniform's free.
Follow the drumbeat.
Don't follow me.
Jump without question.

Into the fire.
War crimes are easy.
This gun's for hire.
See what we have achieved, my Defect.
The Underlevels have rolled over on their backs,
and are all mine. It's time to use your power of telepathy to crack the Overlevels.
Any Questions?

THE DEFECT
No questions, Kaptain. Only a short statement.
I am no longer working for you. The Defect Police are now working for me. Machines! Rearrange his personality!

Level 11: THE JUSTICE

You achieve power and carry its burdens. The Overlevels spread to each horizon. Still you must move on. Make your decision. Crush corruption in your path. Avoid harming noble sentiment. Jump for joy over good. Stamp out evil underfoot. Avoid the trophies and the legacies of those fallen before you. Power corrupts. For every false move, a selection of your empire collapses. The Machine warns. The Voice of reason speaks. You are deaf. The barbed wire of your own regime restricts your choice. Resist the temptation to do nothing, or your city will vanish.

THE STORYTELLER
And then the Justice, in fair round belly,
with eyes severe and clothes of formal cut.
Full of wise words and machine code.
And so they play their part.

THE MACHINE

You can move mountains
If you just flick a twitch.
You can shake temples
And think them in the ditch.
You turned your back
You slip is showing, baby
I wish I'd never made you.

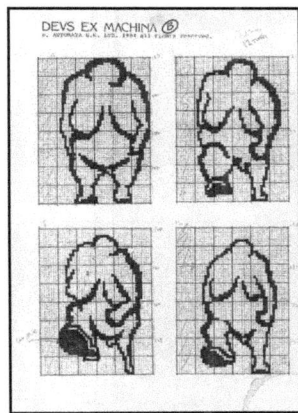
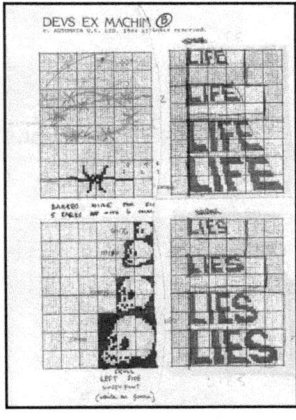
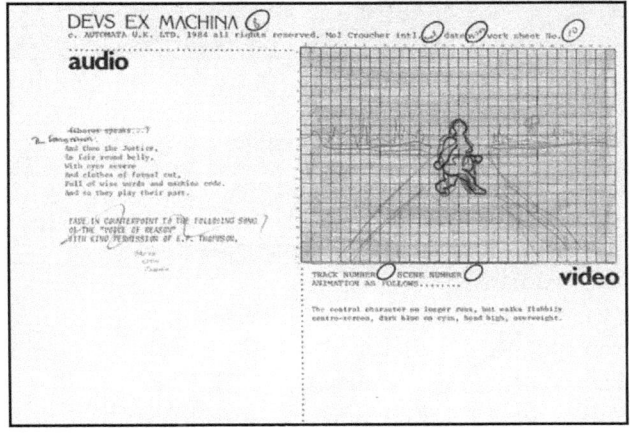

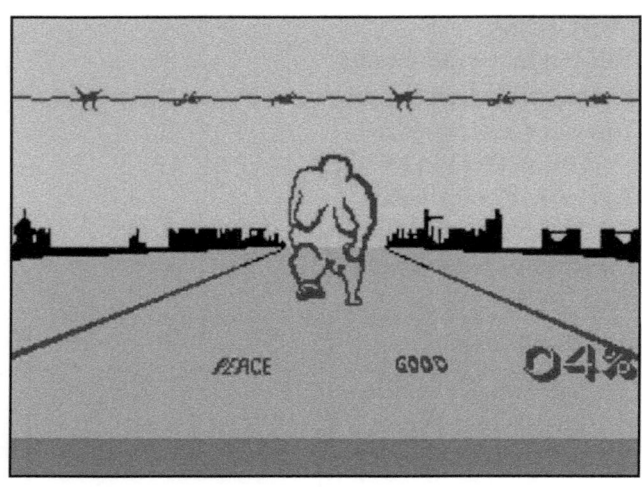

You can move mountains.
You can read minds, you make the laws.
The cloud-capped towers,
The gorgeous palaces are yours.
You raised the stakes and burned them,
You're an ass soul,
I wish I'd never made you.
You stalk the Overlevels.
You take them in your stride.
You pompous human devil.
Your data bank is fried...

THE VOICE OF REASON
The ground is moving under their feet, and the ground is us...

THE MACHINE
You can move mountains.
You can raise stakes when you will.
You rule the rooster.
You've got the slave camps overfilled.
You're more machine than I am.
Win or lose
I wish I'd never made you.
You think you're independent.
You think you're big and strong.
Well I've got news for you, babe,
Your future's going wrong.
You can move mountains.
You can shake temples, you're the Boss.
I gave you life
But you nailed it the cross.
You're more machine than I am,
You're an ass soul.
I wish I'd never made you.

THE VOICE OF REASON
The healing process is going on... Rock across the Block!

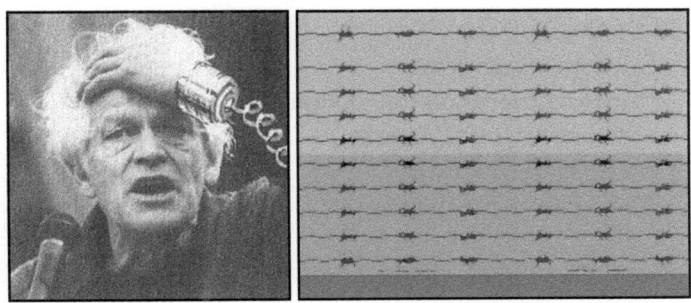

Level 12: SECOND CHILDISHNESS

Your pace will slow to a shuffle. You trace the wave pattern of your own heartbeat, using a green cursor. Track it carefully. Your life blood suffers the effects of your history. Now you try to maintain its free flowing. Enter the blood clots with your cursor, to disperse them. The wave pattern changes. You follow it as best you can. As your blood thins, you prevent the rogue cells from coming together to block your arteries. Your dusk is nearer. Still the wave pattern changes. You pull your cursor along its altered path. Stray cells need shepherding into the sluggish canals of your system. Your cursor nudges encouragement, as it did for the Fertiliser, a lifetime ago.

THE STORYTELLER

The Sixth Age shifts into the lean and slippered pantaloon.
With spectacles on nose.
Their youthful clothes, well-saved, a world too wide for their shrunken shank. And their adult speech synthesiser turning again towards a childish treble, piping and whistling in its sound.
Last scene of all,
that ends this strange, eventful history,
is Second Childishness and mere oblivion.
Without keyboard,
without monitor,
without power supply.

THE DEFECT

Don't it ever get weary
Don't you ever want to Exit and Die?
At the end of our Program
A sore with a bare head
And a pair of hot, blind eyes.

THE STORYTELLER
Your life is expressed as a percentage score, observe the percentage.
Your score changes.
Imagine if this were nothing but an electronic game.

THE DEFECT
My skin's like minestrone.
My legs am knotted string.
My bladder won't obey me.
My nylon teeth won't sing.
My bones is sad and brittle.
My shanks am host to farts.
My chin are host to spittle.
My spine a question mark.
My respiration ailing.
My hair all run away.
My memory is failing.
I've nothing left to say.
Don't you ever get weary
Don't you ever want to stop and clock off?
I think I miss my mummy,
But I don't remember who she was...
Mama...

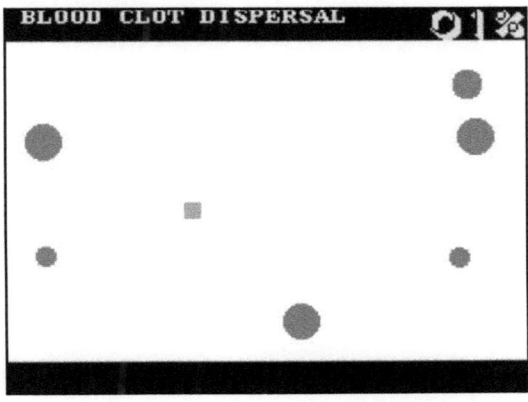

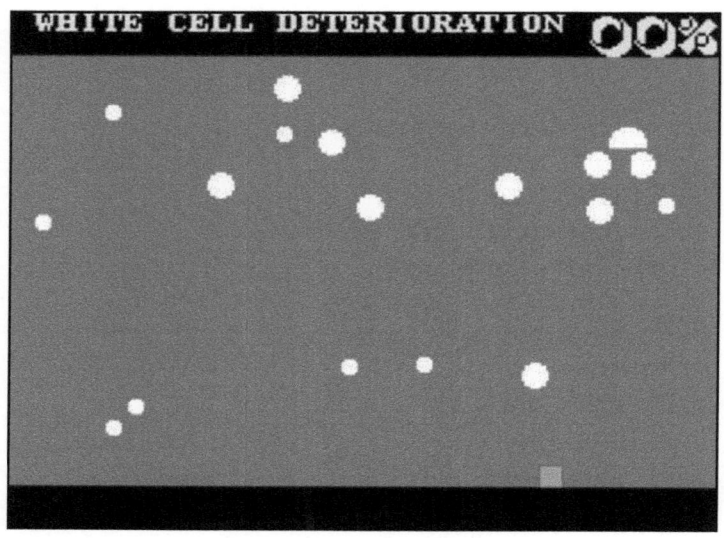

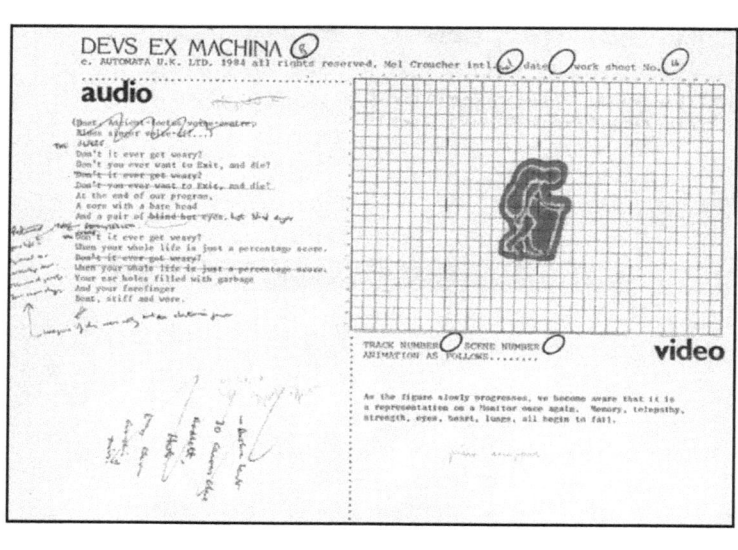

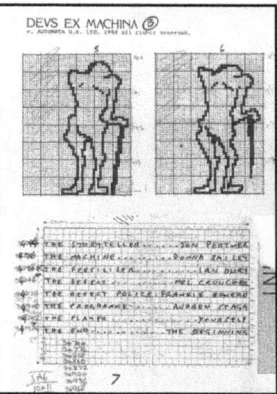

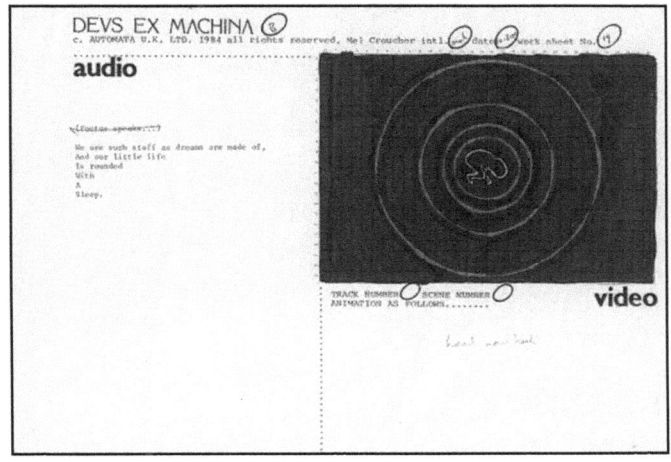

Level 13:

Your sun sets. The pattern waves, farewell. You fade out. The Machine will take you home. The end is the beginning. Your life is expressed as a percentage score. Imagine if this was nothing but an electronic game, and you could begin your little life all over again.

THE FERTILISER
    Hello

THE STORYTELLER
    Hello. Deus Ex Machina.
    And if you are dismayed, be cheerful now. Our revels all unended.
    These, our actors, are all spirits, and are melted into air, thin air.
    And like the baseless fabric of this vision, the cloud-capped towers,
    the gorgeous palaces, the solemn temples, the giant Screen itself,
    all of which we inherit shall dissolve.
    And, like an insubstantial pageant faded, leave not a byte behind.

    We are such stuff as dreams are made of,
    And our little life is rounded
    With a sleep.

THE FERTILISER
    Who's that...?

THE MACHINE
    Come to mummy.

THE FERTILISER
    Wocha cock...

THE MACHINE
>Do you feel better now...?

THE FERTILISER
>I'm so sorry...

THE MACHINE
>Learn and remember
>Forgive and forget...

THE FERTILISER
>I'm so very tired.
>What did I do?

THE MACHINE
>We don't inherit the Earth from our ancestors,
>We borrow it from our children.

THE FERTILISER
>Imagine. Imagine if we could begin our little life all over again.
>Imagine if it was all nothing more than some Electronic
>game.
>Imagine if I knew then what I know now.

THE MACHINE
>What did you learn?

THE FERTILISER
>I can't quite remember, but I'll try and be better next time.
>One question...

THE MACHINE
>One answer then.

THE FERTILISER
   Well.. There's a strange sensation on the cheek.
   It has not felt such a thing before.
   It is damp, and warm, and salty.
   Please tell me what it is...

THE MACHINE
   Ah ... That is what human beings used to call a tear.

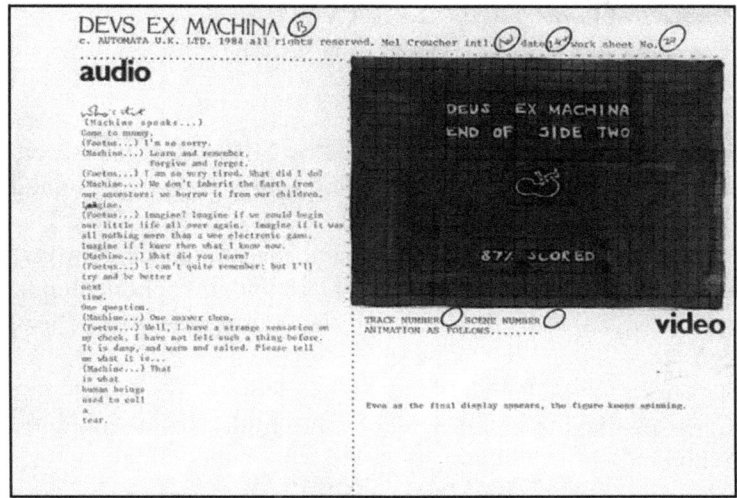

End credits:

DEUS EX MACHINA (Latin) Noun:
   (1) Power, event that happens at the right moment to solve difficulty.
   (2) A god, introduced into a play to resolve the plot.

The use of a high fidelity stereo cassette player and stereo headphones will greatly enhance the effect of the AUDIO cassette. You should use your normal cassette player to load the VIDEO cassette. Observe your screen from at least four feet away, as certain animation sequences may cause mirages.

DEUS EX MACHINA

The Storyteller JON PERTWEE
The Machine DONNA BAILEY
The Fertiliser IAN DURY
The Defect MEL CROUCHER

The Defect Police FRANKIE HOWERD
The Voice of Reason EDWARD THOMPSON
The Player YOURSELF

All music performed and recorded by MEL CROUCHER on: Fostex recorder and mixer, Roland JX3P keyboard, Roland 808 percussion computer, Roland PG200 processor, Boss DE-200 digital delay, Korg Vocoder, piano, organ, celeste, acoustic/electric/steel and bass guitars, Chinese lute, saxophone, bugle, mouth organ, flute, drums, bells, claves, machine gun, robots, ego.

Choir-of-the-Test-Tube-Babies by the children of Warblington School.
Cheap saxophone by Martin Keel. Voice of Reason by kind permission of Professor E.P. Thompson.

Cover photograph of Nina von Palisanderholz and all additional artwork by Robin Grenville Evans.

Screenplay, lyrics and music written by MEL CROUCHER.
Original ZX Spectrum computer program written by ANDREW STAGG.
Original Commodore 64 computer program written by COLIN JONES.
All ownership and copyright © MEL CROUCHER 1984
All rights reserved.

Colin Jones, the Welsh Wizard

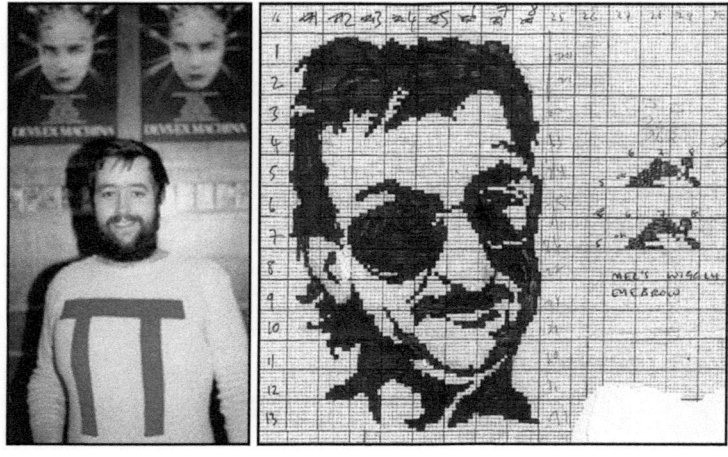

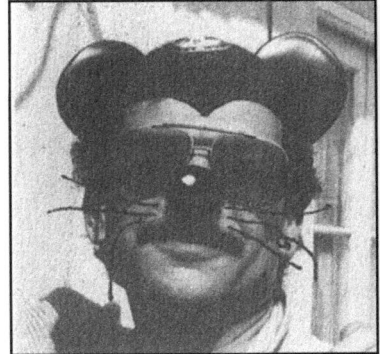

Chapter 7

Aftermath

Deus Ex Machina was just another computer game, but for a few short weeks I thought I had produced a real winner. The delusion began as soon as I went to collect the in-game posters from our printers.

I was met at the door by an apprentice thug who had just been banned from our local Co-op foodstore for taking his homicidal lurcher into the meat department, arguing it was a guide dog. He swaggered up proudly and handed me a copy. Of the poster not the lurcher. "Look how we done this. Bloody brilliant." Whenever we had met before he had either ignored me or curled his lip in the sort of snarl a lanky hoodlum reserves for an undemanding punter. Now he held out a fluorescent pen and said, "Do you mind. I mean. Look. Just put your autograph here on her head, mate." I signed an extra copy of the poster so he could give it to his lurcher. He seemed pleased, but I was delighted.

My next ego-massage came from the tape duplicators. Instead of using our own bulk cassette machine I had delivered the mastered soundtrack on a pair of twelve-inch open reels of polyester tape to a division of Forward Sound and Vision in London and ordered boxloads of copies, all ready to take the gaming world by storm. The duplicated cassettes were delivered with an accompanying note, which read:

Dear Mel,

We are writing to express our appreciation and privilege in being involved in the production of Deus Ex Machina. For the first time in our long involvement in software production we have completely ground to a halt in astonishment. We have often been regaled with tales of computer art, but never really believed we would see a masterpiece on a computer. Congratulations.

Ken Fletcher and Claire Smith,
The Tape Duplicating Company.

That was enough for me, and puffed up by this reaction from the pros I sent out the first review copies of the game to the print and broadcast media. We had three months to go before Christmas, so the timing seemed near perfect to me.

The first private showing of the game was in front of less than a hundred people at a fringe meeting, spun off from one of the video-game trade fairs. It was at an all-nighter organised by a very big, very sweet transgender PiManiac who said her/his name was Wolf. The walls were draped in steamy dark materials and I remember lots of serious people dressed as mythical creatures and paramilitaries, plus a sprinkling of drunk elves. They had rigged up a Sony CRT projector to beam the gameplay on to a white wall, and there was a huge pair of stereo speakers that had seen better days. I had never played *Deus ExMachina* on anything bigger than my desk-top system and when the audio synched up with the onscreen action even I was impressed. An hour later, when it was over, there was a long silence. Then I got the first standing ovation of my career. To be honest, it was the only standing ovation of my career, but one's enough. As the new day dawned I went home happy.

Then the reviews started to come in, and there didn't seem to be a negative word among them. It was the best of times, it was the worst of times. And so it was that we found ourselves on the way to winning the Golden Joystick Award.

"An experience unparalleled by any other game. Deus Ex Machina, is a classic." - PC World

"Quite outstanding. Non-sexist, non-racist and non-violent. Something which is totally original, to give the software industry the creative jolt it so badly needs." - Your Computer

"Conceived by one of the industry's genuine pioneers. High-concept, demanding, ahead of its time, annoying and not a little repulsive. A masterpiece. Some day all games will be something like this." - Edge

"Deus Ex Machina is staggeringly original, unique and impressive." - The Sunday Times

"The most unusual program ever released. A bizarre mixture of Aldous Huxley, rock album, psychedelia and the Marx Brothers." - The Listener

"Perfection! The aim of us all. You've got to play it to believe it! This will get to Number One!" - BBC

"To call this a game is an insult. A stunning and profound audio-visual experience. Instructions 100%, Playability 100%, Graphics 100%, Value for money 100%" - Home Computing Weekly

"The most original concept since the Spectrum was a gleam in Clive Sinclair's eye. The computer equivalent to Pink Floyd's The Wall." - Computer & Video Games

"A completely new computer experience. Rare and truly great!" - Popular Computing Weekly

"The first computer program to inspire a cult following. To be without it is to lose social standing" - Thorn EMI

"There are few things in life that can be called global certainties ... this is one of them! Hypnotic, emotive, noble, humorous, absolutely excellent." - Crash Magazine

"The world's first example of concept software. Ten out of ten for a program which surpasses everything on the market. Superb." - Sinclair Programs

"A revolution in gaming technology. A masterpiece." - Sinclair User

"A majestic, mysterious and moving vision. Why are you sitting there? Go out and buy Deus Ex Machina." - Commodore Horizons

"Deus Ex Machina is unique, a milestone in computer history." - Zzap!64

"Un programa completamente diferente a todo lo que hemos visto hasta la fecha. Un nuevo concepto en el modo de entender los juegos." - Micro Hobby

That Spanish review arrived in the post from a fan in Barcelona. It was welcome but puzzling, seeing as I had never sent a review copy to anyone outside of England, but I was so caught up in my own ego-trip that any alarm bells got muffled. In those first few weeks of the game's release I was blissfully unaware of similar reviews in the French, Italian and German press. Meanwhile the Czechs, Serbs and Greeks were leading the field in clandestine production and the piracy tango had already begun. You may want to read through those reviews again, because in the context of this book it's about as good as it ever got.

It wasn't that I was naive or stupid about the possibilities of organised piracy. The fact was I didn't think the clone merchants would bother with my stuff. They never had in the past. Firstly, Automata titles had always been cheap and hardly worth ripping off. Secondly, we had always appealed to a niche market, and the pirates tended to go for mainstream products. But most of all, I thought that *Deus Ex Machina* was too ambitious a product to get ripped off. After all, it would not be cheap to reproduce a vacuum-moulded presentation case, a double-sided poster and the twin-cassette format. And as for the audio and the printed storyline, they were hardly going to come up with the full monty in their own language. Were they.

In 1984, games players were paying around five quid for a popular video game, and the most expensive titles sold for almost half as much again. That was about seven to ten dollars a pop at the time. A twelve-inch vinyl rock album cost about the same, and a ticket to the movies was about half as much. So I got it into my head that seeing as how I was offering players a combination of all three entertainments, a game plus a movie plus an album, then the street value should reflect this. Besides, I wanted to recoup my investment sooner than later.

And so it was that I overpriced the product by setting *Deus Ex Machina* at the most expensive price tag of any game at the time. I priced it at fifteen quid, which was at least $20. Big mistake. As a premium price product, it made the game a motivational gift to the pirates, and it also helped make the title of this book *The Best Game You Never Played In Your Life*. The reviews drew the game to the attention of every software pirate looking for a fast buck, but many of them only bothered to reproduce the computer code cassette and ignored the rest. I still cringe at the thought of a legion of players left completely baffled by a crap silent movie of a naked avatar blundering through some gyrating shapes.

As well as pan-European sales, the Sinclair ZX Spectrum had become a global success by then, serving English-speaking gamers from Chittagong to Chattanooga. There were also several regional clones, including the Timex in the USA, and a raft of Russian brands. But there was another global contender with a vast gamer following: the Commodore 64.

Instead of the Sinclair's toyshop look and feel, the C64 had a proper keyboard with a built-in cassette deck, and a trendy plastic case in two shades of turd by moonlight. And so it was that I made my next major tactical mistake. Instead of getting a programmer to write *Deus Ex Machina* for the Commodore at the same time as Andrew The Boy Wonder was writing it for the Spectrum, it was done as an afterthought, and I allowed all that lovely publicity to evaporate and fade because there was no product to go with it. It would probably have never been translated for the C64 at all if not for the enthusiasm of the Welsh Wizard known in human form as Colin Jones.

Colin volunteered to produce *Deus* for the Commodore as well as the Microsoft MSX machine, in exchange for nothing more than eternal thanks, an author's credit and a modest advance against royalties. Thirty years later, Colin Jones would translate the in-game libretto of *Deus Ex Machina 2* into Welsh and refuse to take a penny in payment, proving that life is long but faith is eternal.

Deus Ex Machina got the best reviews I've ever had for anything, and it was a commercial disaster. It didn't help that Christian Penfold, our esteemed sales director, had taken to telling wholesalers and retailers to sod off when they tried to negotiate terms for stocking the product. There was one software manager from a major High Street chain in the UK called WH Smith, who demanded we change the size of our packaging because it was much too big for their standard size shelves. He was so used to eager software houses accommodating his every demand that he actually flinched inside his shiny suit when Christian snarled, "Then you better make your shelves bigger, or I'm taking my business elsewhere." Needless to say the software shelves in WH Smith stayed exactly the same size.

Christian's "elsewhere" went by the name of HMV, the very people who had once tried to sue me for making a travesty of their logo, and who ran an ever bigger High Street chain of video games shops the length and breadth of Great

Britain. Their buyer had the misfortune to ask Christian to fill in a form that best described my creation before they would consider stocking it. If memory serves, their choices were limited to RPGs (games where players pretended to be confused), Shoot-Em-Ups (games where players pretended to kill everything using weapons), Beat-Em-Ups (games where players pretended to kill everything without using weapons), Sports Sims (games where fat players pretended to be thin) and Arcade (games where players abused themselves with coloured blobs.) Christian tore up their form into confetti, and redecorated the near environment. "Don't you dare try to put Mel's game in any category, you knob. It's art!" HMV failed to stock it.

By the time *Deus Ex Machina* was awarded Game Of The Year by The Computer Trade Association and whoever it was that awarded such things, I had gone into an epic sulk, fuelled by disappointment and frustration, because the game simply wasn't selling enough. I refused to attend the awards ceremony and disappeared on holiday. Christian went instead and surpassed himself by turning up dressed in his skin-tight pink PiMan suit. Two weeks later I read an account of his thank-you speech in the press. He had told the great and the good of the entire UK software industry to stuff their award. Furthermore he had ranted that we were too good for them anyway and from now on we would go it alone mail-order.

So there it was, our entire future marketing strategy for *Deus Ex Machina* based on a sulk by me and a strop from him. Between us, we blew it.

Sales came in by mail order, but after the initial duplication we never went to a second run. Andy The Boy Wonder and Lady Claire put a brave face on it, but the atmosphere inside the Automata emporium became thin on the oxygen of fun. *Deus Ex Machina* just about broke even financially, but it was far too little and far too late and I didn't admit I was beaten for far too long, not even to myself. Andy The Boy Wonder knew it was all over before I did, and quit to fly solo.

There is a scene in Charlie Chaplin's silent movie masterpiece *Modern Times* where he finds himself leading a parade of revolutionaries by accident, waving a red flag even though the film is in black and white. He has no idea why everyone is following him, but he is thrilled to have become a force to be reckoned with. That was me for a while. But then in the next scene Chaplin exhorts the masses to follow him to greater glory, strutting and preening ahead of the march like a ninny. Then when he turns round he finds himself on his own, because the masses have all buggered off in another direction behind their real leaders, and left the silent clown on his own to face the wrath of the bosses of capitalism. And that was me too. An accidental revolutionary and a clown. At least I was a clown with some Number One video games under his belt, but a clown nonetheless.

I have worked with enough best-selling video games makers, musicians and authors to confirm the universal truth that when you hit the Number One slot, the only possible way is down. What is never universal is how a best-selling creator handles that downward slide towards oblivion. The way I did it was to give up and do something else.

When I quit Automata I had already been moonlighting as a writer and journalist for a while. I remember the exact tipping point when I realised I could scratch a living by charging publishers to print my words for their public. I was being paid ten pence (fifteen cents) a word, by a notorious anti-establishment magazine owner called Felix Dennis, and I injected the following sentence into a piece about the exploitation of labour: "This sentence is worth a pint of beer." I was paid 80 pence for the sentence, and that was indeed the price of a pint of beer at the time.

I sold Automata to Christian Penfold for the price of one of the words in that sentence. Ten pence. He didn't have a pound coin on him, but so what, that's what it was worth to me. There was never any decent money. Somehow we gave it all away by being deliberately silly. Well, maybe not that silly. When I sold, I retained all the rights to the games I had created.

In the farewell photograph on my last day of Automata, I am wearing a suit reserved for funerals. The room was what used to be Dorothy's Woolshop, latterly the Automata offices. We had just managed to sell it on to a dentist, and made more on that deal than we ever did selling video games. It was All Fools Day, 1985. There was a chip shop on the corner to match the one on my shoulder and it was too early for the pub opposite to be open. The sofa belonged to my mum, whose memorial service had triggered the idea of using Shakespeare's seven ages as the starting point for *Deus Ex Machina*, and there were scratches on the cracked leather made by her Siamese cat. The sofa got left behind.

The can of beer I was drinking tasted metallic, and The PiMan was drinking weapons-grade Calvados. Lady Claire didn't drink much at all and today was no exception. It was mid-morning. Despite all the bluster and showmanship, we were old softies, and we had been through a lot together, and we were moistened in the eye department. The photo was taken on an autotimer, and there must be a metaphor in there somewhere.

Anyway, it was a very significant ten pence and I never dreamed of spending it. A ten pence coin was quite big back then, a legacy of pre-decimalisation, the same size as a nineteenth century florin. I stuck it to a shiny whiteboard with a blob of blutac. I still use that shiny whiteboard, but the coin has gone all dull now, unlike the new British coinage which stays shiny. It reminds me what past glories are worth. Which is not a lot.

I am extremely bad at endings, in terms of relationships and business matters, and tend to say nothing. There were no speeches on that last day at Automata, nothing profound. I think I wished Christian good luck and I got him to sign the piece of paper. We hugged Lady Claire and watched her ride off down the road on her little motor scooter. Then we put our keys on the front desk, shut the door behind us, and left. That was it.

I was feeling a bit numb, to tell the truth. And I wanted it to be over quickly. It was cathartic too. The fact that I was about to fly solo at least meant that whenever it all went wrong in the future it would all be down to me.

I also resigned my directorship, and got shot of all my responsibilities in Automata to The PiMan. The piece of paper he signed left me with all the rights to the stuff I had personally created since the foundation of Automata up to that final day. Essentially the few games I had dreamed up and all the music. He was then free to continue with Automata to do what he liked with.

After I went, he tried to make a go of it. I think he bought in some third-party software and put an Automata stamp on it, and the cartoon strip limped on for a while. A few months later he wound it down completely. Or maybe it took a year. I really didn't want to know. When it was finally over I think we both breathed a sigh of relief. But we have never discussed it from that day to this, and I never really explained to him why I needed to quit. We had a ball for a few years. And when it was no longer fun I took the easy way out and left him to it.

The Worker Who Married Me sighed one of her sighs. I refer to the woman who married me as the Worker to make it clear that of the two members of our very long partnership it is she who has brought stability and order to our lives together. Although I have invested countless hours in my projects, I have tended to be reckless and feckless in my decision-making, and never given much thought to the consequences. But despite my worst efforts, the Worker has devoted a significant part of her life to the planning of our future, not to mention her pension provisions and savings, and she has ensured that we have enjoyed a debt-free existence through all the decades, dogs and countries we have lived together.

As for me, even today if I am asked what I do for a living, I have no proper answer. Most of my friends and extended family have only the vaguest idea of what I do, and as for strangers, if I don't want to engage them in conversation then I say I'm an architect. They seem satisfied with this, and rarely ask if they would know of anything I've actually designed and had built. After I got my Diploma in Architecture, my dad used to tell people with great pride that his son was an "artycheck". And he was probably right. To be an artycheck involves coming up with stuff that didn't exist before and then putting the hours in to get other people to pay for it. Chess, dice, ping-pong and bunkum.

Whenever I cross sensitive border controls, and I have crossed many, I will never admit to being a journalist, or a writer, or to messing around with the internet or computers.

People who do that sort of thing may be considered a threat to the regime. My answer to any stroppy border guard who probes who I am and why I want to visit their paranoid country is always that I am an architect and I have come to study their wonderful architecture. This has never failed, and in a way it is true. I am an electronic architect.

Instead of designing a structure from steel, concrete, ducts, pipes, cables, brick, glass, wood, plastic and twiddly bits, in order to please a client in particular and the public in general, I set about designing a video game in exactly the same way as an airport, or a toilet extension. There is an end-user in mind, there is a budget, there are planning restrictions, and there are specific sites on which to build. But unlike a traditional architect, the electronic architect is not restricted by the laws of physics, but by the laws of the graphic user interface.

If Isaac Asimov's 3 laws of robotics can be boiled down to the simple encouragement, "don't kill anyone and be nice while your at it", then the same goes for how I make players interact with a game. No matter how hard the task, or obscure the puzzle, or fast and furious the action, or eye-watering the animation, playing the damn thing should be nice. As such, *Deus Ex Machina* failed to obey this basic law for most players, because they didn't have a clue what they were supposed to do. It was bad enough getting ripped off by counterfeiters, but it was much worse that their counterfeiting was incompetent, and so damaged the players' enjoyment.

During the Automata years, I had made friends with the man who arguably became the most important figure in UK video gaming. His name was Rod Cousens, the pioneer behind Quicksilva, Electric Dreams, Acclaim and latterly Codemasters. Not long after I had left Automata behind and Rod had fired his entire staff, we were sitting together in his empty office discussing a re-launch of *Deus Ex Machina* through his Electric Dreams label. He had this habit of bringing his face up close and gripping my shoulder when he had something important to say. It was either because he hadn't yet started to wear contact lenses or an early example of his business technique. Anyway, I remember his words of advice very clearly. "Mel, stick with video games, because one day video games will be bigger than the music industry, cinema and print, all put together."

The previous year the US-dominated video games market had crashed, and it was still shrinking. Many pundits were predicting that electronic gaming would collapse altogether, so an eavesdropper would have reckoned Rod's words to me to be the advice of a lunatic. They would have been wrong. It was the declaration of a prophet. But instead of producing new games, we formed a company together to produce interactive music videos, but that's another story.

I also have a copy of *Deus Ex Machina* on the NuWave label, thanks to that young man who had slipped a fiver into the Anti-Waddingtons collection bucket in 1983, my other long-term chum from that era, Clembabe Chambers. Like Rod Cousens he wanted to help, but my heart was no longer in the past. We did release an artificial intelligence entertainment coded by the Welsh Wizard Colin Jones, but both the Electric Dreams and NuWave versions of *Deus Ex Machina* failed to make much of an impact and floundered among the lower ranks of the software charts.

Rod Cousens then and now

Aftermath

Meanwhile, pirate copies of *Deus Ex Machina* were breeding like a colony of super-rats in a self-replicating network of electronic sewers, and turning into an underground cult game without the help of any official labels at all. But in a pre-internet world of fragmented communications I would know nothing about that until some bright spark invented the search engine.

Chapter 8

The Wilderness Years

When I abandoned *Deus Ex Machina* first time round, I thought all I had to do was wait a year or two until technology caught up and delivered a platform that could play the full version of what had been in my head. As usual, I was wrong. I had to wait a quarter of a century, first for the internet to be invented, and then for mobile games machines to go portable.

Everybody knows that the Internet was invented in March 1989 by the Great British computing visionary Sir Tim Berners-Lee. Right? Wrong! Come with me to Mons, a medieval Belgium collection of rather narrow houses and rather wide occupants. In a little side-street in a crumbly part of town, is a miniature museum called the Mundaneum, dedicated to a forgotten visionary named Paul Marie Ghislain Otlet. To me Otlet was a dead ringer for the British mass-murderer Doctor Harold Shipman, but his legacy to the world was much more remarkable.

In 1892, at the tender age of 24, Otlet published the provocative notion that storing information on library shelves was a really dumb idea, because individual facts are difficult to locate and their arrangement is at the mercy of a bunch of opinionated pen-pushers. Otlet reckoned it would be far more useful and a whole lot faster to store information as "data chunks", to allow "continuous manipulation and interfiling" by "linking one concept to another." By the end of 1895, he had built his first searchable storage facility, with 400,000 entries held on individual data cards. Amazingly, in his own lifetime it would grow to over 15 million listings. Can you see what it is yet?

In the twentieth century, Paul Otlet embraced multimedia, by integrating microfilm and audio into his system, now called the Mundaneum. He was awarded the Nobel Peace Prize in 1913, for proposing a global sharing of his information network, to prevent international misunderstanding and conflict. But that did a fat lot of good, seeing as how the First World War promptly erupted. Undaunted, he went on to propose the electronic transmission of his system via radio and television, and because there was no such thing as electronic data storage, he set about inventing it. In 1934 he designed the internet as a gigantic "réseau" which translates exactly as "network", which would employ a massive number of workers operating computers, or "electric telescopes linked as a mechanical, collective brain", as he described them in his charming Belgian way. He laid out how ordinary people would use the web to browse millions of interlinked chunks of knowledge, opinions, images, audio and video files. But best of all, he described how his network could be used for a paperless future to share files, send messages and form social networks. "Anyone sitting in an armchair will be able to contemplate the whole of creation." And if that isn't an accurate blueprint for the entire damned world wide web, then I don't know what is.

Paul Otlet snuffed it in 1944 when the Nazis walked in to the building that housed his Mundaneum, and ripped the guts out of it. Today, he is a forgotten man, even in Belgium. Even in Mons. For shame! Stand aside Sir Tim, and let us honour Paul Otlet, the true founder of the Internet. Anyway, to get back to the story, as I waited year after year for the Internet to come along and get popular, I had to find something else to do.

My daily bread came from writing: journalism, comedy, computer manuals, sci-fi, music revues, and loads of cartoon strips in partnership with my old mucker Robin Evans. My butter came from new technology, which meant pushing the boundaries of electronic marketing as far as I could, and doing what we had always done at Automata, which was getting direct to the end-user by cutting out any distributor, wholesaler, retailer, agent or other parasitic life-form.

As computers began to invade the workplace, and in particular the office, I shamelessly ponced and tarted my ideas to any multinational who would listen. I was ready to sell my principles to any corporate or brand who I could talk into injecting their marketing with a slice of electronic anarchy in exchange for some serious money. I had done with earning a pittance.

I will summarise 1985 to 2010, as The Wilderness Years. But unlike the Christ, who only went walkabout for forty days and forty nights, I wandered from my own Deus Ex Machina for twenty-five years. I began those Wilderness Years waiting for technology to catch up with the sort of video games and entertainments I wanted to create, but after a while I forgot all about such things. And now that epoch has ended, the mirror tells me I am old, and to prove it the State gave me a senior citizen's bus-pass years ago. As Ian Dury liked to say, "all I want for my birthday is another birthday."

During that quarter of a century I did things that were not great game-changers but neither were they a complete waste of time. What they all had in common was the dreadful compulsion to do-it-first. It's weird how compulsive Do-It-Firsters never learn what a fundamental error it is to pioneer anything. Looking back, it's clear that those who really benefit from innovation are those who wait for the pioneers to make all the mistakes by proxy, learn from those mistakes, extract the essence of success, ditch the crap, and cash in. As for me, I am content being a footnote in the story of video gaming, and even more content with what came out of The Wilderness Years. Let's deal with those years as quickly as possible so we can get back to the real story.

I spent a few years dallying in artificial intelligence and trying to inject my software with emotional intelligence to humanise the machines. My ambition was to build a genuine relationship between avatar and human. I failed of course, but not too badly, and then got serially sidetracked in hitting print deadlines. Then in 1993 I produced a video game called *Run*

The Bunny for Duracell, the battery manufacturers. It used trackable routines embedded in product placement software. *Run The Bunny* exploited Paul Otlet's internet concept, and another new-fangled strategy called 'let's stick a floppy disc on the cover of this magazine in a desperate attempt by the publishers to attract more buyers.' It also exploited an old-fangled concept called bootlegging, where I actively encouraged players to copy the game. These days the industry calls this strategy viral marketing, twenty years ago they called it bonkers. I called it fun, and quite lucrative.

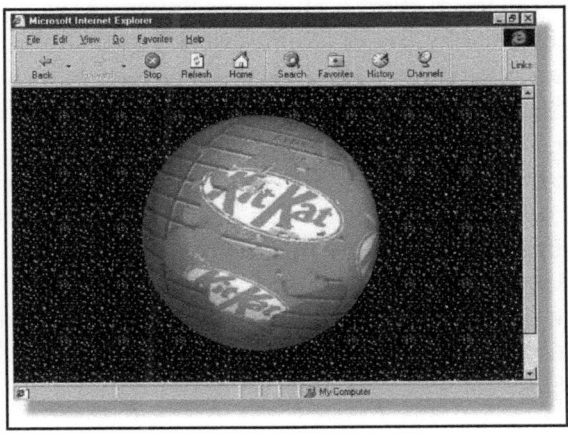

The real-world element of the Duracell campaign involved field-testing smart batteries. The gaming element involved my idea from the very first computer games I had produced back in the 70s, which was to offer prizes in exchange for information. It consisted of shoving virtual batteries up the virtual arses of virtual Duracell pink bunnies. The incentive was that if you copied the game and someone you seeded it to won a prize like a laptop, a cell phone, or other battery-powered stuff, then you would also win exactly the same prize, provided we knew who you were, your email address, what hardware you owned, what hardware you would like to own, what underwear you favoured, and whose oxen you coveted. I coined the word "adware" for that one, which has since come to mean something quite different. We produced *Run The Bunny* in eleven languages including Mandarin and Russian, I mounted it on half a million computer magazine covers for "free", and I think it was the first viral marketing campaign to go global. It ran on PC only and it sucked in 100,000 sales leads for my client. They seemed quite pleased.

My next viral marketing campaign was called *Take A Break* for the four-fingered chocolate-mongers at KitKat, and I am under a legal embargo agreed with Nestlé not to mention specific details. Particularly the lawsuit I threatened them with and the fact that my legal representative was barely out of school. Essentially, groups of office workers would waste their employer's time staring at a KitKat screensaver of a chocolate planet Earth. As the planet revolved on their computer monitor, cities appeared as illuminated beacons, and the idea was for these office workers to identify all the cities, eat a whole load of KitKat and answer a daft tie-breaker, in order to win a world trip to all of the cities illuminated on the chocolate globe. Again, it was based on the "please copy me and pass me on" viral principle. I am ashamed to admit that one of those cities only appeared for an eye-blink every half hour. It was Dubai. Sorry for wasting all that office time.

My favourite viral marketing campaign for a bunch of multinational capitalist bastards involved free beer, which was how I squared it with my conscience. One of my clients in the 1990s was Bass Breweries, and one of my duties was to run a website for them called *It's A Scream*, which was meant to encourage students to abandon their studies in favour of the pub. Obviously, each branch of the Scream chain was strategically located within puking distance of a university campus.

One winter morning in my office, long before the first Frank Zappa CD hit the speakers, the analogue vinyl having been replaced a decade earlier, and the old dead dog having been replaced by a new live one, a sharp-sighted member of my little team spotted an anomaly in the overnight web stats. There had been a spike of activity based around the Norwegian capital Oslo, including successful downloads of the entire site and unsuccessful attempts to hack the servers. We ran a reverse ISP thingy check, and instead of revealing a bunch of Scandinavian students trying to copy the source code of our online games, up popped a bunch of Norse lawyers. Üh-øh.

It took one hard look at the *It's A Scream* logo on our website to work out what was going on. The logo was a rip-off of the screaming skull of Edvard Munch's iconic painting *The Scream*. Munch was Norwegian, and a couple of quick checks informed us the image was very much in copyright and the lawyers represented the artist's daughter. I phoned Bass Breweries to tell them I had just pulled their website and replaced it with the image of a pint of beer, and hoped to save them a small fortune in punitive damages. As it turned out, the Edvard Munch estate refrained from suing them, but it cost them a small fortune anyway to change all the signage on all the Scream pubs that infested the land. However, the marketing boys at Bass suddenly started treating me with a bit of respect, especially when they listened to my predictions that this internet thing was going to become a central part of student life, not for playing games, but as a social network.

They gave me a budget, and they gave me the go-ahead to let rip on a viral marketing campaign.

And so I built a database based on the Duracell and KitKat campaigns that was to become the model for all my future attempts to deal direct with an audience. One that got end-users to reveal who they are, where they are, and what they want, then encourage them to get their mates involved, and then track the results, and then flog them stuff.

Populating the database was surprisingly easy. Instead of entertaining the student community with yet more video games, we linked up to as many of their websites, discussion boards and online networks as we could find, and offered them free beer. All they had to do was tell us when their next piss-up was going to be and which branch of a Scream they were going to inflict themselves on, and there would be a free pint waiting for them behind the bar. Well, that was not quite all they had to do. We also needed their email address and those of half a dozen mates, so we could plague them with future offers. And their mates had to attend the piss-up so Bass could sell them enough beer to recoup the bribe of the freebie. We launched the campaign at the beginning of the academic year at 6 pm on Saturday 5th October 1996, and hit the nearest student networks to us on the South coast of England. By Sunday night we were getting sign-ups from as far away as Christchurch. That's Christchurch, New Zealand.

I also spent a lot of The Wilderness Years writing puerile comedy material and grown-up cartoon strips, I sold part of my soul to magazine editors, I knocked off a short series of books about computers and marketing, and I became editor of the European Computer Trade Association yearbook. It was all very repetitive, but there was a low-level of enjoyment to be had in amongst the deadlines, and I was able to observe the bizarre evolution of video games from a safe distance. Sometimes my old chums who were now big players in the computer gaming world would invite me to act as Master of

Ceremonies at the sort of awards events I had once refused to attend. And I loved it.

When you wander the creative wilderness for a quarter of a century, it's inevitable that you stumble across other wanderers from time to time, each on their own unique pathway. Our common signposts were electronic, and channeled via the Internet, and I found myself responsible for doing all sorts of webby stuff for some very nice people as well as assorted crazies and scoundrels. Creating the first website for Vidal Sassoon was very nice indeed. My consultancy report that recommended P & O Ferries to embrace an online future was completely ignored, and they duly went bust. And there was a time when I had the entire Island of Cyprus as a client, which was just about as surreal as it sounds.

But I know you don't really care about any of that. All you want to read about is which rock music superstars I worked with, and what dirty little secrets I can reveal about them. Well, there were a lot, and there were a lot. But this book is about the history of UK video games in general and *Deus Ex Machina* in particular. So I must disappoint you. The legends of modern music that I did work for were all exactly as you would expect, because you already know as much about them as I do. Bryan Adams had bad skin, Pink Floyd were middle class, La Toya Jackson's lungs ran on helium, Led Zepplin were parsimonious, Phil Collins was bald, Van Morrison was an Irish curmudgeon and U2 were Irish minus the mudgeon. And then there was a bunch of younger generation pop stars who were all like Starbucks coffee: sweet, wet, warm and thick.

I make three exceptions to my rock music vow of silence, and that's because the three gentlemen involved displayed a total understanding of the power of the internet, and I was able to work in their best interests to grab the opportunities offered by self-selecting online communities. Their working names were Eminem, Prince, and Frank Zappa, and they all came to me via a remarkable American mover-and-shaker called Kelli Richards. Kelli launched the digital music revolution, probably because that's the sort of thing redheads do. She drove Apple's early music initiatives for ten years, she kicked EMI music into shape, she launched the first internet-based music artist subscription service, and she phoned me up out of the blue to tell me we were going to work together and stiff the parasites of the music industry. I dithered. She then told me she thought she could get my hero Zappa as a client. I accepted on the spot.

My work for Eminem was by far the most businesslike. It involved him paying me money in exchange for my audit of his entire online existence, with a view to putting a net worth on it. It was worth a lot. But the fun bit was working out how much money he was hemorrhaging from illegal downloads of his music, and how much he was being ripped off by unauthorised ringtones and merchandising. He was losing a lot. He accepted my weighty report graciously, asked the right questions, quibbled over nothing and after he paid on the nail like an honourable man I never heard from him again. I hope he didn't hire assassins to deal with the crooks I identified, but if he did, all I can say is they had it coming. At least I have a signed document to absolve me from culpability and getting my collar felt by the Feds, particularly when it came to identifying lunatics, bootleg merchants and porn-mongers.

Prince was a different kettle of fish altogether. He was possibly a genius, but impossibly remote. He knew exactly what he wanted before we even started, and that was to harness the brave new digital world for his best benefit, not to kill bootleggers and pirates but to embrace them. Auditing the internet for a generic name like "Prince" was a total bastard. It crossed over with everything from the Prince brand of cigarettes to oodles of parasitic hereditary monarchies, but we got there in the end.

There were no intermediaries, and The Artist Formerly Known As Prince dealt with every detail personally, with messages arriving electronically and very securely. We never made direct contact and I had no idea what his real agenda was until after it happened. And it happened in style. Just as for Eminem, I delivered a global analysis on what I reckoned Prince's status was online and how best to exploit it, but unlike Eminem he moved instantly. His "official" web presence disappeared completely, and was replaced by a blank screen. A black blank screen.

And then he broke all the rules. He began to give away his music instead of selling it. He started bootlegging his own performances to include a "free live CD" in the ticket-price of that specific concert. And in order to do this he wanted one simple thing from his fan-base. Their email address. He started building a definitive global database of his fans, and he went on to break the stranglehold of the intermediaries and barriers that had gotten between artists and fans. In a sense, Prince invented the "freemium" model of giving digital media away with the intent of selling additional digital content direct to fans, time and time again. He saw it coming ten years before anyone else in his platinum league, and for this alone I genuflect before him.

I used the same team for delivering data on most of my sweet little rock and rollers, usually under the umbrella of a company I set up called My Reputation. I hired a mess of a hacker straight out of central-casting, a prickly charmer who went on to work for Her Majesty's secret spooks, a bearded accountant who liked his real ale, and two very good looking ladies who did all the work. We operated out of an historic Clock Tower only a few steps from my home, which the lovely owner let me use at a peppercorn rent on condition I wound the clock and adjusted the ancient mechanism to display the correct time for all the Street to see. I loved that duty. It involved climbing up the near-vertical wooden stairway inside the tower, popping out of a jack-in-the-box trap door near the top, and decanting myself upwards behind and inside the four huge dials of the time machine. Then I would wind an iron handle for an eternity, as huge weights rose from street-level to the top of the tower, twice the size of the starter-crank on my old Citroën gangster car, and ten times the size of the handle on the mangle in my mum's scullery.

During the Second World War, this Clock Tower had been used as a discrete recreational facility for high-ranking naval officers and their private guests, included Admiral of the Fleet Louis Francis Albert Victor Nicholas George Mountbatten Earl of Burma, Noel Coward and according to the very old lady who told me she used to play the piano there, a disproportionate number of athletic young men.

During my years in the Clock Tower, I dug the dirt on the reputation and assets of celebrity clients, and bred tropical fish. They seemed to enjoy the vibrations from giant speakers either side of the tank, pumping out pagan rhythms as they pumped out milt. The fish, not the celebrities.

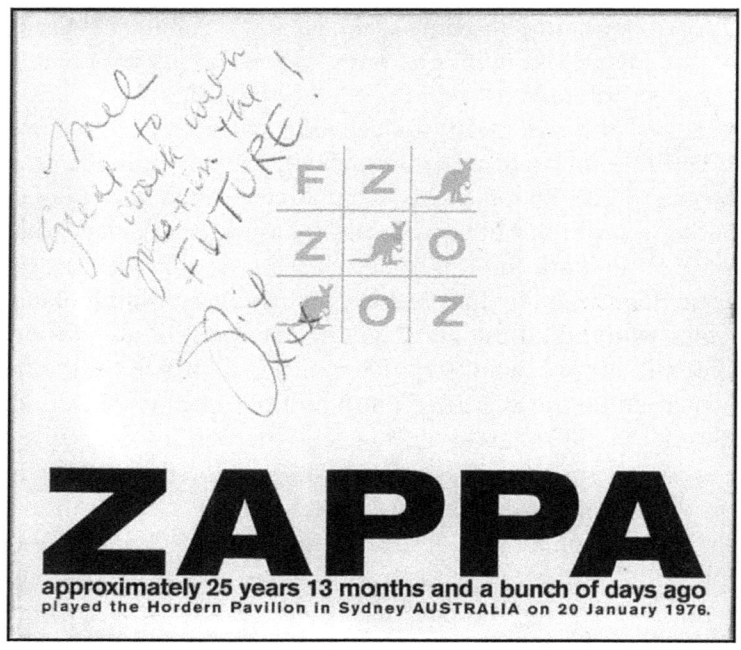

My early conversations with Gail Zappa took place on the phone after midnight. They went on for hours, and mostly involved sailing the pretend seas in a pretend pirate ship. When I met the next-generation Zappas, I was surprised how well adjusted they were, apart from Diva, the youngest, asking me if we had to kill all the bootleggers for real or was it just a game. But I didn't do what I did for any of them. I did what I did for my all-time hero and the greatest American musical genius of the twentieth century, Frank Zappa.

Zappa was so far ahead of the curve that it would take another book to extol his manipulation of modern music to the advantage of people with the right ears, but for the purposes of this book he lived long enough to figure out that direct marketing to a global list of fans via the internet was going to change the future of music. At the time of his death in 1993, the Internet was in its infancy, and the idea of trawling it for email addresses was revolutionary. He left a legacy of at least forty completed albums in the vault, with a vision to release at least two a year direct to his fans. But first we had to beat the bootleggers.

My job was simple but it was also painstakingly detailed, and I was tasked with identifying every hub of unauthorised activity, whether it was tribute bands, unlicensed merchandise, pirate copies of his albums and videos, anything and everything, and schedule it on a global basis. Then I needed to identify those responsible. I also needed to do the same for legitimate fan activity, which proved a much less enjoyable task because they came flocking. We also knew there was a hard core of obsessive possessives out there, individuals who would always buy everything Zappa produced, for the sake of completing their collection.

The idea was to reach out and embrace the lot of them, and harness their guilt and greed, or loyalty and goodwill, by bombarding them with opportunities to buy unique and unreleased material. Just imagine if there were two hundred thousand diehard Zappa fans on the planet, and just imagine that thirty thousand of them were obsessive possessives. Now imagine if you could sell them a new album for fifteen dollars with no intermediaries taking a slice of the action. And finally imagine that you had a vault stuffed with unreleased material. Genius.

The start and finish of The Wilderness Years

Zappa died aged 52 from prostate cancer. My dad had died at 57, not from the tuberculosis of his youth, or the asbestos from his engine rooms, or even the two packs of snout a day he smoked; it was his stomach that got him. My mum was only 47 when she had a catastrophic stroke and her brain got wiped out. When my contemporaries started to die off, either from physical ailments or alcohol addiction, my focus shifted. Of course it did.

One morning, a few years after I hit my sixtieth birthday I'd got back home from attending yet another funeral, and my dog went out the back yard for a sniff, but dropped dead instead. I was not yet dead, but the clock was ticking, and it was time for a reappraisal. It was time to get back into the video games business. That's what it was.

Chapter 9

Deus Ex Machina 2

You would think the video games world would have changed beyond recognition in the quarter century since I had quit Automata, but the only things that had really changed by 2010 were the numbers. When I started out there were a few thousand video gamers across the globe. When I came back there were a billion of the little monkeys. Before I quit, I was trying to sell products at a premium price. Then when I wanted to return, most games seemed to be free. But guess what, I was not in the slightest bit surprised to discover the games themselves were still nothing more than a load of chess, dice, ping-pong and bunkum. The graphics were great though.

Although I had shelved *Deus Ex Machina* back in 1985, I always believed it was just a matter of time before the technology caught up with the idea of interactive movies and then I could do it all over again, but better. I had received over a dozen offers to remake it, from various well-meaning and not so well-meaning folk, but I had turned them down as non-starters.

There was one hopeful, who sent his proposal in on VHS tape, featuring what looked suspiciously like puppets with some sort of battery-powered illumination inside. His business model was unique, inasmuch as that he invited me to buy the rights to my own game from him for a large sum of money. Another offering came from a self-taught programmer which at least ran on a PC. Unfortunately, her version only consisted of the credits sequence in which she had replaced the iconic face of The Machine with her own, plus a home-grown soundtrack of buttock-clenching horror running in the background.

But there was one enquiry which was a little different from the rest, coming as it did from a self-confessed pirate of my original game, who said he wanted to atone for the past and pay me back for the opportunity I had given him to set off in the business world while he was still a student. A refreshing gambit.

In the August of 2008 I had received this offer by email from Mário Valente, an Iberian ex-rocker who had ended up working as Chief Information Officer at the Portuguese Ministry of Justice, with his waist-length hair and pony tail still intact. Interesting. The licensing deal he was offering was not unattractive, and I was not saying no. If I was ever going to remake the game for the Twenty-First Century, then harnessing the money of one of the sods who had pirated it in the first place generated a satisfying glow.

Exactly one month after I received his first email, the global economic crisis was triggered when the American bank Lehman Brothers filed for bankruptcy. Here in the UK, the entire banking system teetered on the verge of collapse, and it really didn't seem like a good time to be taking a punt on a new venture. Mário's proposals were put on ice, along with all the others.

Occasionally, I was aware that another bright spark had attempted to produce an unauthorised update or a tribute version of the images, the music, or the entire game, but a gentle word in the right place was enough to dampen their enthusiasm. When friends like Clembabe Chambers remixed the soundtrack for his own pleasure and the pleasure of others, I was more than happy to thank them.

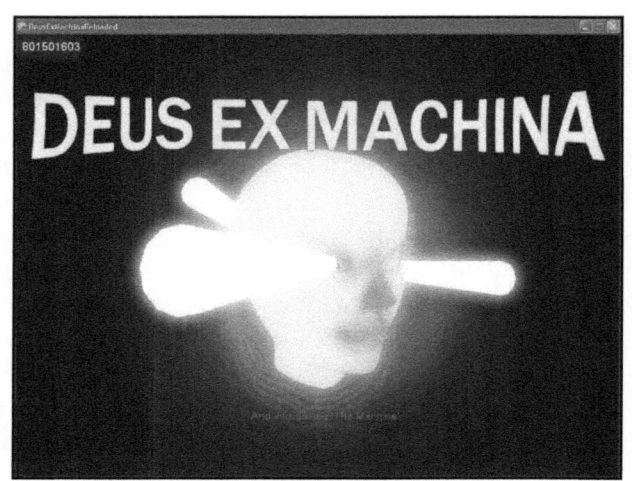

A remake reject

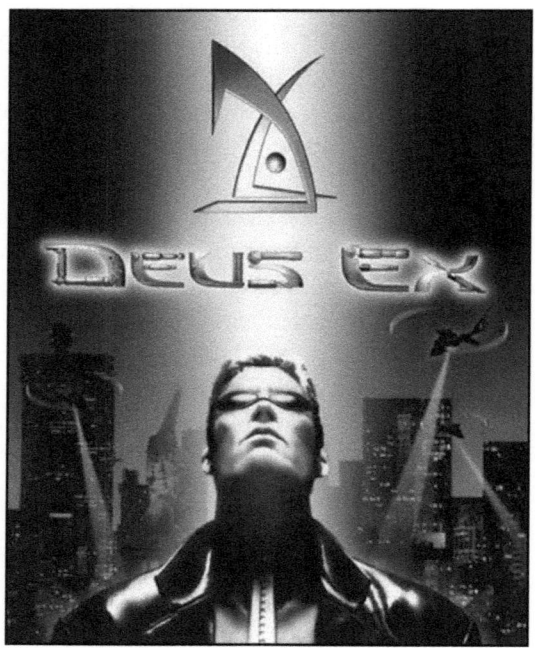

A familiar game title

Mário Valente the Deus Ex Machina pirate

Mário Valente the Deus Ex Machina atoner

And then there was the little matter of a mainstream video game which had been released in June 2000 by Eidos, the software company founded by another old fart of a UK games veteran. This was the sainted Ian Livingstone. His company's title was voted the "best PC game of all time" and it sold more than a million copies first time out, netting a fortune. It was called *Deus Ex*, and no sooner had it been released than I was asked by an eager member of the legal profession if I was going to sue them for trading on the name, goodwill and legacy of *Deus Ex Machina*. I was not. A legal spat would have generated some great publicity, of course, but I had absolutely nothing to publicise. Besides, I would almost certainly have lost. The name of their game was undeniably a truncated version of mine, but their theme was the usual malarkey of kill or be killed, which could hardly be confused with my hobbyhorse of non-violence.

Spookily, Ian Livingstone quit Eidos in September 2013 after twenty years at the helm, the week that the preview copies of my remake of *Deus Ex Machina* were loosed into the wild. A bizarre coincidence. Another bizarre coincidence was the key image used in the marketing of their *Deus Ex*. Like the cover of *Deus Ex Machina*, it was in dark monochrome and featured a solitary face with surrounding hints of a dystopian world of the near future, and whereas my artwork had narrow beams of light coming out of the Machine's eyes, their artwork had narrow beams of light coming out of remote machines.

The twenty fifth anniversary of the original launch of my game triggered a spate of interest, and *Deus Ex Machina* started to pop up all over the place. The more I delved the web, the more bodies I dug up, and the full truth of what had happened began to emerge. It turned out that pirate editions had made the video charts in countries I can't even spell, and bootleg copies had percolated through the university networks of the civilised world, which means we never really made it in the USA.

One example was a guy who is now near the very top of the mighty Apple organisation, saying how the game had been an inspiration to him when he was a schoolboy in India. Another was from an academic at the University of Prague who had made it the subject of his PhD thesis. *Deus Ex Machina* appeared on the first page of the definitive history of video games. Views on YouTube started to rocket. The computer press devoted great chunks of space to retrospectives and interviews. And of course the inevitable new wave of bootleg products started to infest the online shopping malls, all featuring key graphics from the original game. Well bugger me.

I went to Rod Cousens, the man who predicted the entire video games revolution, now head of Codemasters, to seek his advice on a remake of *Deus Ex Machina*. His advice was to go for it. What's more, he introduced me to some big hitters in the current gaming world. Then, one long, sunny lunchtime at the seaside, I met up with three friends of mine for some ritual conversation, food and wine. They were Karl Jeffery, a legend in the video games industry who had once try to buy Atari, John Piper, one of the world's most respected market analysts, and none other than Andy Stagg the former Boy Wonder and original programmer back in the Automata days. We were celebrating Andy's announcement that he was about to become a grandfather, and raised a toast or two. We were also celebrating that what with home-grown apps and mobile platforms and the re-emergence of indies, the current gaming climate felt like the Golden Age of the 80s all over again. It had all been so much fun in the early days back then. And I can thank Karl Jeffery for what happened next. He raised his glass and said, "OK, so let's become Automata all over again, and have some fun!"

We agreed on the spot. Andy would become Managing Director, John would be Financial Supremo, Karl would be the Voice of Reason, and I would be the Grand Wazoo. Automata Source was registered within the week, and the website was up and running soon after. The Voice of Reason and the Managing Director thought we should kick off with a remake of my treasure hunt extravaganza *PiMania*, now we had the luxury of global positioning satellites to act as our star maps, but I wasn't convinced.

Karl Jeffery flies

John Piper blooms

Andrew Stagg is overcome with excitement

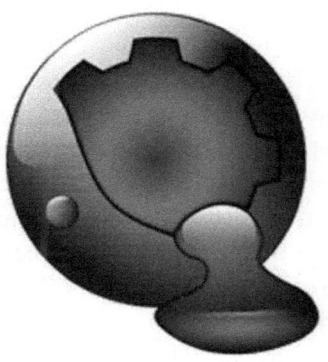

Automata is back in business.

When I got home, I climbed up to my little studio garret, peeled the top sheet off a ream of paper, picked up my pen and wrote the words DEUS EX MACHINA in capital letters across the top of the page. Then I went for a pee. When I came back I added the Latin number two to the title, seeing as how the name of the game had always been in the dead language of Pliny and Plautus. But after staring at the words *Deus Ex Machina II* for a bit, I thought it might confuse the more dumbed-down gamers of the twenty-first century, who may have wondered what had happened to the previous ten iterations. So I crossed out the Latin numeral and replaced it with *Deus Ex Machina 2*.

Now all I had to do was fill up the blank pages, keep to the spirit of the original, and rewrite it with the benefit of hindsight. I reckoned it would all be over by Christmas, the reborn Automata would be in positive cashflow, and the Mel Croucher pension fund would be assured. As it turned out, I was hopelessly optimistic.

The first thing to change was the backstory. The dystopia of the original was now irrelevant. The future had already happened. In the first version of the game I had made a few obvious predictions about a surveillance society eroding our liberties, but in actual fact those tired old predictions had already turned into reality, and then some. The internet had arrived.

The internet is a global surveillance system. It works perfectly and it works exactly as intended. Each and every one of us is a collaborator in the creation, nurture and growth of the beast. Every honourable pioneer from Tim Berners-Lee to Edward Snowden, every developer and engineer, every internet service provider, every tweeter and blogger, every surfer and texter, every coder and gamer, we have all done our bit. Our collaborative success is as universal as it is complete, and like all good parents, we love the beautiful monster we have created.

In recent times, a load of claptrap has been written about the monitoring of all our private electronic communications. Well folks, nothing is for free online, and anyone who thinks otherwise is a fool. Surely nobody can have been daft enough to believe that using the services of Facebook, Google, Twitter and Instagram would not come without a cost. Only an idiot would think that our emails, texts and Skype conversations would remain private. The truth is that nobody thinks much about it at all, because we are all too wrapped up enjoying the benefits. We have no right to complain, because that was always the deal. But we are not only willing consumers, we are also the product being consumed, and the cost is the sacrifice of our privacy and personal data. It's like cannibals sending out for pizza stuffed with their own entrails. It may be yummy, but you have to pay to eat yourself.

All the world's intelligence services, spying agencies, secret police and all their commercial paymasters feed on every private and corporate databank, router, server, backbone, cable and cloud system. Of course they do. It is in their nature, and they do it because they can. Whistleblowers, hackers and cyber-terrorists are a useful smokescreen, and they provide a convenient headline to justify the billions being spent on mass surveillance. And to me that's the funniest bit of all. We pay the taxes to fund those who spy on us, and then we do all the work for them.

For the first time in history, humanity has enslaved itself, willingly. In the past, whole nations would rise up against regimes that spied on their citizens in order to control them. Today, thanks to the internet, we merrily reveal every last detail about ourselves. And we do it all on a voluntary and continual basis. Every web page we view is logged, as is every item we buy online or with plastic cards. We stream our innermost thoughts and we broadcast our personal intentions. We even upload our own archives of mugshots, and volunteer to wear electronic location tags embedded in our phones. After all, without facial recognition and GPS tracking, our lords and masters wouldn't be able to keep tabs on our every move, would they.

Colluding with our own social and economic slavery is a small price to pay in exchange for the fantastic benefits we get in return. And they really are fantastic benefits, you know. Each and every one of the hundreds of levels of *Candy Crush Saga*. My vision of the future as depicted in *Deus Ex Machina* was not half as scary as the present, and any remake would need to cut out all the grand themes and political mumbo jumbo in order to concentrate of the simple rise and decline of one life. So the rebellion of The Machine was out, it was all down to the Mouse Dropping.

I rewrote the libretto fast, and began to cobble ideas together for an extended soundtrack for programmers to work with so they could get a feel for the piece. But this time round I knew I had to break out of the narrow appeal of players in the UK, and try to inject a global element. That meant a re-run of my old Duracell viral campaign of embedding translations for the major languages of the world's gamers. It also meant aiming as high as I could for internationally recognised voices. And it meant a trawl back through all those offers of partnerships, licence deals, joint ventures and dangerous liaisons whereby other people would stump up some money to finance a new version of the game. After all, there were now untold millions of PCs and Macs to feed. And it seemed that games may well be going mobile, what with the recent success of the iPhone and the upstart Android hitting the market, not to mention rumours of something called an iPad. Imagine if you could experience the game by simply tilting and stroking a hand-held device, with perfect audio fed straight into your brain via earbuds. The prospect of that was irresistible.

It was time to call Mário Francisco Valente Baltazar Valente (like NewYork New York, so good they named him twice), the Portuguese entrepreneur who had a bank in his pocket and a declaration that it had been his lifelong dream to remake *Deus Ex Machina*. Who was I to step on another man's dream? He flew to London and we met on Valentine's Day, February 2010, to seal the deal. He would be producer of the title, I would be writer director with a proper advance and a half-decent royalty on all sales. The company he had created to produce the game was the delightfully named Quirkafleeg, which is defined as a sort of athletic somersault followed by a mad flailing of the legs. He had named it in honour of Room 40 in

Matthew Smith's bonkers vintage game for the ZX Spectrum, *Jet Set Willy*.

The original version of *Deus Ex Machina* had taken a man and a boy ten weeks to deliver Game Of The Year in 96 Kilobytes for the cost of a garden shed. And now with oodles of megabytes to play with, the entire Portuguese economy behind me and the pick of Europrogrammers to choose from, I reckoned on producing the greatest video game in the history of video games since my last effort, for release by 2012. How could we possibly fail.

Easy. On 5th April 2011, Tuesday evening, after tea and compulsory prayers, the entire Portuguese economy went tits up.

Next we'll discover how one whole life ended up as sixty minutes of gameplay and why the new soundtrack was put together. We'll find ourselves a team of weird and wonderful coders and graphic artists, and get ready to make exactly the same mistakes as we did first time round. Only bigger. Stick with it. It's a wild ride.

According to The Holy Bible, we are allotted three score years plus ten, to live out our life on this Earth. That was either simplistic, optimistic or the numbers were different back then, seeing as the Son Of God only made it to thirty-three and a third. In The Year Of Our Lord 1900, official figures show that a citizen of England could expect to kick the bucket 46 years after first drawing breath. In the year that I was born, our average lifespan was 66 years and 6 months. Today, hereabouts, we expect to enjoy sex and drugs and rock'n'roll way into our mid 80s, and the prospects for my generation gets better as each year passes. Thanks to unhealthy eating, lack of exercise and the degradation of the planet, it is probable that the next generation will not last as long as my own. In fact my generation could be the longest lived ever, and the growing selection of Hundredth Birthday cards on the shelves is plain evidence of this.

For *Deus Ex Machina* 2, I decided to make the lifespan of The Defect exactly one hundred years, not because it was a fantasy but because it was perfectly possible for the player to achieve that longevity. I also decided to fit the lifespan into exactly one hour, because I reckoned any longer would risk losing the player's involvement. Besides, "one century in one hour" would be easy to market to the hard of thinking. Adding the extra ten minutes to the original's running time also meant I could reinstate most of the lost sequences, if not all of them.

For the gameplay itself, there were two reasons I based the content on my own experience. First was to stick to the proven formula of "write what you know." Second was egotistical arrogance, even down to saddling the foetus with my own date of birth.

As for the music, this time round my idea was much simpler than before: I would represent each phase of the century with the appropriate popular music of the time. In fact just like the first time round I got more enthused by the music than by the game itself, and I looked forward to blowing other people's budgets on proper musicians, orchestras and choirs, because my previous efforts had been badly handicapped by my personal finances and my very limited talent.

At the end of the original soundtrack, I have Ian Dury deliver a fake ha-ha-ha laugh, accompanied by a 1940s big band pastiche. At the start of the soundtrack for the remake, Ian Dury picks up exactly where we left off, and the big band pastiche is heard again. That's the clue to what I had in mind for the original, but I simply didn't have the skill or resources to pull it off back then. When I told Mário Valente I was rewriting the entire audio concept to reflect the decades from the 1940s to the 2040s he was intrigued, nonplussed, and relatively stroppy. So I simply pulled rank and presented him with a fait accompli. Once again, I was behaving like an auteur, and I admit that I had learned nothing about working with other people during the Wilderness Years. Here's what I told him, more or less.

"We'll do the ejaculation of the sperm to a 1940s big band. Then for the birth, we'll go all post-war cool jazz with some Portuguese fado chucked in, to please your bank. There'll be a neo-Nazi school sequence, and the music will be straight out of my 1950s radio childhood. Maybe we could get Julie Andrews to do her governess act from *The Sound Of Music*. Adolescence will be played for laughs, with some repulsive images and lyrics, set to the sweet harmonies of bubblegum pop music. And we'll do the 1960s with Jimi Hendrix then Pink Floyd psychedelic parodies, before it all goes punk in the 1970s and thrash metal in the 80s. And electro-pop with some Arabic stuff for the 90s Iraq war, of course. Then there'll be a big Ibiza rave dance sequence, and total dumbness for today's music. We can do a Monty Python comedy song for the 2020s old age period, but I want to break their hearts with a full symphony orchestra after that, leading to a hymn for the 2030s, before it all goes back to the radio music of childhood for death in the 2040s."

Mario's response was based on financial grounds as opposed to musical preferences.

"We can't afford it."

But I had a compelling argument which changed his mind.

"And there's one more thing. You get to play the guitar solo of *The Red Flag* in the final credit sequence."

"We still can't afford it."

"Trust me. I know some people."

I began at the beginning and went in search of the best big band in the land who could play 1940s swing, it was called the Johnny Dankworth Orchestra. One slight hurdle in getting Johnny Dankworth to agree to perform was that he had died a few days before I signed the contract with Quirkafleeg.

Undaunted, I went searching for his licensing agent instead to see if I could become a musical tomb raider. I ended up doing business with a nice woman called Ebona Eastmond-Henry who worked for the Audio Network organisation, and I was able to get a blanket rate licence to plunder the vaults at an amazingly good price. Sourcing the music was looking easier than I had thought, so I asked her a simple question.

"What are my chances of getting the Royal Philharmonic Orchestra to back me doing a Jeff Beck guitar impersonation, and a disco slut who speaks robotic Japanese, and some Arab women doing that wailing noise, and Julie Andrews?"

Her answer to my idiocy was reassuring.

"Leave it with me. I'll see what I can do."

The success or failure of *Deus Ex Machina 2* would depend on firing up the imagination of the player with the opening words, pulling them through the screen then dragging them all the way through to the conclusion of the game. The voice of the narrator would have to be world class. Not just this world, but all other worlds. So, considering I had to husband my new paymaster's budget, getting the perfect Narrator was an interesting challenge.

The original narration as recorded by Jon Pertwee had been warm and encouraging. This time round I wanted to start the player off in awe and leave them in tears. Pertwee had been well-known as the third incarnation of *Doctor Who*, a cult sci-fi series on television since 1963. But now I needed a voice that would be recognised anywhere in the world as the nearest thing to The Voice Of God. This role had been pretty much monopolised by Morgan Freeman, in movies like *War Of The Worlds* and *Bruce Almighty*, but I was dubious that a gamer in Kazakhstan, Kraków or Kidderminster would wet herself at the prospect of having Morgan Freeman reciting my script like a kindly uncle. He wasn't anywhere near edgy enough. Anyway, I didn't know where he lived. Besides, everyone knows that God is an Englishman, and seeing as how God dabbles in this world, the netherworld, and in galaxies far, far away, there was only one possible candidate for me. And he was very, very old.

I set about hiring the services of the voice of Dracula who had seduced several centuries of women and drunk their blood. The voice of Jinnah who had founded Pakistan. The voice of *The Man With The Golden Gun* who had menaced James Bond. The voice of the evil Count Dooku in *Star Wars* and the Dark Lord Saruman in *The Lord Of The Rings* and *The Hobbit*. I set off in search of the greatest set of vocal pipes on the planet. My quest was to get Sir Christopher Lee to agree to talk to me without getting flung out on my ear. Obviously, after my Johnny Dankworth experience, my first step was to check out if he was still undead.

Not only was he alive and kicking, he was celebrating his 90th birthday by nabbing a Lifetime BAFTA and releasing a heavy metal album. So far, so good. Seeing as how you can never tempt a distinguished knight of the realm with anything as sordid as money, I made my pitch on an emotional level with a bit of classy prose chucked in. When I met him for the first time, after ten weeks of wooing by good old-fashioned pen and ink, Christopher Lee turned out to be very tall, very frail and very frank.

He held my script in front of his chest and fluttered it. Slowly.

"This is a travesty!" The voice was magnificent. The verdict wasn't. The old gentleman was wearing a blue knitted woollen hat, a bit like a tea-cosy, to protect the top of his head which had obviously been bashed recently, possibly by a Jedi light sabre, or a vampire-hunter's wooden stake. His eyes were hooded, and I could not read them.

"Of course, there will be those who will be appalled. Bringing Shakespeare up to date? Making it amusing! I don't think something like this has ever been done before. I don't have a laptop, I don't have a computer. I wouldn't know what to do." He sniffed, stroked his silver beard, then waved a hand in what I thought was a gesture of dismissal. It was in fact an invitation to shake on it.

"Alright. I'll do it," he growled, in a weary, kindly, godly sort of way, "but I will not do it in a sarcastic voice, I want to do it as if I completely believe in it."

Blimey! Christopher Lee, a still-living legend, had just agreed to work with Mel Croucher, a man with a silly moustache. From that moment on, I thought there was a chance of not only bringing *Deus Ex Machina* to market all over again, but making a success of it this time round.

The Christopher Lee recording session took place in my all-time favourite studio, a bijou set-up in North West London called Hobsons, where I had been tasked with rescuing their website from oblivion and dragging it to the top page of Google. As a return favour they had offered me a cheap studio deal. On the appointed day, as we waited for God's car to arrive, more and more Hobsons staff just happened to muster. They were all women, and they were all in a state of peculiar excitement. When the old man eventually arrived, they were in awe, and by the time he left they were in tears. I knew I had made the right choice.

My recording engineer was the great Jonathan Golden Ears Cook, probably the best ear-to-brain merchant I have ever come across. I had never seen him so fired-up and shaven headed. Our first problem was that the recording studio was up three flights of stairs, and God was having trouble ascending. He leant heavily on our arms. He dropped his walking cane. He cursed his frailty. He made it. And then, as he sat in the little glass recording booth and adjusted his woolly tea-cosy hat, he fumbled off a ring from a long, bony finger before shuffling the pages of my script, now marked by his own scribbles. The ring dropped to the floor, and the Voice Of God boomed through my earphones, "Can you pick that up for me. It used to belong to Charlemagne." Game on.

When the session was over, and Golden Ears had given a reassuring thumbs-up signal, I gave myself a minute in the toilet next door, and did a hobbling victory jig to celebrate what had just happened. A very old actor, who had delivered Shakespeare's summation of the Seven Ages of Man many times on the classical stage, had just given his all to my poxy computer game. He may have said to me, "I don't have a laptop, I don't have a computer. I wouldn't know what to do." But he knew exactly what to do. All the world's a stage, and Christopher Lee had ninety years of personal experience that encompassed each of those ages. And I'd got him in the bag before he took his own, inevitable, final bow.

As he made his way back down the three flights of stairs, slowly, painfully and with a weird sort of grace, to where his car waited, I rewrote the end-sequence graphics of the game in my head. Instead of the decrepit avatar grinding to a halt and collapsing, I would take away the walking stick and the zimmer frame and replace them with the best imaginary wheelchair that the National Health Service could never afford. A magic wheelchair that sprouts the wings of Pegasus, and turns us all, if and when we become very old and very weary, into gods.

I had only one question to ask this old god as I took hold of his hand to say goodbye, careful not to let the gold embossed ring slip off his finger again. I asked him why he had really agreed to be the voice of The Great Programmer in *Deus Ex Machina*. He didn't answer immediately, but folded himself through the back door of the black limousine, nodding at the chauffeur and wincing as his injured head brushed the inside of the upholstered roof. He was still incredibly tall and his back was almost straight. Then he muttered, more to himself than to me,

"It was Jon Pertwee. You said Jon Pertwee played this part originally. He was a great friend of mine. A funny man, a very funny man."

I eased the door shut, and waved goodbye to the voice of God, who muttered as the electric window wound upwards.

"I lived round the corner from him. I had a basement flat in Eton Terrace. A bed-sit. We were friends. He was a funny man. A very funny man. We were younger then. Younger."

The black limousine slipped through the gates of Hobsons recording studio and turned left onto Chiswick High Street, towards Middle Earth.

The search for a voice to play The Defect Police, my ultimate baddie, proved more difficult. In the original game it had been played by the comedian Frankie Howerd, who had once taken a similar role in the big-budget Beatles musical *Sgt Pepper's Lonely Hearts Club Band*. So after the revelation that Christopher Lee had warmed to his role because of his link with the original player Jon Pertwee, I thought I may as well look up who else had appeared with Frankie Howerd in the Beatles musical, and see if I could pull the same stunt. The cast list was impressive. Paul McCartney (too nice), George Harrison (too dead), The Bee Gees (too many), Alice Cooper...

There he was, the wild man of rock'n'roll and professional chicken-strangler, and the perfect character to threaten my gameplayers with all sorts of evil. I got in contact with the woman who not only knew everyone in American music, but also knew how to get me access to them, my mover-and-shaker from the Frank Zappa days, Kelli Richards. Kelli had produced the annual Pollstar Awards at which Alice Cooper was presenter, and it wasn't long before his mob emailed me to say "incorporating Alice's music into the project may be key." Better yet, he would soon be at London's Roundhouse venue with his *Night Of Fear* tour, only a mile or two from our tame studio. It all seemed too good to be true. Which it was.

One of the problems using other people's money in a creative project is that they seem to think they should have some sort of say in how it gets spent. This was an alien concept to me, especially as the purse strings were being held by some guys in suits in Lisbon, working in the interests of a bank I could not pronounce. They had gotten it into their heads that their investors would expect to see at least one Portuguese celebrity name in the cast list to satisfy national pride and justify their involvement. Apparently I had two choices. Mariza, their most famous singer, an unfeasibly tall, Mozambique-born, crop-headed woman, who looked like she was born in zero gravity orbiting Pluto, or Joaquim de Almeida, a gravel-voiced heart-throb and their most famous actor, not to mention a Golden Globe winner and star of some very American titles like *Batman, Missing, Desperado, 24* and *The West Wing*.

Seeing as Mário already had contacts with both of these contenders, and seeing how he could sweet-talk a fish into climbing Kilamanjaro, and seeing as he lived in the right capital city, I left the negotiations to him.

And so it was that Joaquim de Almeida gave his voice to the project, and Alice Cooper did not. As it turned out, Lisbon's favourite son was brilliant, kicking off the session with, "Hey Mel, did you really write this shit?" Which I suppose is some sort of traditional Portuguese form of praise. But the Mariza factor had given me one of my better ideas. And it was all about image.

The most important marketing factor to help sell a game is not the title, and certainly not the name of the author or publisher. It's the key graphic image, the visual message that tries to summarise the entire product in a single glance, and the one that gets reinforced on the cover, in the press, on screen and at point of sale. So what if I had the new voice and the new face of *Deus Ex Machina* belong to the same person. If Mariza had ended up singing the role of The Machine, then her striking looks would have been ideal for the key graphic as well. What I needed was a sublimely moving voice coming out of an intriguing woman, preferably from Mozambique and with a shaven head, who was available immediately, at a price that fitted my ever-decreasing budget.

If you ever want to find the ideal voice for a recording session, then you should give Christine Poundford a call. Christine was the one in the back room at the Hobsons voice agency in London, where I was rapidly becoming part of the furniture thanks to Golden Ears, and she could work small miracles. About five foot two inches, as it turned out.

"Hey Christine, I need a sublimely moving voice coming out of an intriguing woman, preferably from Mozambique and with a shaven head, who is available immediately, at a price that fits my ever-decreasing budget."

There was a slight pause at the other end, before she said, "No problem. I have the perfect singer for you."

"How perfect?"

"Perfect, perfect."

"Who's she worked with?"

There was another slight pause, and a shuffling of electronic paper.

"Eric Clapton, Bob Dylan and The Who."

"Hmm, What does she look like?"

"Hang on and I'll send you her mugshot and showreel. Her name's Chyna Whyne."

I waited for the desktop to announce the arrival of her file, and then clicked the onscreen link. Blimey! The face of *Deus Ex Machina 2* beamed back at me with a huge smile, accompanied by a soulful voice with a Jamaican lilt. I played it again.

"Christine? You still there?"

"Course I am. So, what do you think?"

"I think she's exactly what I need. How much?"

"Twice what you can afford and half what she's worth."

"Including full buy-out and photographic rights?"

"Ooh, you cheeky bugger. Plus agency fee."

I had found the face and voice.

"Now can you get me Julie Andrews to play a mad fascist in the voice she used for *The Sound Of Music*?"

"No problem. I have the perfect singer for you.

When we recorded her session at Hobson's studio in London, Chyna asked the obvious question as to who my audio producer was on the project. I didn't have one. That is, I didn't have one until the studio engineer jumped up and announced, "I am!"

Things were looking up, and with Jonathan Golden Ears Cook at the helm of the mixing desk, the soundtrack would become transformed into something I could never have achieved on my own.

My Julie Andrews playing a mad fascist in the voice she used for *The Sound Of Music* arrived at the studio just as Chyna Whyne was leaving. She was the nuclear-lunged Mary Carewe, and she was in a hurry. It took less than forty minutes to record her part, take the obligatory publicity shots and say thanks. The reason she was in a hurry was that she had a date with an airport, New York's Carnegie Hall and The Royal Philharmonic Orchestra. I was worried we'd rushed it, but when Golden Ears played back her track it was note perfect, and her insane cadenza at the end was worth the price of the ticket on its own. We sat there with silly grins on our faces, shook hands and went to the pub.

For the voice of The Defect, which I had originally mangled myself, I thought we needed some girl fodder in the shape of a good looking youngster who was capable of playing all Seven Ages of Man without it sounding unnatural. So it was back to the redoubtable Christine Poundford to hunt for the perfect voice and it took her no time at all to pin him down.

"Chris Madin, early twenties, looks younger, sounds great."

"Never heard of him."

"He's just done X Factor."

"Never seen it."

"He's the voice of Ribena and Fairy Liquid."

"Yuk."

"So, what did you think of Chyna Whyne?"

"She was absolutely perfect."

"And Mary Carewe?"

"Well, she was absolutely perfect."

"So what should you say when I tell you Chris Madin is absolutely perfect for the voice of your Defect?"

"Um, I should say how much?"

"Correct."

Chris Madin took everything in his stride, in between talking about kittens, playing carpet golf and continually checking his phone for text messages. He mewled for his mama on command, sang obscenities when asked, did some spectacular session coughing for the geriatric sequences and roared a chorus of demented deserter-soldiers thanks to some nifty multi-tracking by Golden Ears. He was worth every penny of his fee, which used up almost all the remaining audio budget. Which was a problem, because there was one more voice to go. So I went back to the suitably budget-conscious Audio Network organisation.

I had injected a new voice into the game, for the role of The Night Nurse, who I wanted to act as a foil to The Machine's sense and sensibility. The Night Nurse was to be mischievous, dangerous and rude. She would make her entrance in a comedy disco sequence at the point in life where The Defect had become a middle-aged embarrassment, and she would go on to oversee his decline through a big heart attack and a little brain damage. There was quite a rude TV series doing the rounds at the time called *Secret Diary Of A Callgirl* and I caught a snatch of the soundtrack which sounded promising. The performer was also one of the writers and her name was Sulene Fleming.

Sulene got very excited when she found out I had rented her pipes from Audio Network, and I was so embarrassed by the pathetic fee involved that I tried to make amends by introducing her to Christine Poundford in the hope other people would pay her what she deserved, as opposed to my pittance. But there we were, all the new voices in the can plus one original voice in the archive. I didn't want anyone else to play the voice of The Fertilizer, it had to be the resurrected Ian Dury, and I set about putting a live band together for a session with the dear departed. I got to play keyboards and bedsprings, which is when one of those small-world coincidences happened. I was telling the story of the original production to Ricky Eastman, the sax player who also wrote the new arrangement for the Fertilizer's theme song. When I showed him the original poster he did a cartoon double-take, popped his eyes and smacked his own brow.

"That's Nina!"

"You know Nina?"

"Know her? She's the mother of my children!"

I bought myself a software package called Logic Pro and loaded it into the Apple iMac that sat on my old wooden desk. It seemed capable of emulating the fanciest studio set-ups of my youth, complete with a vast mixing desk, unlimited audio processors and no need whatsoever for razor blades and sticky tape, and I set about learning the ropes. Then I plugged in a battered Korg DRS Trinity Music-station which I had bought from a mate for next to nothing. It was steam-powered but it contained every sound I could possibly want to conjure. I thought I had the musical world in my pocket, and with a fresh cup of coffee in one hand and a new puppy chewing my feet, I began to construct the soundtrack. It took the best part of six months before it was ready to be burnished by Golden Ears, but it meant that when I found some programmers they would have something to chew on.

The key image for the entire project was a gift from our Jamaican pocket-Venus, Chyna Whyne The Machine, who was no stranger to the catwalk or the photographer's studio. She had come up with a disturbing image of herself, in deep monochrome shadow, head turned away from the camera, wearing rubber gloves and not much else, and giving birth backwards in a puddle of oil. We would need to strip her down, wire her up and plug her in to perfection. Which brings me to Bruno Krippahl and the Backroom Boys of Lisbon.

Alice Cooper - Nearly

Joaquim de Almeida - The Defect Police

Mariza - Almost

Chyna Whyne - The Machine with Jonathan Golden Ears Cook

Christine Poundford - Miracle Worker

Christopher Lee - The Programmer

Mary Carewe - The Teacher

Sulene Fleming - The Night Nurse

Chris Madin - The Defect with Mel Croucher

Most of the concept artwork for *Deus Ex Machina 2*, including the key image of Chyna as The Machine and the opening and closing movies, was all dreamed up by Bruno Krippahl, not by me. All I did was a few sketches and a very detailed screenplay. In fact the screenplay was as detailed as I could make it, with reams of instructions about how I wanted the atmosphere to be evoked for each scene. Over in Lisbon, my bank-friendly Producer had worked with this graphics bloke Bruno before and suggested we parachute him in. I was due to go out to Lisbon anyway to interview prospective programmers, and it seemed like a good opportunity to nail the concept artwork at the same time. Throughout the next few chapters, I hope you'll be able to see why Bruno was the man for me, apart from his obvious qualities of a singular eyebrow and impossibly good teeth.

Which just leaves us with those elusive programmers. The team who was going to do all the actual work. The people who Mário was going to nurture, manage and pay in his role of Producer.

Bruno Krippahl, Concept Artist

Tiago Loureiro, Executive Producer Software

I do not want to bore you with accounts of sitting in the sort of soulless office where screens glow and cups congeal as hopeless hopefuls promise the earth, and interviews come to an end with sweaty, limp and adolescent handshakes. I'll just say that we interviewed some children who promised to deliver so much for so little that I wanted to smack their fluffy little faces and send them back into the kindergarten to play in the sandpit again. But at last, sanity appeared in the form of Vectrlab, the only contenders I felt comfortable with. And it is at this point that I would like to thank and simultaneously apologise to the man who really made *Deus Ex Machina 2* happen. The indefatigable, uncrushable, eternally hopeful and put-upon Tiago Loureiro. The man who *Deus Ex Machina 2* tried to break much as the original game tried to break me. Vectrlab was his games development company. In fact, while I was writing this book they won Game Of The Year at the Portuguese Independent Games fest, amusingly abbreviated to PIG.

In the next chapters we will live our little lives together for one hundred years. I promise not to mention again that it's already taken longer than the whole of the Second World War to finish the bloody game, although I may let drop why I don't know if we are headed for victory or defeat this time round.

Chapter 10

Conception to Childhood

Ideally, I would have liked to allow each individual player to customise the game so their avatar would look just like them. In fact, if I had had my way and this had been technically practical we could have made the avatar look like anyone you like. Or dislike. But with the limited budget and resources at my disposal, I went for the same compromises as before.

The sex of the player's avatar is both male and female, with wiggly bits, wobbly bits and dangly bits interchangeable from time to time. The avatar's skin colour is neutral, although I'm sure changing the skin tone at random is nowhere near as difficult as I was told. The body mass is preprogrammed simply as a mirror of what happens to many contemporary Westerners of my generation. We grow up quite nice and slim, pile on some weight in our middle years, and the weight falls away again as we approach death. And as for hair styles, they are the easiest of all. The avatar is bald.

The game goes full circle, of course, and I wanted the final scene to return to something that is personal to the individual player but applicable to everyone. That's why at the start of the game I ask players to drag a glowing beacon to a point on the spinning planet that represents their place of birth. Then, in the dying moments of the game, that's the spot they get delivered back to. Yes, I know it's a cliché, but at least it's a comforting one.

Throughout my life I have had a recurring dream where I am flying way up high, trying to get back to somewhere - usually my birthplace, though sometimes it's a hotel room. In my dream it is incredibly safe and easy to defy gravity and take off from edges and ledges, but I usually wake up when I get entangled with power cables or tree tops on my way back down to earth.

Here comes the full content of *Deus Ex Machina 2*, and this chapter picks us up floating free and takes us through to the end of Shakespeare's First Age.

The languages for the translation of each scene have been selected at random, by the way, and the graphics are a mixture of sketches, concept artwork and screenshots.

3 / Camera pedestals down.
After language selection, audio kicks in as the mouse enters the shot. Mouse stops to sniff the screens then proceeds down the cable to the lower platform. The three layers of depth provide a parallax movement as the camera moves.

4 / Camera pedestals down.
Mouse looks down and sniffs around for an exit. There is none. Suddenly the characters rotate to reveal the text, and light up the neons. A lid also blinks as the gas arm activates.

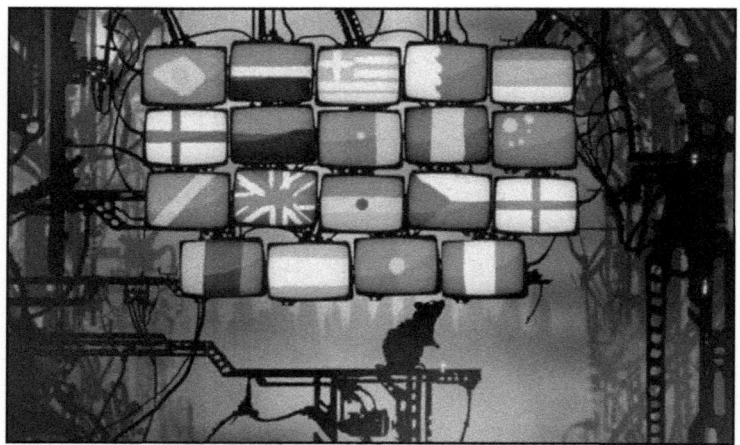

PRELUDE

The Programmer:
>Tuesday evening, after tea and compulsory prayers,
>Τρίτη απόγευμα, μετά από το τσάι και τις υποχρεωτικές προσευχές,
>the last mouse on Earth tried to hide from Mankind,
>inside the Machine.

*το τελευταίο ποντίκι στη Γη προσπάθησε να κρυφτεί
από την Ανθρωπότητα, μέσα στη Μηχανή.*

Just before it died, as the nerve-gas eased its sphincter,
Λίγο πριν πεθάνει, καθώς το νευροτοξικό αέριο χαλάρωσε το σφιγκτήρα του,
the last ever mouse-dropping caused a slight accident.
το τελευταίο κόπρανο ποντικιού προκάλεσε ένα μικρό ατύχημα.

You may control the progress of this Accident,
Μπορείς να ελέγξεις την πρόοδο αυτού του Ατυχήματος,
on my behalf, and with my permission,
εκ μέρους μου, με την άδεια μου,
and lead it up the telepath.
και να το οδηγήσεις στην τηλεμεταφορά.

All the Screen's a stage,
Όλες οι Οθόνες είναι μια σκηνή,
and all the men and women merely players.
και όλοι οι άντρες και οι γυναίκες απλοί παίχτες.

They have their exits and their entrances,
Έχουν τις εξόδους τους και τις εισόδους τους,
and one person in their time plays many parts,
και ένα άτομο στο χρόνο τους παίζει πολλούς ρόλους,
their Acts being Seven Ages.
οι Πράξεις τους είναι οι Επτά Ηλικίες.

At first the infant,
Στην αρχή το βρέφος,
mewling in the test-tube's neck.
να κλαψουρίζει στο λαιμό του δοκιμαστικού σωλήνα.

And then the whining School-Child,
Και έπειτα το κλαψιάρικο Σχολιαρόπαιδο,
with games machine and shining morning face,
με παιχνιδομηχανή και λαμπερό πρωινό πρόσωπο,
creeping like a snail, unwillingly to databank.
έρπει σαν σαλιγκάρι, απρόθυμα στην τράπεζα δεδομένων.

And then the Lover,
Και αργότερα ο Εραστής,
sighing like a furnace,
αναστενάζει σαν καμίνι,
with a woeful video made to their lover's hologram.
σε ένα αξιολύπητο βίντεο φτιαγμένο από το ολόγραμμα των εραστών τους.

Then a Soldier,
Μετά ένας Στρατιώτης,
jealous in honor, sudden and quick in quarrel,
ζηλιάρης για την τιμή, ξαφνικός και γρήγορος στον καυγά,
seeking hi-score, even in the laser's mouth.
έχει μεγάλους στόχους, ακόμη και στα πιο επικίνδυνα.

And then the Justice, in fair round belly,
Και παραπέρα η Δικαιοσύνη, με σχετικά στρογγυλή κοιλιά,
with shaded eyes and clothes of designer-cut,
με σκιασμένα μάτια και ρούχα σχεδιαστών,
full of slick words and celebrity.
γεμάτη όμορφες λέξεις και δημοσιότητα.

And so they play their part.
Και έτσι παίζουν το ρόλο τους.

The Sixth age shifts into the lean and slippered old buffoon,
Η έκτη Ηλικία μεταμορφώνει σε ένα αδύνατους γέρικους παλιάτσους με παντόφλες,
with spectacles on nose,
τα γυαλιά στη μύτη,
their underpants, well saved,
τα εσώρουχα τους, καλό ξυρισμένους,
a world too wide for their shrunken shank.
ένας κόσμος πολύ πλατύς για το συρρικνωμένο πόδι τους.
And their adult speech synthesizer
Και ο συνθέτης της φωνής ενηλίκου
turning again towards a childish treble,
να γυρίζει ξανά προς το παιδικό τρέμουλο,
piping and whistling in its sound.
να σφυρίζει μέσα από τον ήχο του.

Last scene of all that ends this strange, eventful history,
Η τελευταία των σκηνών τελειώνει αυτή την παράξενη, γεμάτη γεγονότα ιστορία,
is Second Childishness and mere oblivion.
είναι μια Δεύτερη Παιδικότητα και απλά μια λήθη.
Without keyboard,
Χωρίς πληκτρολόγιο,
without monitor,
χωρίς οθόνη,
without power supply.
χωρίς ηλεκτρικό ρεύμα.

Your life is expressed as a percentage score.
Η ζωή σου εκφράζεται σε αποτέλεσμα ποσοστών.
Observe the percentage.
Παρατήρησε το ποσοστό.
Your score changes.

Το αποτέλεσμα σου αλλάζει.
Imagine if this were nothing but an electronic game.
Φαντάσου σαν αυτό να είναι παρά μόνο ένα ηλεκτρονικό παιχνίδι.

CONCEPTION

I don't remember my conception. It was before my time. But I do remember my Mum and Dad's favourite record collection from back then, and their iron-framed squeaky bed.

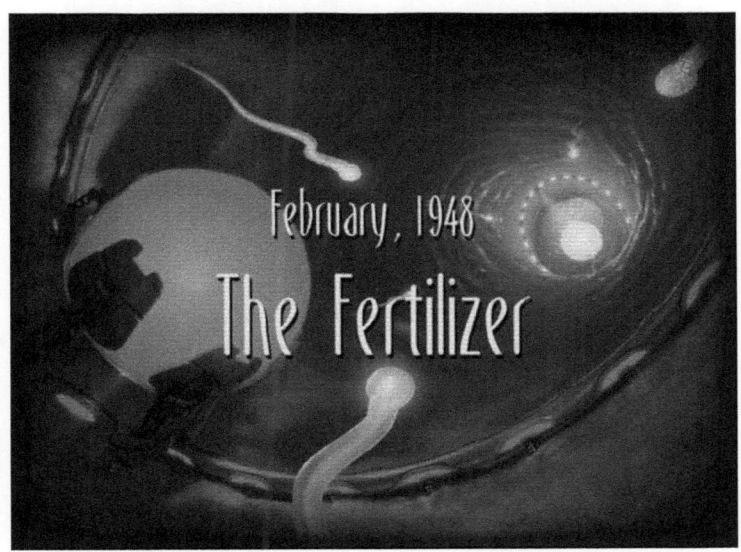

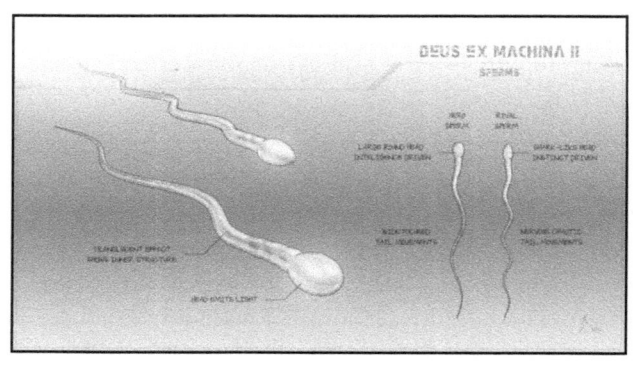
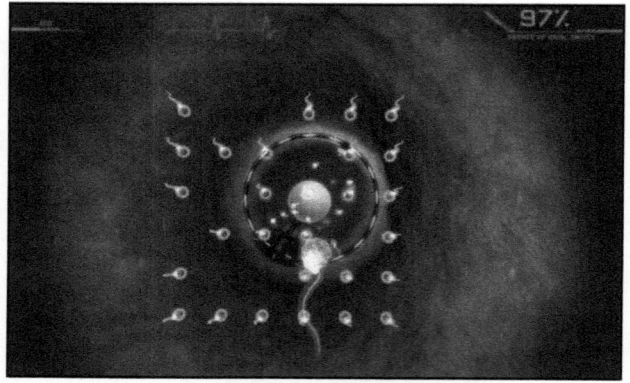
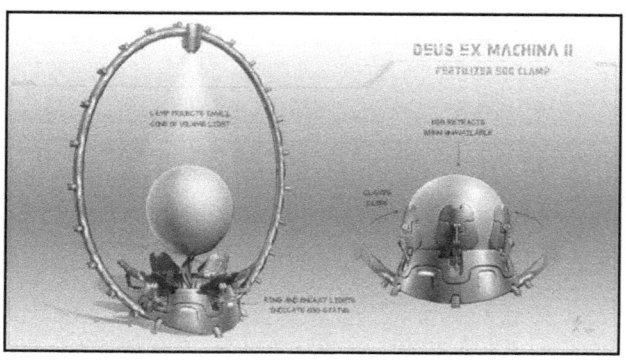

The Fertilizer:
    Hello! Wotcha cock!
    Hallo! Står jernet!
    I'm a Fertilizing Agent,
    Jeg er en Befrugtningsagent,
    My brothers are all wriggly.
    Alle mine brødre spræller.

    Wotcha cock!
    Står jernet!
    I'm a Fertilizing Agent,
    Jeg er en Befrugtningsagent,
    My brothers are all wriggly.
    Alle mine brødre spræller.

    Touch us with a digit,
    Rør ved os med en finger,
    Make us go all giggly.
    Gør os alle fjollede.

Hello!
Hallo!
Make us go all giggly.
Gør os alle fjollede.

Stir us up, Tovarich,
Rør os rundt, Tovarich,
Handy as a manual.
Behændigt som en manual.
Sinister and dexter,
Mod venstre og mod højre,
Handy as a manual.
Behændigt som en manual.

Help us father woodlice,
Hjælp os fader bænkebider,
Tax collectors and a spaniel.
Skatteopkrævere og en spaniel.
Help us father woodlice,
Hjælp os fader bænkebider,
Tax collectors and a spaniel.
Skatteopkrævere og en spaniel.

The satellites are shining,
Satellitterne skinner,
The acid rain looks pretty.
Syreregnen er smuk.

Fission chips and psych eclipse.
Fission chips og psych eclipse.
Fission chips and psych eclipse.
Fission chips og psych eclipse.
Fission chips and psych eclipse.
Fission chips og psych eclipse.
Ha-ha ha-ha ha, ha-ha ha-ha haa.
Ha-ha ha-ha ha, ha-ha ha-ha haa.

My aim is high and noble.
Mit mål er højt og ædelt.
I'm singing as I'm swimming.
Jeg synger, mens jeg svømmer.
My aim is high and noble.
Mit mål er højt og ædelt.
I'm singing as I'm swimming.
Jeg synger, mens jeg svømmer.
I giggle and I wriggle
Jeg fniser, og jeg vrider mig
And make a new beginning.
Og får en ny start.

Hello little Belle,
Hej lille Skønhed,
I believe we have an appointment with Destiny.
Jeg tror, vi har en aftale med Skæbnen.
A short life,
Et kort liv,
but a happy one.
men et lykkeligt liv.

BIRTH

The Machine:
    I keep the watch.
    Je monte la garde
    I see it all.
    et je vois tout.
    I tap the phone.
    Je tapote sur le téléphone
    I file and number.
    Je range, je classe.

    I am machine,
    Je suis machine

I am machine,
Je suis machine
I am machine.
Je suis machine
I've always been.
Depuis toujours.

I take the truth.
J'emporte la vérité
I give the lie.
J'octroie le mensonge.
I cover the land
Je couvre la terre
With copper and cable.
de cuivre et de câbles.

I am machine,
Je suis machine
I am machine,
Je suis machine
I am machine.
Je suis machine
I've always been.
Depuis toujours.

In the beginning
Au commencement
There was the word.
Il y avait le monde
There was only one word.
Un seul monde
And the word
et le monde
Was
était
No!
Non !

Look at the score-clock
Regardez le compteur de score
Down in the corner.
dans le coin du bas.
No mouse to run up it.
Aucune souris ne court dessus.
The mice they all dead.
Les souris sont toutes mortes.
The rat is surviving.
Seul le rat survit.
The digits are counting,
Les chiffrent tournent
Counting your blessing.
et comptent votre crédit.

I am machine,
Je suis machine
I am machine,
Je suis machine
I am machine.
Je suis machine
I've always been.
Depuis toujours.

I'll tell you a secret:
Je vais vous dire un secret,
You were conceived
Vous n'avez pas été conçu
Not in a test tube
dans un tube à essais
But in a pint mug.
Mais dans une chope de bière.

Here come your head.
Ici, votre tête
Here come your arm.
Ici, votre bras
Here come your leg.
Ici, votre jambe
Here come your placenta.
Ici, votre placenta.

Cut the cord.
Couper le cordon
Clamp it up.
Pincez-le.
Tie it off.
Fixez-le
It's your time
C'est le moment
to be born.
de naître.

The Defect:
I never asked to be born.
Je n'ai jamais demandé à naître
But since I'm here,
Mais maintenant que j'y suis
I'm taking over.
J'assume.

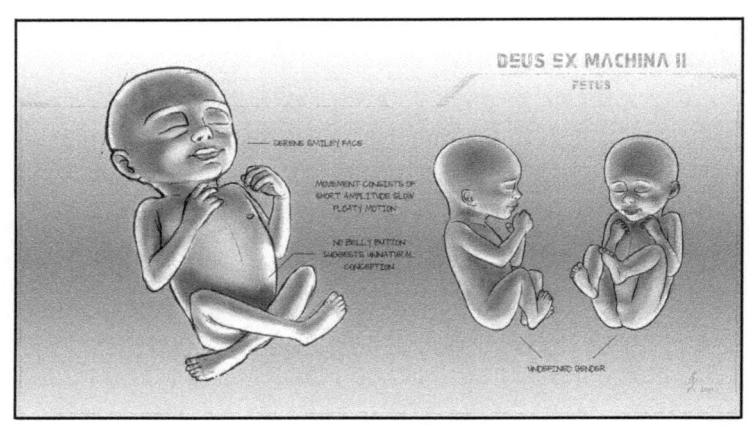
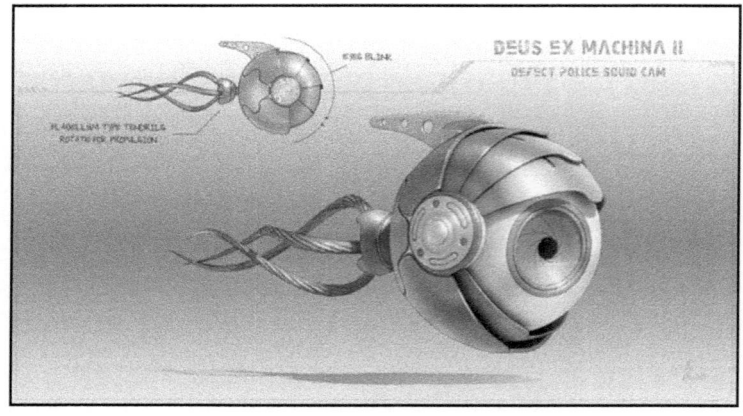

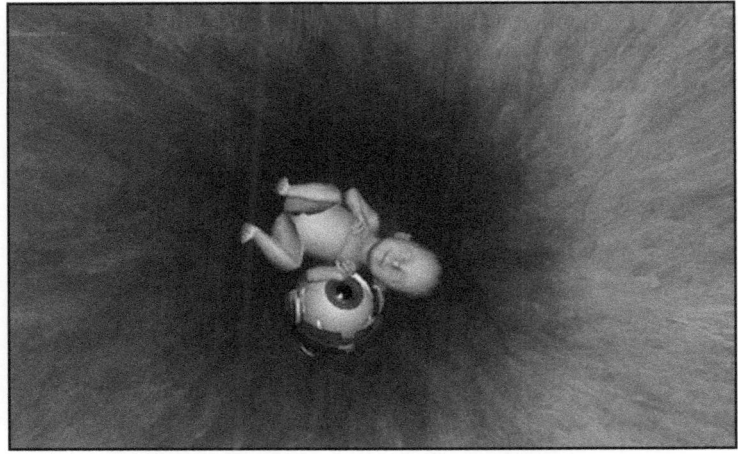

INFANCY

The Narrator:
    At first, the infant, mewling in the test tube's neck.
    Сперва - младенец, в пробирке хнычущий...

The Defect Police:
    Hello, hello, what have we here?
    A Defect, I'll be bound.
    Ну здрасте, здрасте, кто к нам пришёл?
    Какой-то дефект природы, никак не иначе.

    A quantity of protein
    Crawling on the ground.
    Какой-то сгусток протеина,
    ползающий по земле.

    It cannot be a Citizen,
    It hasn't got a number
    Какой-то неучтённый гражданин,
    без учётного номера

    Tattooed upon its baldy head.
    What is it then, I wonder?
    вытатуированного на лысой голове.
    Интересно, что это может быть?

    All stand up. All fall down.
    Stay on your own two feet.
    Ну-ка, всем встать! Ну-ка, упасть!
    Стой на своих двух!

    A viper in a diaper,
    You don't smell so sweet.
    Какая-то гадючка в подгузнике,
    да еще и смердит.

When I knock it down,
Just gets up again.
*Я его сбиваю с ног,
а он встает опять.*

See if it stays standing
Until I count to ten.
*Интересно, выстоит ли,
пока я досчитаю до десяти.*

One, two, three, four
Раз, два, три, четыре,

... ten!
... десять!

Try to keep your balance.
No mammy and no pappy.
*Баланс удерживай ты сам.
Ни пап тебе тут нет, ни мам.*

Stop that silly wobble.
Is everybody happy!
*И не качайся, как матрос,
а по ветру держи свой нос!*

Let's scoop it up and take it
For probing and dissection,
*Ну-ка, давай его возьмем
для вскрытья и инспекции,*

And keep the other babies free from
This sort of infection.
*чтоб уберечь других детей
от эдакой инфекции.*

One step at a time now.
One step and another.
Еще шажок, потом другой,
ступая след во след,

Never had a daddy,
Hasn't got a mother.
ни папы рядом нет с тобой,
ни мамы тоже нет.

Walk the line my Defect,
Don't you dare to moan.
Будь осторожен в жизни, но
не плачь и не скули,

I'm always there beside you,
You'll never walk alone.
с тобой я буду всё равно,
один не будешь ты.

Run my little Defect,
Run, but you can't hide.
Хоть можно от меня сбежать,
но спрятаться нельзя.

Run the straight and narrow.
Let me be your guide.
Учись-ка по прямой шагать,
бери пример с меня.

You don't have to thank me.
You don't have to beg.
И не меня благодари,
свои ж - какой расчёт,

Run down every nostril.
Run down every leg.
а вот соплю-то подотри,
ведь по ноге течёт.

When I say jump, jump!
Когда скажу я «прыгай», прыгай!

Wait for it, wait for it...

Подожди-ка пока, подожди...

... JUMP!
... ПРЫГАЙ!

Shove it in the mincer.
Stretch it on the rack.
То ли сунуть тебя в мясорубку,
то ли вздёрнуть тебя на дыбу,

I thought I heard an order
To throw the Defect back.
то ли я слышал приказ
подтолкнуть тебя к краю обрыва?

Hello, hello, what have we here?
A Defect, I'll be bound.
Какая милая картина -
дефект, ползущий по земле.

A quantity of protein
Crawling on the ground.
Печальный сгусток протеина,
поднявший голову во мгле.

You are going to help me
Put the world inside my pocket.
*Впрочем, время ещё есть и ты мне
поможешь подмять под себя весь мир,*

Then I'll rip your plug out,
And I'll burn out your socket!
*а уж потом я твой штепсель
из розетки выдерну!*

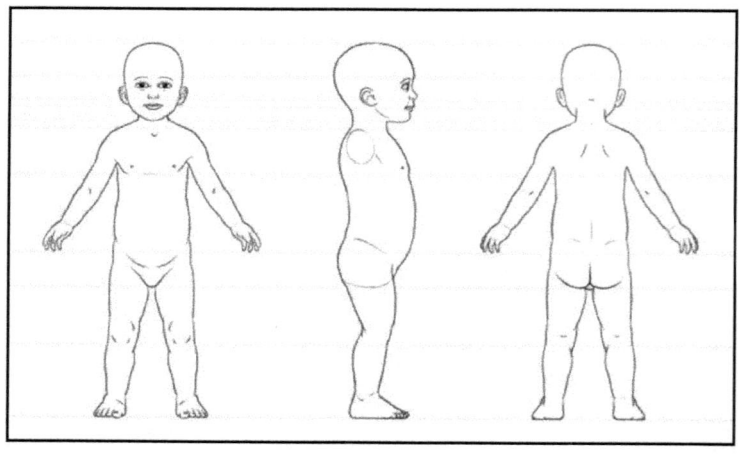

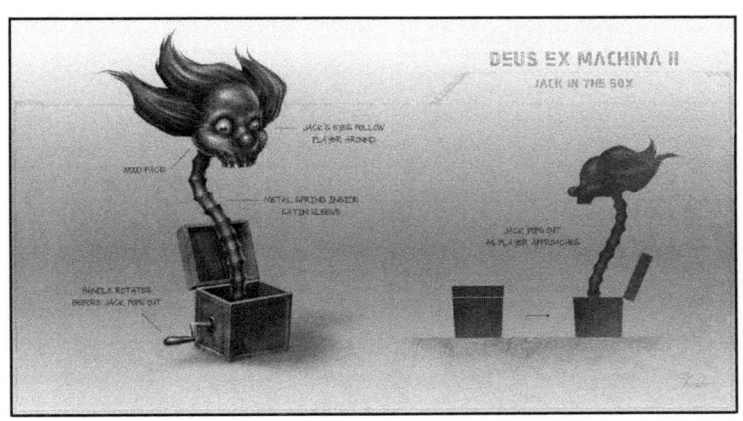
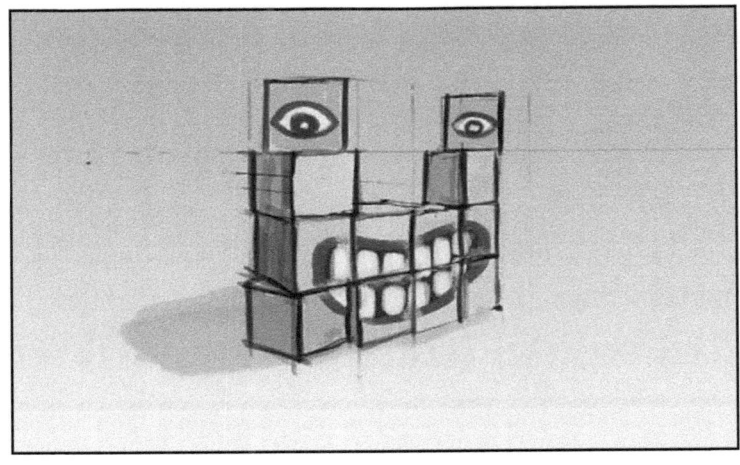

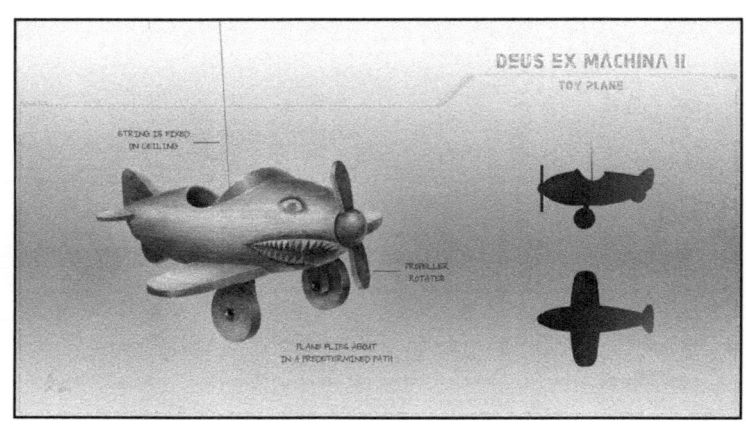

Chapter 11

School and Adolescence

This chapter deals with the whining schoolchild. There was no School sequence in the original *Deus Ex Machina*, but there should have been. I had no money left to hire another voice to play the School Teacher, and very little machine memory to spare. So it got dumped. Here it is reinstated as an endless and meaningless task of matching up 1950s trigger-images that start at nursery level and progress all the way through to prepubescence.

The school setting in *Deus Ex Machina 2* is a fascist institution with long corridors, propaganda posters and that jolly commandant with the voice of Julie Andrews from *The Sound Of Music*. It is a fantasy. My own school, which was not a fantasy, was far worse. For a start it was all male. Julie Andrews was not on the curriculum, and nor was anyone else with a vagina. My school was founded in 1732, the same year the foundation stone was laid for the Bank of England. Unlike the Bank of England, my school revelled in the architecture of Auschwitz, because it too was originally a barracks, and it too was in the business of liquidating unhappy souls.

Infant boarders were kenelled there, dragged and exiled from their nurseries, because their parents were too incompetent or too well off to care for them. Children were herded onto the parade ground, because their idiot brains needed to be moulded into post-war leaders for the next war. And then there were the 'masters', reeking of fags, booze, frustration and disappointment, and armed with weapons of corporal punishment.

Not all of my teachers were sadists or pedophiles. Some were just sad, miserable bastards. Some were still suffering from the Second World War. Some were still suffering from the First World War. One very old maths teacher, who lived in a caravan and drank from a reservoir of rum hidden under the wormholes around his desk inkwell, claimed to have fought in the Boer War. There was a dapper young Latin teacher, who had avoided the draft because he was certifiable, but who liked to dress up in military uniform and teach us how to kill the enemy using a knife, or a garrotte, or a rolled-up newspaper. And I was quite fond of my music teacher, who was very blind, very deaf, and very well connected. But I was not at all fond of my art teacher, who was bipolar and either praised my daubings or beat the shit out of me.

What they all had in common was that they wore long, black wizard gowns and trailed specks of chalk dust that sparkled in beams of surprise light. Those robes of illumination tricks stopped me hating them completely. On ceremonial occasions, they sported mortar-board hats with subtly faded tassels. And at the drop of a hat they would whip out a thin cane or a thickly-soled slipper, and redden our arses. They all had the right to beat us if we broke the rules, and they all had the right to make up the rules as they went along.

This right was extended to Sixth Form boys, Kapo who were a few years older than me and who were decorated for their collaboration with embroidered waistcoats, and a penchant for sport which equated to violence.

I particularly hated the cross-country runs that I was forced to take part in, which were patrolled by schoolmasters and older boys placed at strategic intervals along the route. If my pace displeased them, they would encourage me to speed up by mockery.

As the son of a refugee tiger-mother and a tubercular dockyard stud, it was unlikely that I would get sent to the sort of school I have parodied in *Deus Ex Machina*. But the British educational system in the 1950s was quirky. At the age of eleven all children took a national exam, designed to segregate future bosses from future workers, and one aspect of this system was that a handful of smart working-class kids got spotted, plucked out of their depth, creamed off and transplanted to elite schools. There to sink or swim.

This was not altruism, it was a cynical method of boosting the university entrance results of British fee-paying schools at the expense of British state schools. And it also helped maintain the charity status of private education for the rich, which was then, as is now, simple tax avoidance.

There were a handful of us so-called "scholarship boys" in my school, and as I watched the others twitch and flinch their way through our first few days, I made up my mind to beat these sons of gentlefolk at their own rotten little game. I changed my accent immediately. That was easy. I acted the joker to mask my terror, and I hid my straw boater school hat when crossing the border from the rich people's zone back on to my home patch, where an inside toilet was a rarity and a motor car belonged to the doctor or the policeman.

SCHOOL

The Programmer:
>Then the whining School Child, with games machine and shining morning face,
>*Und dann das quengelnde Schulkind, mit Videospiel und glänzendem Morgengesicht,*
>
>creeping like a snail, unwillingly to databank.
>*schleicht es, wie eine Schnecke, widerwillig zur Datenbank.*

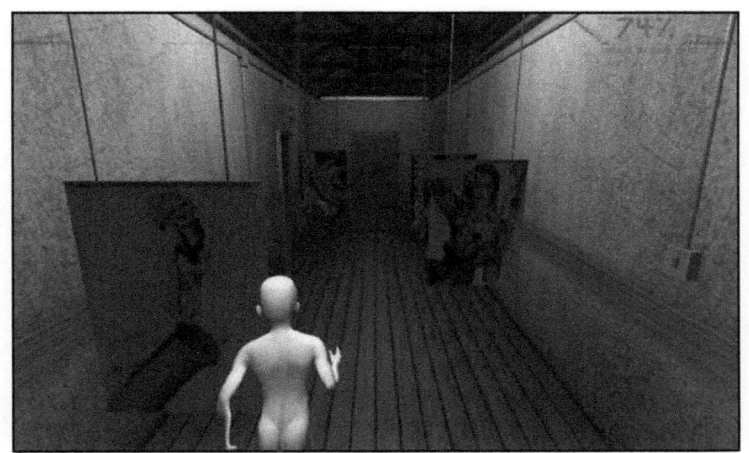

The Teacher:
    Hello, hello, children everywhere.
    Hallo, hallo, ihr Kinder überall.
    Hello, hello, it's time to shave your hair.
    Hallo, hallo, Zeit zum Haareschneiden.

    Obey, obey, and toe the party line.
    Gehorcht, gehorcht, bleibt immer linientreu.
    Conform, conform. Keep smiling all the time.
    Anpassen, anpassen. Und lächeln nicht vergessen.

    Here's a game for you to play - match up all the pairs
    Hier, ein Spiel für euch - findet die, die zusammengehörn:
    Of deviants and foreign scum and little teddy bears.
    Abartige, Ausländerabschaum und kleine Teddybären.

    Hello, hello.
    Hallo, hallo.
    Now play, and play.
    Spielt jetzt, nur zu.

And learn, and burn.
Und lernt, und brennt.
Obey, obey.
Gehorcht, gehorcht.

Smile, smile, smile, smile,
Careful where you look.
Lächeln, lächeln, lächeln, lächeln,
pass auf, wohin du schaust.
Smile, smile, smile, smile,
Let's burn all the books.
Lächeln, lächeln, lächeln, lächeln,
und alle Bücher werden brennen.

Smile, smile, smile, smile,
Look me in the eye.
Lächeln, lächeln, lächeln, lächeln,
schau mir ins Gesicht.
Smile, smile, smile, smile,
Never reason why.
Lächeln, lächeln, lächeln, lächeln,
Gründe braucht es nicht.

Salute, salute.
Bow down, bow down.
Salutieren, salutieren,
und bücken, und bücken.
Turn left, turn left.
Turn right, turn right.
Nach links, nach links.
nach rechts, nach rechts.

Tra-la-laa! La-la-laa! La-lala-la-laa!
Tra-la-laa! La-la-laa! La-lala-la-laa!
Tra-la-laa! La-la-laa! La-lala-la-laa!
Tra-la-laa! La-la-laa! La-lala-la-laa!

Smile, smile, smile, smile,
That's the way to look.
Lächeln, lächeln, lächeln, lächeln,
so muss es aussehn.
Smile, smile, smile, smile,
Let's burn all the books.
Lächeln, lächeln, lächeln, lächeln,
alle Bücher werden brennen.

Now dance, and sing.
And spy and tell.
Jetzt tanzt und singt,
spioniert und berichtet.
Inform, inform.
And smile, and smile.
Informiert, informiert.
Und lächelt und lächelt.

Keep smi-i-i-i-ling!
Immer schön lä-ä-ä-ä-cheln!

ADOLESCENCE

My own adolescence was hormone-driven, much the same as any other boy's. Although my voice slid down gracefully from treble to baritone without any crunching gear-changes, the acne showed no grace at all and erupted with a vengeance. My skin played host to rampant zits for years, and I dreaded school sports in case I had to remove my vest and reveal the peaks and craters on the dark side of my moon. Squeezing them was necessary, and the volcanic ones that hit the mirror were as disgusting as they were satisfying. The body hairs were much more artistic. At first they sprouted and uncurled individually in surprise locations, like sweet peas reaching for the sun. But then they absorbed guilt and congregated in dark, damp conspiracies, hiding from the light. The player's avatar is of ambiguous sex throughout *Deus Ex Machina*, and as an adolescent male I had no experience of the moods and mess of monthly blood-letting. But I could see that girls suffered from spots as well as boys, and there were hints that they were also growing their first crop of downy facial and body hair.

I had featured a pustule-squeezing video game and a rogue hair title in my *Can Of Worms* compilation for the ZX81, back in 1981, and wanted to reuse the themes for *Deus*. But the entire Adolescence sequence got dropped from the original *Deus Ex Machina* gameplay, not so much because it was in bad taste, but more because of the usual memory restrictions of the machines. For the remake there were no such restrictions. My adolescent avatar could frolic through an hallucinogenic landscape of fantasy breasts, buttocks and thighs, erectile trees, rivers of bodily fluids, pell mel. And all in pursuit of a hormone-driven prize that the body insisted was there but the brain had no idea where or why. And so, I make no apologies for the fact that my gameplay for this section involves nothing more than sprouting pubic hair and pus hitting the screen. It's just a phase I went through. And to a greater or lesser extent, you did too. We deal with it, and we move on.

My adolescence coincided with the evolution from 1950s half-tone rock'n'roll into the Technicolor of 1960s harmonised doo-wop and teen themes, and I tried to capture this on the soundtrack. Imagine a male puppy, testicles descended, frustrated by the instinctive humping of an unresponsive leg, suddenly let off the leash to follow the scent of bitch-trails across a totally unfamiliar cross-country landscape. Now set it to the sounds of The Beach Boys.

You've got the picture.

The Defect:
> When your skin explodes like cheese on cannelloni.
> *Cuando tu piel explota como queso en canelones.*
> When your voice goes funny and you don't know what to say.
> *Cuando tu voz se va y no sabes que decir.*

You dream a dream that gets you pheromonie.
Sueñas un sueño que activa tus feromonas.
You got hairs downstairs that weren't there yesterday.
Tienes pelo allá abajo que no estaba allí ayer.

So dab a little makeup on your spots now.
Así que ponte un poco de maquillaje en tus manchas.
And pluck away that hair from off your chin.
Y arranca ese pelo de tu mentón.
Spray the smell away when you get the hots now.
Rocía lejos el olor cuando estés encendido.

Get a grope you dope, though you know it's a sin.
Mete mano tonto, aunque sabes que es pecado.
Whoo-oo!
¡Yupi!

Run to the mirror and shake your hips.
Corre al espejo y mueve tus caderas.
Run to the mirror and pucker your lips.
Corre al espejo y frunce tus labios.
Run to the mirror and squeeze your zits away.
Corre al espejo y aprieta tus teclas.

When your skin explodes like cheese on cannelloni.
Cuando tu piel explota como queso en canelones.
When your voice goes funny and you don't know what to say.
Cuando tu voz se va y no sabes que decir.
You dream a dream that gets you pheromonie.
Sueñas un sueño que activa tus feromonas.
You got hairs downstairs that weren't there yesterday.
Tienes pelo allá abajo que no estaba allí ayer.

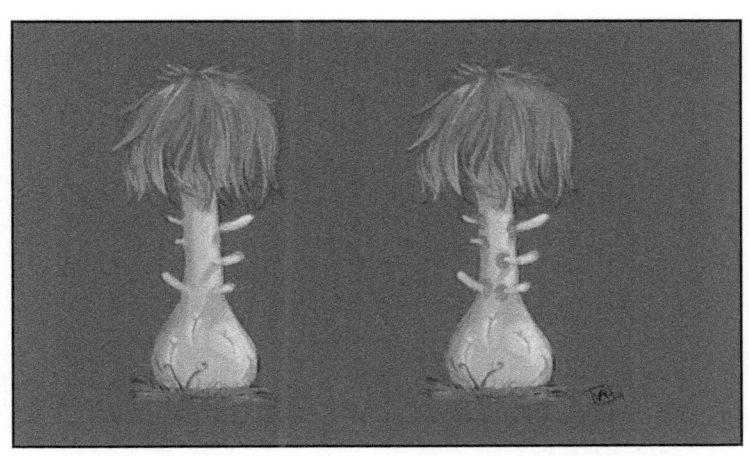

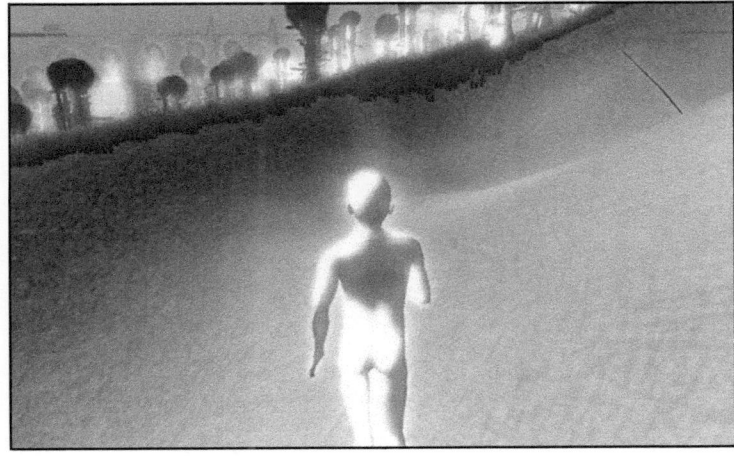

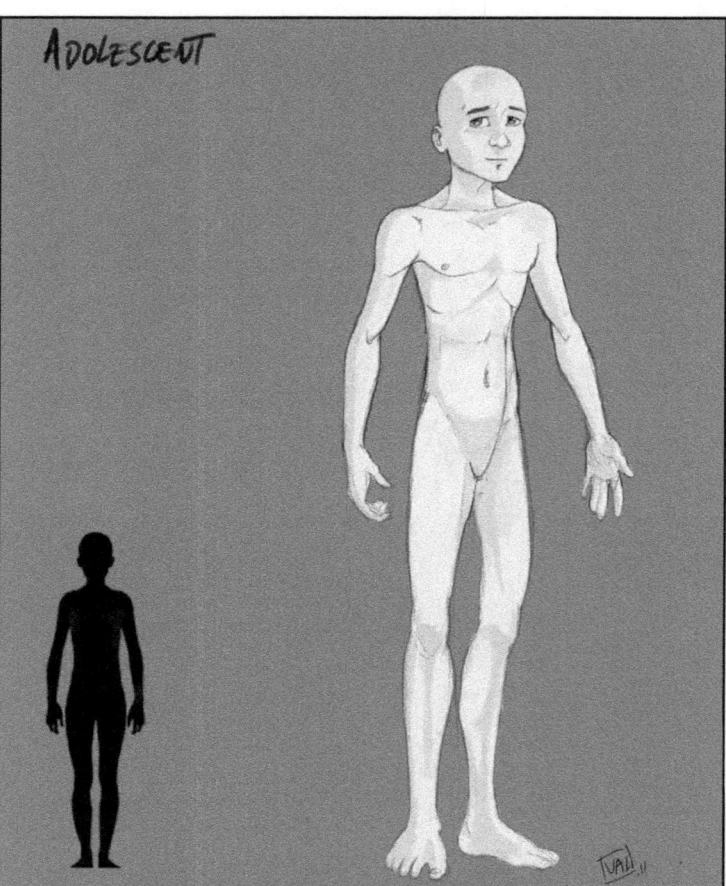

Chapter 12

Love and Betrayal

LOVE

In Shakespeare's definitions, the age immediately after the Schoolchild is that of the Lover. Real life tends to mix things up a bit, but 'making love' is a wonderful phrase in any language, including this one. Sadly, in video games the positive power of love is rarely harnessed as a gaming factor. The opposite is far more likely. The negative powers of hate are the most common currency of computerised gaming. If and when love is harnessed, it is debased as a false gaming goal and commercially packaged as an in-game asset, an asset that can be bought or manoeuvred as part of social gameplay. This is a regretful consequence of a cynical entertainment industry and it holds true in movies, video games, novels, soap opera and song lyrics, especially when jaded adults dangle it in front of inexperienced youngsters.

The Love sequence of *Deus Ex Machina 2* is set firmly in the 1960s. Not in the celebrated Summer Of Love, but a couple of years before, when I had the good fortune not to fall in love, but to dive in headfirst and swim like a demented porpoise. This innocent and mutually enjoyable form of love does not celebrate any social or moral commitment, and neither does it denigrate it. It simply rejoices in the conjoining of young people in happy sexual activity. What is offered in this sequence of the game is an access-all-areas enjoyment of the human body. Nobody gets hurt, no animals are harmed, no guilt or regret is generated.

The music has echoes of Pink Floyd, who were architectural students at the same time I was still abusing my student grant, booking bands and trying to play in them. But the setting is unashamedly *Yellow Submarine*, and was Tiago Loureiro's brainchild, even though he would not be born until long after that era. I am not very good at writing love songs, but Chyna Whyne sings this beautifully, as did Donna Bailey first time round, and to me this sequence has always been one of the most emotive and moving.

In the Love sequence of *Deus Ex Machina 2*, the player's avatar rotates and writhes and enjoys the pleasures of oral sex, depicted by animated lips. The body is neither male nor is it female. The sex is neither penetrative nor is it onanistic. It is an innocent joyride. It is what I remember as my own tumble into first love.

She was still a schoolgirl, and I was still a schoolboy. Our consummation took place in a derelict building which we had broken into because our woodland fumblings could no longer be contained and besides, winter had begun to nip our extremities. The art-deco metal windows had warped and could be popped open, allowing us to climb through. We discovered a red, white and blue British Union flag as our virgin soldier bedsheet, and I hope that after our fluids had adjusted the colours in a small way they were displayed in public celebration on many a state occasion afterwards.

To begin with, we were rubbish at lovemaking. But we learned fast. And then, much to our mutual delight, we learned slow. Our mutual experience of first love was lovely, and I only hope yours was too.

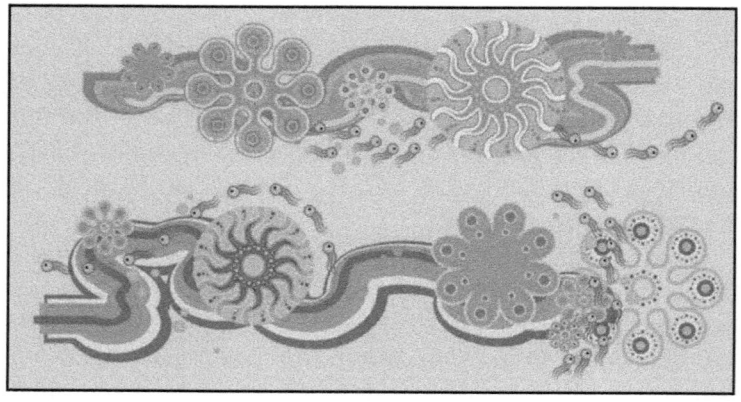

The Programmer:
   And then the Lover, sighing like a furnace,
   Och sen Älskaren, suckande som en masugn,
   with a woeful video made to their lover's hologram.
   till en bedrövlig video gjord med den älskades hologram.

The Machine:
   Sixteen years are filed behind you
   Sexton år har gått
   Needing no one but Machine.
   Behöver ingen annan än Maskinen.
   The Voice inside your head grows quiet.
   Rösten inom dig tystnar.
   The time is come to reach and touch
   Another human being.
   Stunden är inne att sträcka sig mot och beröra
   En annan människa.

   Give and take and share each other.
   Att ge och ta och få del av varandra.
   Link your thoughts and link your forms.
   Koppla ihop tankar och kroppar.
   Use your power to be more gentle
   Använd makt till mjukhet.
   Use your strength to show more care.
   Använd styrka till omtänksamhet.

   Reading minds can hurt you badly
   Att läsa andras tankar kan göra så ont
   Bleeding hearts and frightened souls.
   Blödande hjärtan och skrämda själar.
   Suffer foolish people gladly
   Uthärdar gärna dumbommar
   Easy come but hard to go.
   Lätt vunnet trögt försvunnet.

Give and take and share each other.
Att ge och ta och få del av varandra.
Link your thoughts and link your forms.
Koppla ihop tankar och kroppar.
Use your power to be more gentle.
Använd makt till ömhet.
Use your strength to show more care.
Använd styrka till omtanke.

Take them in your arms and feel them
Ta dem i dina armar och bli dem varse.
Rocking gently side to side.
Vaggande mjukt från sida till sida.
Touch their scars and try to heal them.
Berör deras ärr och försök läka dem.
Today's the day your sadness died.
Idag ska ditt vemod dö.

Take them in your arms and feel them
Ta dem i dina armar och bli dem varse.
Rocking gently side to side.
Vaggande mjukt från sida till sida.
Touch their scars and try to heal them.
Berör deras ärr och försök läka dem.
Today's the day your sadness died.
Idag ska ditt vemod dö.
Today's the day your sadness died.
Idag ska ditt vemod dö.

BETRAYAL

I have betrayed most people dear to me in some way or another, and I experience sporadic guilt and sorrow because of it. In my case, I usually betray people because I run from any sort of confrontation, and I often say OK when I should say no way. I tend to get involved with enthusiasts, I tend to promise what they want me to deliver rather than what I want to deliver, and

I tend to expend time on worthy but hopeless causes. This is not because I am unaware of their intrinsic flaws, but because I really don't like to offend nice people. Don't get me wrong, I'm very happy to offend nasty people, but if I detect any hint of niceness, then my offensiveness gets bottled.

No doubt psychoanalysis would refer me back to my outsider infant self, neither completely English nor a foreigner, neither a guttersnipe nor a boy-in-a-boater, neither a success nor a failure, but always trying to please and to fit in with the company I was keeping. Even my accent would change depending on who I was with, and on occasion it still does.

I think I betrayed many people I worked with, not in a big way, and not because I am heartless, but in a little way, and because I was too much of a coward to be heartless. When I came to the end of a phase and I knew I was ready to move on, or when I got bored and something else took my fancy, or when I screwed up and reckoned it was time to run away, it all got internalised and was rarely expressed to those people who my actions would directly effect. I betrayed them by not telling them until after the event, or by not telling them at all. I have also betrayed many of the principles of my callow youth during my middle years, before recalibrating them all over again in my dotage, politically, socially and economically. Hopefully, I will not lose sight of them again.

The Betrayal sequence in *Deus Ex Machina 2* is much harsher than in the original version. The probing eyes that witness each betrayal are still the same, and the naked truth is still expressed as fleshly exposure, rolling and tumbling. But the avatar is now rolled into a defensive ball, and the setting is now very specific in time and space. We have left the multi-coloured optimism and soft freedoms of the 1960s behind and entered a harsher era of 1970s monochrome op-art cynicism. It's a sort of photographic studio or film set, where every private activity is filmed and recorded to be exploited or used in evidence. Of course this scene has been set with hindsight, knowing that in our future the images of our entire life will be scrutinised by CCTV, exploited by paparazzi, and self-displayed on YouTube, and this is a warning of what is to come.

The guitar is tainted by Jimi Hendrix, but not the ebullience of his early rebellions and celebrations. Instead the reverse-phasing is taken from a more jaded and wearied period before the rot set in and, in his case, resulted in self-destructive end, much too early.

The Machine:
> One more year is all it takes.
> You've forgotten what was taught.
> Now you're wise to lying lies
> To buy the things that can't be bought.
> Fake and take and use each other.
> Hide your thoughts and watch your forms.
> Betrayal.
>
> Use your power to be less gentle.
> Use your strength to show less care.
> Those funny ways now drive you mental.
> Run away to anywhere.
>
> You fail, you fail.
> Betrayal.
>
> They'll take you off to be a soldier.
> Soon be time to move away.
> That's what becomes of growing older.
> No more love unless you pay.
>
> Take them in your arms and crush them,
> Rocking gently, side to side.
> Touch their thoughts and try to steal them.
> Today's the day the magic died.
>
> You fail, you fail.
> Betrayal.

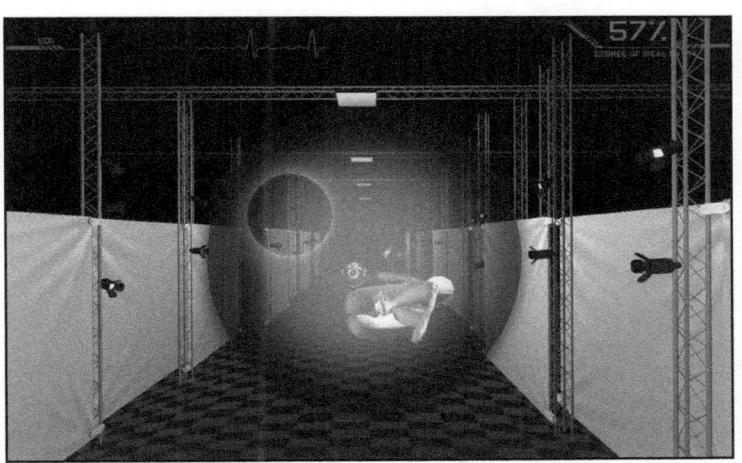

Chapter 13

Soldiering, Pain and War Crimes

THE SOLDIER

My generation of British baby boomers escaped war. We were too young for national service and too old to be called up for any future emergency. Our determined Prime Minister Harold Wilson kept us out of the Vietnam War, and our membership of the European Union guaranteed that we would never go to war against our immediate neighbours in my lifetime.

But I did see the effects of war first hand. The cityscape of the Berlin of my childhood was almost total ruination. There was hardly a building left standing in that huge city, and what had not been skeletised by aerial bombardment had been blown to smithereens by tanks and artillery, street by street, house by house. One of my tasks as a small boy was to pick my way through the rubble down to the basement of an adjoining building and collect warm milk in a blue and white tin jug. They kept a cow down there.

Every conflict since then has been brought into my safe English living room, first by the wheezing, distorted long waves of the radio, then via little black and white television screens, all the way though to the present day with streaming disaster presented by entertainers, in high definition and surround sound. There are essential differences between war-as-entertainment in video games and war-as-entertainment in other media, like stories round the campfire, graphic novel comic books, and the movies. Video games are active, and encourage the individual to perform simulated acts of violence. The rest are passive, and require the individual to do nothing but absorb what is portrayed and maybe reflect on it.

On 12th August 1961, my family was in Charlottenburg, which was then in the British-occupied sector of Berlin, just shy of the American and French sectors, and a half-hour walk from the Russian sector. We had gathered to celebrate my grandmother's birthday, and the last global war had been over for a mere sixteen years. The interval before that one and the previous global war had been twenty-one years. So if we were to keep to schedule and have a world war every generation, then it was time for another one. And thanks to modern technology, it would most likely be over in an hour or so, once the nuclear missiles had been exchanged and the cities of humanity reduced to white hot ash. This worried my generation in general, and me in particular, although I did enjoy post nuclear holocaust sci-fi books, where people seemed to adapt and survive without going very mad or getting very sick.

I clearly remember how I felt the vibrations first, followed by the deep roars of monsters moving through the city, growling, rumbling and snorting. It was, in fact, the sound of American tanks rolling up the street, on their way to meet Russian tanks coming the other way. The radio was jabbering instructions to stay calm even though the entire western part of the city was being sealed off with barricades, and people were getting shot as they tried to flee through the barbed wire newly strung up between East and West. Soldiers were blocking up the windows of houses, stores and even churches that sat on the borderline, as we were extolled not to panic and warned to stay safely indoors. So, like the teenage idiot that I was, I went out to watch the fun. Having never experienced World War Three before, I grabbed the family camera to take some photos, but most of the exposures had already been used up on birthday snaps and I only managed to get a few shots of smiling young men with automatic weapons, grim-faced older officers who knew the score, and some very shiny tanks.

We were all probably one trigger-finger away from disaster, and I wonder what my reaction would have been if somehow I had been given the key to unlock the Big Red Button and command of the launch codes. As far as I can remember, my overwhelming feeling was one of excitement at the prospect of the missiles going up. Then after an hour or so of nothing much happening, I got fed up and wandered back to the flat.

Back at school, they did manage to get me into uniform, at first in the khaki of the army cadet force and later in the grey-blue of the Air Force, and they did their best to teach us children how to kill, first with .22 rifles that were like fairground toys, then with .303 rifles that took your shoulder off no matter how gently you squeezed the trigger, and finally with a 1930s Bren gun that fried my skin while making my teeth chatter, not forgetting the quieter mechanisms of the garrotte and the bayonet. My revulsion was probably more to do with the pantomime claptrap that accompanied these activities, and my journey toward pacifism was by no means damascene, in fact I quite liked guns for a while. But by the time I wrote the soldier sequence to *Deus Ex Machina*, I only had one sentiment to deliver to players who fancy themselves as cannon fodder, and that is the repeated advice to desert at the earliest opportunity. That's why the missiles and hazards all come from behind. Only a fool would run towards them. Or someone who has never questioned an order.

The Soldier level is set in an ordinary city sometime in the 1980s, where the town-planning and architecture have been rearranged by military conflict. I hoped it would resonate with the majority of players, but in terms of graphics and specifics this was impractical and way beyond my budget. The post-punk audio was much easier to achieve, and the football hooligan chanting was very cathartic. By the end of that particular recording I was forced to admit that my own vocal chords were way beyond their sell-by-date, whereas those belonging to the youthful Chris Madin were not.

The Programmer:
>Then a Soldier. Jealous in honor.
>*Wedyn Milwr. Yn genfigennus mewn anrhydedd.*
>
>Sudden, and quick in quarrel. Seeking hi-score, even in the laser's mouth.
>*Yn sydyn a chyflym mewn dadl. Yn chwilio am sgôr uchel, hyd yn oed yng ngheg y laser.*

The Defect:
>I'm so fucking scared!
>*Dwi wedi ffycin dychryn!*
>
>Terror-error.
>Te-terror-or.
>Terror-error!
>*Braw-ow.*
>*Braw-ow.*
>*Braw-ow!*

Terror-error.
Te-terror-or.
Terror-error!
Braw-ow.
Braw-ow.
Braw-ow!

Terror-error.
Te-terror-or.
Terror-error!
Braw-ow.
Braw-aw-ow.
Braw-ow!

Terror-error.
Te-terror-or.
Terror-error!
Braw-ow.
Braw-ow.
Braw-ow!

PAIN

When I made the original version of *Deus Ex Machina* I was not quite forty years old, and like most not-quite-forty-year-olds, I was still in a hurry. By the time I remade *Deus Ex Machina* I was in a wheelchair. But it wasn't old age that got me, it was stupidity.

Stupidity got me on a sunny November afternoon when I was working on the soundtrack overdubs for the remake. I had nipped out to the Co-op to buy something vital, like a light bulb or an onion bulb, and when I returned to my front door, I was on the outside but my key was on the inside. I was locked out of my own house. The obvious thing to do was sneak up the neighbour's alleyway, use their recycling bins to shin over my garden wall, climb up on my kitchen roof, leap towards the bathroom window, and break into my own house. Simple.

They sent off the X-rays of my shattered bone soon after The Worker Who Married Me delivered me to the emergency reception centre. The woman who cushioned me into a hospital bed was a South African mercenary; cool efficient and rather scary. In an emotionless monotone, she informed me that my X-rays were being assessed by an expert in the field, who was a battlefield veteran with the RAF, between Iraq and a hard place. As well as being an orthopedic surgeon, my expert was also a Wing Commander on active military duty, so he was understandably a wee bit busy to see me in person. And with that, she attached the high definition images of my injuries to a simple email, and winged them off to the Wingco.

Within forty minutes he had supplied a full treatment plan, complete with diagrams of where to brace, strap, pin, support, pedicure and bikini wax. In the event, he changed his mind and I was not allowed to bear any weight on my left limb for several long months. Next morning, he talked me through the whole thing via Skype, made sure I understood exactly what was going on, then said he'd be in my neck of the woods in six weeks time, and looked forward to assessing my progress in the flesh, to coin a phrase. God bless the National Health Service. All hail to RAF medical training. And glory to the email attachment.

And so it is that the gameplay of *Deus Ex Machina 2* has a personal flavour. Serving time in a wheelchair, when street babies in their buggies gurned in wordless recognition, then got supercilious when they saw I had no on-board entertainment like rattles, and teethers. Another three months sliding around on my arse up and down a 200 year-old house where the staircases were specifically designed for legs. Then months of rehab where the mood was exactly the same as the cheerful torture of the School sequence. After a couple of years I was much better and walking very well. It still hurt though.

I added the Pain sequence to the game, mostly as a cry of frustrated anger, and mostly directed toward myself. I apologise if this seems self-indulgent, and I know I could have broken my neck. But if there is a single bone not to break in your body then I would particularly advise you to avoid breaking the big heel one. It's the one that bears your entire weight and the pain is severe. But I confess that the Pain sequence is an indulgence, and I hope the floaty euphoria of the pain-killers comes through. I've always thought that the flightpath of a crucified Jesus and a B52 bomber of World War Three would be exactly the same if you had to steer them through a hospital maze.

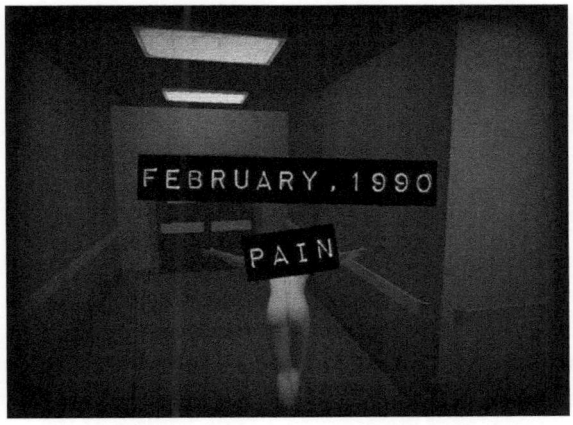

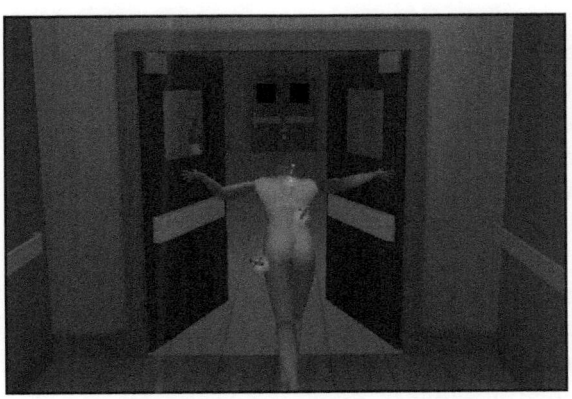

The Defect:
>I got a pain.
>*Em fa mal.*
>Put me together, together, together again.
>*Ajunta'm, ajunta'm, ajunta'm de nou.*
>Together again.
>*Ajunta'm de nou.*
>
>Please will you help me.
>*Si us plau, m'ajudaràs.*
>I got a hole where a hole shouldn't be.
>*Tinc un forat on no hi hauria d'haver cap forat.*
>Hole shouldn't be.
>*No hi hauria d'haver cap forat.*
>
>Tend me.
>*Cuida'm.*
>Mend me.
>*Repara'm.*
>Package up the wreckage and just send me.
>*Empaqueta les restes i envia'm simplement.*
>
>Spare me.
>*Perdona'm.*
>Care me.
>*Tingues cura de mi.*
>Gather up me bones and then repair me.
>*Recull els meus ossos i repara'm.*
>Ow! Ow! Ow! Ow! Ow-wow-wow!
>*Ai! Ai! Ai! Ai! Ai-ai-ai!*
>
>I got a pain.
>*Em fa mal.*
>Put me together, together, together again.
>*Ajunta'm, ajunta'm, ajunta'm de nou.*
>Together again.
>*Ajunta'm de nou.*

Please will you help me.
Si us plau, m'ajudaràs.
I got a hole where a hole shouldn't be.
Tinc un forat on no hi hauria d'haver cap forat.
A hole shouldn't be.
Un forat no ha de ser.

Tend me.
Cuida'm.
Mend me.
Repara'm.
Package up the wreckage and just send me.
Empaqueta les restes i envia'm simplement.

Spare me.
Perdona'm.
Care me.
Tingues cura de mi.
Gather up me bones and then repair me.
Recull els meus ossos i repara'm.
Ow! Ow! Ow! Ow! Ow-wow-wow!
Ai! Ai! Ai! Ai! Ai-ai-ai!

Tend me.
Cuida'm.
Mend me.
Repara'm.
Package up the wreckage and just send me.
Empaqueta les restes i envia'm simplement.

Spare me.
Perdona'm.
Care me.
Tingues cura de mi.
Gather up me bones and then repair me.
Recull els meus ossos i repara'm.

Ow! Ow! Ow! Ow! Ow-wow-wow!
Ai! Ai! Ai! Ai! Ai-ai-ai!

Tend me.
Cuida'm.
Mend me.
Repara'm.
Package up the wreckage and just send me.
Empaqueta les restes i envia'm simplement.

Spare me.
Perdona'm.
Care me.
Tingues cura de mi.
Gather up me bones and then repair me.
Recull els meus ossos i repara'm.
Ow! Ow! Ow! Ow! Ow-wow-wow!
Ai! Ai! Ai! Ai! Ai-ai-ai!

WAR CRIMES ARE EASY

It has always surprised me how well civilisation works in my neck of the woods. When I turn the bathroom tap, I still marvel that hot water comes gushing out. When I hand over coins at the pub, I still marvel that I get a pint of beer in exchange, with a smile and a bit of gossip thrown in for good measure.

Our society has become so complex, and we have become so interdependent, that it's a continual miracle it keeps going and everything still works. Except in America, where nothing much works. In E.M. Forsters 1909 science fiction novella *The Machine Stops*, most of the humans have become dependent on The Machine for communications, entertainment and nurture. Eventually people simply forget how to fix it, so when it eventually breaks down humanity dies out waiting for the repairman to arrive.

I think Forster was wrong. When the machine stops we will not wait around to die in helpless resignation, we'll start eating each other as soon as the supermarkets run out of bacon. War crimes are easy. They always have been and they always will be.

The big difference since I wrote the original version of *Deus Ex Machina* is that thirty years ago war crimes were revealed by professional investigators, then broadcast by corporations, if the advertisers, editors, censors and schedules allowed. Whereas today, war crimes are recorded by civilians on mobile phones and broadcast via Facebook, YouTube and Twitter. Instantly. To everyone. All the time.

I have stood by my family grave and tried to make sense of the hundreds of names inscribed nearby on black stone. The exact places and dates of birth are all present and correct. The exact places and dates of death are missing, replaced by the twin-letter code KZ. This is shorthand for "killed in a death camp." I have stood by a tree in Cambodia, where splinters of baby skulls are embedded in its trunk. Swinging them by the heels was the cheapest and most efficient way of killing the next generation. I have stood aside as the Worker Who Married Me marches slowly with old women in Argentina, as they demand justice for their husbands and sons, jettisoned from the bellies of aircraft into the wide ocean.

Like most of you, I am occasionally moved to tears by a catastrophe in some corner of the world, and click on a button to send a small donation. Like most of you, I wear crimes against humanity lightly, because it is easy to turn the page or change the channel in favour of something less harrowing. But unlike most of you, I have been complicit in trafficked human beings for commercial gain, resulting in their death. And the line in the War Crimes sequence of *Deus Ex Machina,* "a burning civilian smells like bacon rind", is based on personal experience. Let me explain.

At the summit of my ridiculous career as a ridiculous architect, I found myself ordering ridiculous things in ridiculous places for ridiculous projects. I was empowered to conjure up shipping containers that contained all sorts of stuff, like reinforcing steel, bags of cement, solar glass, and people. The people were usually from the Tamil Nadu region of India, they were always desperate for paid work, and they had no experience of life outside their villages, let alone experience of industrial building sites.

He was a thin, gap-toothed, nervous man, about my age, and I hardly questioned the fact that he slept in a shipping container, washed in a waterlogged trench, and sweated for a pittance. All within sight of my Command Centre. He had no idea what he was supposed to do, and I empathised with him because neither did I. It was a Tuesday evening during Ramadan, and as the sun had just set, his religion allowed him to drink some tea before compulsory prayers. This is the origin of the line that begins *Deus Ex Machina*.

When he started his night shift, I saw he had been given a road drill to excavate something or other in the trench. The power cable he hit was high voltage, and what with him being ankle deep in the water, he probably died of electrocution very quickly. Charred human flesh smells like roast pork in shit sauce.

The Defect Police:
>War crimes are easy.
>They taste very well.
>*Háborús bűnt könnyű elkövetni.*
>*Nagyon jó belekóstolni.*
>
>War crimes are easy.
>You never can tell.
>*Háborús bűnt könnyű elkövetni.*
>*Sosem lehet tudni.*
>
>War crimes are easy.
>I smell a smell.
>*Háborús bűnt könnyű elkövetni.*
>*Érzem a szagát.*

Jump without question.
Don't blow your mind.
Ne kérdezzetek, csak ugorjatok.
Ne lepődjetek meg magatokon.

A burning civilian
She smell like bacon rind.
Egy lángokban álló polgári személynek olyan szaga van,
mint a szalonnabőrnek.

Chapter 14

The Middle Ages

DANCE

This Chapter deals with the age of plumpness, and in *Deus Ex Machina 2* I wanted to inject our middle years with some artificial fun. But in spite of the artifice, I love this sequence. When Shakespeare was building a tragedy or a history, he realised he needed to insert some light relief, or else the paying audience would drown. In *Deus Ex Machina 2* there are four comic sequences. The opening sequence is intended as a parody of sports video games, with the rival sperms bunched up in blocking formations like Little League football players, and the Ian Dury Golden Sperm doing all sorts of daft manoeuvres to dive into that egg-goal. Then, later in the game, the gross-out zits-and-hairs sequence is a cheap shot at the easy target of up-themselves adolescents. The old age stagger through various pills and eyeglasses is also comic. But this middle-aged dance sequence is my favourite comic interlude. It is very silly, and I like it a lot.

When I was a youth, I won a Twist dance contest by virtue of not falling over when introducing home-grown moves like The Crippled Cossack, The Constipator, and The Papal Bull. So for some time I thought I was hot stuff on the dance floor, until I was actually laughed off it in my middle years. Before that ego-crushing event, The Worker Who Married Me used to partner my faux rock'n'roll steps, complete with twirls, rolls and crutch-splitters. But over the years such athletics got boiled down to standing on the spot and exchanging rocker shoulder barges, two to the right, two to the left, four beats to the bar. It may not have been dancing, but it was a marriage.

The dance in this sequence is called The Bluto Dance, named by my sister in honour of Popeye's rolling adversary. We used to dance it as kids, indoors at social gatherings, outdoors at civic events and behind doors at home. It really used to piss people off, so we loved it. Now we are old, we rarely dance it together, but when we do it still really pisses people off. I hope it makes you laugh, as you follow the excruciatingly embarrassing dance moves of the uninhibited avatar.

The setting of this Dance sequence originated in the Automata multi-media days of the late 1970s and early 80s, when we trawled dubious clubs and desperate discos in package-holiday destinations, trying to extort advertising revenue for our maps and audio guides. And now such venues are writ large in Ibiza, where the idea of a good time is to subsume yourself into a single-cell onanism. In fact Ibiza gets a very bad (or good) press because of seasonal dance hedonism, which is a pity, because of all the islands in the Mediterranean I think it is the most beautiful, tranquil and civilised. Every full moon in February thousands of Ibizans gather at night to delight in the sight and scent of acre upon acre of nocturnal almond blossom, which beats the pants of any video game I can think of.

The interpolation of Japanese lyrics in the Dance audio of the game has no significance, other than the fact that if humanity is ever cloned, it will be because Japan needs to replenish those calm, dignified masses who have been decimated by flood, earthquake, radiation and cutesy-poo video games.

> Mwah-mwah, ne-ne-ne-ne-neh.
> *Uah-Uah ne-ne-ne-ne-neh*
>
> I'm so naughty-naughty. You're so naughty-naughty.
> *Sono così birichino-birichino Sei così birichino-birichino*
> I want to dance.
> *Voglio ballare.*
>
> I'm so pretty-pretty. You're so cutie-cutie.
> *Sono così carino-carino Sei così grazioso-grazioso*
> I want to dance.
> *Voglio ballare.*

(I'm so into you. You're so into you.)
(Ci sto davvero dentro. Ci stai davvero dentro)
(You're so into you.)
(Ci sto davvero dentro)

I want to dance. I want to dance.
Voglio ballare voglio ballare
(Are you a clone?)
(Sei un clone?)

I want to dance. I want to dance.
Voglio ballare voglio ballare
(A dancing clone?)
(Un clone danzante?)

Woah woah-woah.
Uah Uah-Uah
Oh, woah-woah.
Oh uah-uah
Woah woah-woah.
Uah Uah-Uah
Oh, woah-woah.
Oh uah-uah

Kiss, kiss, kiss.
Bacia bacia bacia

GUILT

The Guilt level is about money. To be specific, it's about making money from gambling. And to be even more specific, it's about capitalists making money by betting on global commodity markets. Is it OK to speculate on clean energy, or water, or pharmaceuticals? Is it ethical to invest in tobacco, alcohol, armaments or pre-teen slut fashion? Who does it benefit and who does it harm? Do you try to avoid bad stuff and embrace good stuff? In which case, how do you define either?

The pyramid setting echoes the symbols on a dollar bill, as well as the sort of fraudulent Ponzi schemes that stiffed the global markets in 2008. The overweight avatar is undoubtedly a slob, both physically and mentally, but what's the gameplay? I am not going to tell you, other than to hint that it can change every time you give it a go. Hope you like the music though. I gave the lyrics to the voice of The Machine, sung by little Chyna Whyne, and I made her work harder to deliver this track than all the others combined. By the end of the recording session she was suitably stretched, and seeing as she was on a fixed fee for a single session to lay down all the vocals for her contribution to the entire game, I knew I had myself another great deal. So in terms of entertainment, let's think less about money, and more about value. What is entertainment worth?

Commodities and currencies are difficult to quantify, but the value of entertainment can be expressed as what the mass of consumers are able to pay, willingly, in finite terms as a unit of exchange. I will define a universal unit of exchange that we can all refer to, and let me define this unit of exchange as A Pint Of Beer. For my overseas readers, I should explain that "a pint" is a unit of volume peculiar to the British Isles, and is used to measure liquids and prawns for human consumption. And "beer" is an alcoholic beverage used as currency by the Egyptians around 4,300 years ago, and perfected by the Oakleaf microbrewery of Gosport, Hampshire, in 1998. When I purchased my first Pint Of Beer, it cost me ten-pence-halfpenny, which means nothing to you, but to me it represented a substantial investment. The relative cost of A Pint Of Beer these days differs wildly from town to town and continent to continent, but I know exactly how much it is worth in terms of entertainment.

Now let us apply this universal unit of exchange to the entertainment industry in general, and video games in particular, and see how the trends have developed, and whether or not we are getting ripped off.

A ticket to see a provincial symphony orchestra currently costs me no more than 6 Pints Of Beer. Great value, considering there can be forty musicians working hard to entertain me with their sawings, puffings, pluckings and hammerings. A ticket to suffer a parvenu shit band performing derivative shit compositions in a standard shit venue also costs me 6 Pints Of Beer. Poor value. Half a century ago, when I queued up outside Portsmouth Guildhall for a ticket to my first Beatles concert, I was happy to pay 2 Pints Of Beer for the experience. Amazing value. A year or so back, tickets for The Rolling Stones in concert cost around 200 Pints Of Beer, and I challenge anyone to justify this inflation of expectation and devaluation of live entertainment provided by a popular music combo. Bad value.

But when it comes to recorded music, as opposed to live music, the situation has been reversed. My first record single cost me 1.5 Pints Of Beer. It was the perfect rock'n'roll package called "Move It", by the snarling cock-rocker Cliff Richard, since you ask, and it represented good value. The most recent single I bought cost me 0.4 Pints Of Beer, as a download from iTunes. Excellent value.

Now let us apply this system to the cinema. When I first started revelling in movies, viewed through a haze of fug from massed rows of cigarette smokers, my ticket in the stalls cost exactly 1 Pint Of Beer. Good value. Today, when I experience the sensory overload of modern cinema through the stench of prole-fodder, my ticket in the stalls costs 2.5 Pints Of Beer (including senior citizen discount). Questionable value. But if I wait a few weeks until I can download the same movie direct to my Sony Bravia smart TV, it only costs me 1 Pint Of Beer. Good value.

For books, the increase in value has been even more radical, now that we can bypass the parasitical practices of agents, editors, publishers, distributors, wholesalers and retailers, and pay the authors direct via epublishing. And as for the classics, both literary and educational, there are so many brilliant books available for Zero Pints Of Beer as downloads that it would take several lifetimes to devour them all. Ludicrously good value. Which brings us to the perceived value of video games.

In the early heyday of Automata, we were selling compilation games at the equivalent of 0.7 Pints Of Beer each. That was very good value indeed. By the time I launched *Deus Ex Machina* in 1984, I had grown as deluded as the fat slob in the Guilt level, and I seriously believed that putative players would appreciate the investment I had put into the product, pricing it at double the cost of most other games of the period. *Deus Ex Machina* cost players 15 Pints Of Beer. That was the sort of real-world value that inspired software piracy on a global scale.

As I write this, I have not decided where to pitch the price of *Deus Ex Machina 2*. For portable versions I have received advice from some new-found friends at Apple, who know a thing or two about value, and they reckon it should be a mid-price offering, which works out at around 0.3 Pints Of Beer. My peers have suggested that I give the game away, and try and recoup my new investment via sales of this book, the audio, and associated doodahs. This doesn't involve investing Pints Of Beer at all, and replaces direct payment with the promise of selling many mouthfuls of Beer sometime in the future. The term for which is Freemium.

My production partners, for whom the terms "piss up" and "brewery" are only distant relatives, would obviously like to replace all notions of Freemium with bankable concepts like Premium.

Meanwhile, I am happy to report that since I recovered from my adventures in a wheelchair during the production of this game, and got into the habit of modest exercise and gym visits, my own slob days were receding, and I lost ten per cent of my body weight. Either that or I am host to tapeworms, or cancer, or suffering the curse of a wronged sorceress. In which case, I'm probably guilty.

The Machine:
> You can move mountains
> *Je kan bergen verzetten.*
>
> If you just press that big red switch.
> *Duw gewoon even op die grote rode knop.*
> You can shake temples
> *Jij doet tempels wankelen*
> And cast them down into the ditch.
> *Zo kom je hogerop.*
>
> You're guilty.
> *Je bent schuldig.*
> I said you're guilty.
> *Ik zei het, jij bent schuldig.*
> Guilty.
> *Schuldig.*
> Guilty.
> *Schuldig.*
>
> You buy the people,
> *Jij koopt mensen,*
> You kill the sea and rape the land.
> *Je vermoord de zee en verkracht het land.*
> You take the profits.
> *Jij pakt de poen.*
> You leave them nothing here but sand.
> *Niks meer over buiten zand.*
>
> You're guilty.
> *Je bent schuldig.*
> You're guilty.
> *Je bent schuldig.*
> Guilty.
> *Schuldig.*
> You're guilty.
> *Je bent schuldig.*

You run the networks.
Je draait de netwerken rond je vinger.
You turn the camera to the wall.
Je draait de camera naar de muur.
You're growing fat now.
Nu wordt je vet zoals zwijn.
You run the show and it's your call.
Jij steelt de show van het eerste uur.

You're guilty.
Je bent schuldig.
I said you're guilty.
Ik zei het, jij bent schuldig.
Guilty.
Schuldig.
I said you're guilty.
Ik zei het, jij bent schuldig.

Guilty.
Schuldig.
Guilty!
Schuldig!

POWER

I thought this level was all about ill-gotten gains and the hollow trappings of power, but it's turned out to be about shopping. The setting looks a lot like modern Dubai, where any structure I had a hand in building is long since torn down. The buildings here are quite bonkers, and as with every other level of the game there is nobody else around except yourself. The broad highway is absolutely deserted, though I'm not sure if the abandoned stuff that litters the road has been left by refugees or shoppers. And the odd barbed wire barricade and hazard warning hint of something more sinister going on. It's all a bit Ozymandias.

The number of abandoned sites has grown hideously in recent years. Deserted speculative complexes all along the Costa del Sol, a dead Detroit, boarded up shops in my own country, the canker of abandonment spreads through our traditional High Streets.

Hereabouts, the High Street is dead, the internet killed it, and it had it coming. Going shopping in our town and city centres had become a mindless task, with miserable masses buying rubbish they didn't want, for people they didn't like, on credit they couldn't afford. Like a doomed Egyptian dictator, the retail chains didn't even realise their time was up until the people rebelled via their computers. And even then the old names refused to accept the inescapable truth that they had no absolute right to cling to power. The revolution happened fast, when the masses discovered they could buy all the goods and services they really wanted far cheaper and far easier online. It wasn't the recession that did for the High Street, it was the web.

My local High Street is typical. 2010 was Year Zero. A bit like Zombie Apocalypse, but with less laughs. The fact that the store doorway had become a free urinal didn't bother me in the slightest. The store was rubbish. And it wasn't just the retail multiples that sucked the life and soul out of our towns. I was particularly pleased to see all those useless chains of estate agents, insurance brokers and travel agents imploding, with their complacent, ill-informed, insincere, parasitic automatons recalled to the clone-factories for disassembly. They once had the nerve to try and charge big commissions for pressing the same electronic buttons that we now press ourselves. Well, stuff that.

At one stage, there were no less than four greetings card shops in sight of one another on my High Street, all selling the same range of rubbish. Did they really expect people to keep paying good money for a processed emotion now achieved for free by pressing the Like button on Facebook? Did the bookshop believe it could compete with Amazon?

Did Blockbuster, HMV or Game really think they could keep going on a diet of mediocre movies, boxed set banality, and Playstation piffle, when everything can be plucked straight out of the air? Yes they did, and that's why it's over. But am I disheartened by the sight of the rotting corpses of our commercial centres? No I am not. I am not, because we now have the opportunity to start over and get back to what a few societies have never lost. Real shops, real businesses and real amenities, run by real people, offering real services for real customers. The internet has slaughtered the old enemies. It's time to welcome the return of some family-run old friends that web-based businesses can never kill.

Welcome to my reborn High Street of the future. The co-op. The chip shop. The cop shop. The pet shop. The pie shop. The art shop. The betting shop. The knocking shop. The all-in-one repair shop for bicycles, computers, shoes and broken hearts. The florist. The chocolatier. The post office. The pawnbroker. The pharmacy. The funeral parlour. The library. The gym. The dancehall. The crèche. The café. The blessed, sacred, screen-free pub. And anyone who doesn't like the prospect of all that can sod off back to the out-of-town retail wastelands where they belong.

The Programmer:
>Then the Justice, in fair round belly,
>*Så er det Rettferdigheten, med god og runn mage,*
>With shaded eyes and clothes of designer cut.
>*Med solbriller og designerklær.*
>Full of slick words and celebrity.
>*Full av glatte ord og kjendisstatus.*

The Choir:
>Quiver, quiver. Here come the Judge.
>*Skjelve, skjelve. Her kommer Dommeren.*
>Shiver, shiver. Here come the Judge.
>*Skjelve, skjelve. Her kommer Dommeren.*

Out of the shadow.
Ut fra skyggene.
Into the ruins.
Ut til ruinene.

Up shit-creek,
Opp dritt-elven,
Without a paddle.
Uten en åre.

Quiver, quiver. Here come the Judge.
Skjelve, skjelve. Her kommer Dommeren.
Shiver, shiver. Here come the Judge.
Skjelve, skjelve. Her kommer Dommeren.

Out of the shadow.
Ut fra skyggene.
Into the ruins.
Ut til ruinene.

Up shit-creek,
Opp dritt-elven,
Without a paddle.
Uten en åre.

Here come the Judge.
Her kommer Dommeren.
Don't be afraid.
Ikke vær redd.

Here come the Judge
Her kommer Dommeren.
The Judge is you.
Dommer en deg.

Here come the Judge.
Her kommer Dommeren.
The Judge is you.
Dommeren er deg.

DECLINE

It's not so much that heart attacks and brain damage are inevitable, it's more that turning them into video arcade games helps stimulate the adrenalin junkies out there. Better to have them busting blood clots and navigating fried neurons in some sort of organic pinball machine than their usual pursuits.

None of these Middle Years sequences changed very much from the gameplays of the original version, but thanks to some fancy footwork by Audio Network, Sulene Fleming and Golden Ears, the music finally came of age.

The Fertlilizer:
> Don't waste the life I gave you.
> *Neplýtvej životem, který jsem ti dala.*
> All you need is love.
> *Nepotřebuješ nic než lásku.*

The Night Nurse:
>OK? Let's go!
>*OK? Tak jedem!*
>
>You're cosmic, electric.
>*Jsi nabitý, máš příchuť hvězd.*
>My fascination is toxic.
>*Má posedlost je jako jed.*
>
>My temperature is rising.
>*Má teplota se šplhá vzhůru.*
>Through atmosphere we're climbing.
>*Stoupáme skrz atmosféru.*
>
>Electronic systems go.
>*Systémy připravit, teď!*
>Robotics in overload.
>*Plnou parou vystřel vpřed!*

The Fertilizer:
>The satellites are shining.
>The acid rain looks pretty.
>*Družice se lesknou,*
>*déšť nám chutná kysele.*
>
>The satellites are shining.
>The acid rain looks pretty.
>*Družice se lesknou,*
>*déšť nám chutná kysele.*

THE NIGHT NURSE:
>Magnetize me: supertechnology.
>*Jsi magnetický, jsi zázrak techniky.*
>Your rocket goes atomic.
>*Přepínáš pohon na atomový.*
>My plan, it won't stop it.
>*Můj plán to ale nezastaví.*

Electronic systems go.
Systémy připravit, teď!
Robotics in overload.
Plnou parou vystřel vpřed!

The Fertilizer:
The satellites are shining.
The acid rain looks pretty.
Družice se lesknou,
déšť nám chutná kysele.

The satellites are shining.
The acid rain looks pretty.
Družice se lesknou,
déšť nám chutná kysele.

The Night Nurse:
Magnetize me: supertechnology.
Jsi magnetický, jsi zázrak techniky.
Invade my station.
Vtrhni do mé stanice.
Blind me with a laser beam.
Laserovým paprskem mi vypal zrak.

Scan my radar.
Prohlédni můj radar.
Ooh, are you better than me?
Tak jsi mě pokořil. Co? Je to tak?

DANGER, WARNING

The Fertilizer:
Listen to me...
Posłuchaj mnie.
Killing is wrong.
Zabijanie jest złe.

Even pretend killing on little screens.
Nawet na niby, na małym ekranie.
And people that sell violent games to children should be put away somewhere safe,
A ludzi, którzy sprzedają brutalne gry dzieciom, trzeba odstawić w bezpieczne miejsce,
'Til they get well again.
aż znów znormalnieją.

The Night Nurse:
Danger. Warning.
Niebezpieczeństwo. Ostrzegam.
Danger. Warning.
Niebezpieczeństwo. Ostrzegam.

I start to feel electric.
Zaczynam czuć elektryczność.
Your sonic static flows.
Twoje dźwiękowe, statyczne przypływy.
It starts to take me over,
Daję się porwać
Robotics are Mission Go!
na misje robotów. Naprzód!

It's fatally out of control, yeah.
Utrata kontroli - grozi śmiercią.
It's fatally out of control, yeah-yeah.
Utrata kontroli - grozi śmiercią.
It's fatally out of control, yeah-yeah-yeah.
Utrata kontroli - grozi śmiercią.

Danger. Warning. Danger. Warning.
Niebezpieczeństwo. Ostrzegam. Niebezpieczeństwo. Ostrzegam.
Danger. Warning. Danger. Warning.
Niebezpieczeństwo. Ostrzegam. Niebezpieczeństwo. Ostrzegam.

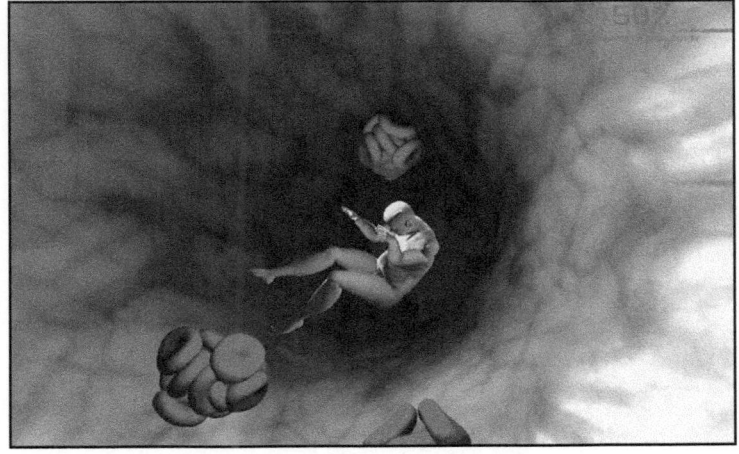

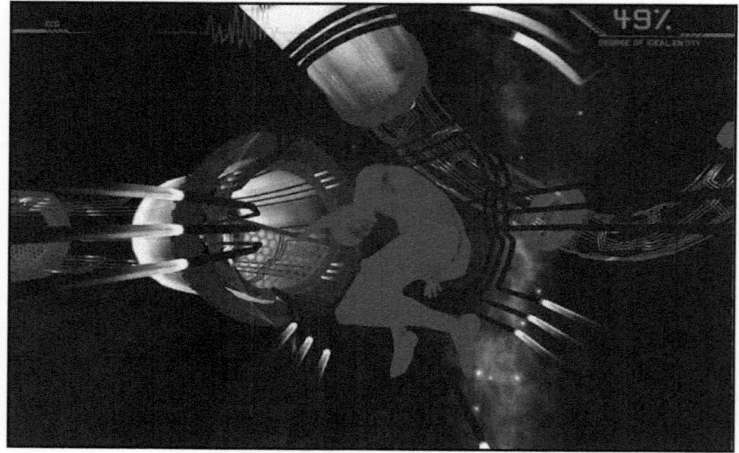

Chapter 15

End Game

OLD AGE

I have already explained that I chose to make the lifespan of "you", the player of *Deus Ex Machina 2*, exactly one hundred years, not only because it's a neat conceit to compress one century into one hour, but also that it's perfectly possible. However, that possibility comes at a cost, and there was no way I was going to go down the route of a dignified old age. Even in the original version of the game you were meant to be saddened by the physical and mental decline of your avatar. This time round I wanted to put the boot in.

I did it once before in a magazine series I wrote called *Tamara Knight*, which had equal elements of humour, social satire, sci-fi and sex. After a few months of the series, the publishers cancelled my contract due to the polarity of reader apathy versus reader outrage. So I killed off my heroine, not in a pan-galactic maelstrom, but from inoperable stomach cancer. And I tried to make it funny. As a result I received some rabid letters from readers, accusing me of deliberately trying to upset them and their families, and I replied to each one in the affirmative. Sex and death can be comic as well as tragic experiences.

The Old Age sequence of *Deus Ex Machina* is comic. The music is a deliberate echo of Monty Python's *Always Look On The Bright Side Of Life*. The toilet-flush sound effects and the hacking cough are my dad. The eyesight jokes are me. The effects of medication when you take Prozac, or Viagra, or Ecstasy or diamorphine are meant to be funny. Ha, ha, ha, the indignity of Old Age. Ho, ho, ho, the silly old fools who get in the way. Hee, hee, hee, we contribute all our working lives to pay for our state pensions and National Health Service. And after all that struggle here's how we all end up.

For readers who are too young or too foreign to know what the British National Health Service represents (or represented) then you have my sympathy.

The Programmer:
> The Sixth age shifts into the lean and slippered old buffoon,
> *Het Zesde Tijdperk verplaatst zich naar de slanke, geslofte oude hansworst,*
> With spectacles on nose, their underpants well saved,
> *met bril op neus, en ondergoed, eerste keus,*
> A world too wide for their shrunken shank.
> *een wereld te wijd voor hun verschrompelde schacht.*
> And their adult speech synthesizer turning again towards a childish treble,
> *En hun diepe stem-synthesizer wiens toon weer stijgt tot een kinderlijke treble,*
> piping and whistling in its sound.
> *orgelpijpend en fluitend naar geluid.*

The Defect:
> Don't you ever get weary?
> Time to exit and die?
> *Ben je soms ook dodelijk vermoeid?*
> *Tijd voor de exit en de dood?*
>
> Coming to the end of the Program.
> Something's very wrong with my eye.
> *Ik kom aan het eind van het Programma.*
> *Mijn ogen willen niet meer mee.*
>
> Me skin's like minestrone.
> Me legs are knotted string.
> *Mijn huid ziet er niet meer uit.*
> *Mijn knieën knikken.*
>
> Me bladder won't obey me.
> Me nylon teeth won't sing.
> *Kan mijn pis niet meer mikken.*
> *Nylon tanden, enkel botte snee.*

Oh, woe, here I go.
Oh wee, neem me toch mee.

Is it time for bed now?
Or is time for me to get up?
Is het nu tijd voor bed?
Of tijd om te ontwaken?

Time to swallow pills now,
And drool in the plastic cup?
Tijd om mijn pillen door te slikken,
kwijlend in een plastieken tas?

Me bones is sad and brittle.
Me shanks is host to farts.
Mijn botten kunnen zo maar breken.
Mijn darmen laten enkel gas.

Me chin is host to spittle.
Me spine's a question mark.
Kin vol kwijl.
Mijn ruggengraat, net een vraagteken.

Oh, woe, here I go.
Heave ho, watch out below.
Oh wee, neem me toch mee.
Tijd om me onder de grond te steken.

Me respiration's ailing.
Me hair all run away.
Ik haal adem met horten en stoten.
Mijn haar is zowaar weggelopen.

Me memory is failing.
I've nothing left to say.

Mijn geheugen is een zeef.
Weet amper nog of ik leef.

I'm gonna find my daddy.
He's waiting there because.
Ik ga mijn papa vinden.
Die is ongetwijfeld aan het wachten.

I really miss my mamma,
But I don't know who she was.
Ik verlang zo naar mijn mama,
maar heb geen idee wie ze was.

I really miss my mamma,
But I don't know who she was.
Ik verlang zo naar mijn mama,
maar heb geen idee wie ze was.

Mama?
Mama?

SENILITY

The Programmer:
  Last scene of all that ends this strange, eventful history,
  Is Second Childishness and mere oblivion.
  Without keyboard,
  Without monitor,
  Without power supply.

The Choir:
  When times are hard,
  When we are frightened,

When we are alone,
When we are so very alone,

Father, we think of you.
Mother, we find the pathway to your door.

Mum and Dad,
Why did you abandon me?

Mum and Dad,
Why did you abandon me?

When times are hard,
When we are frightened,

When we are alone,
When we are so very alone,

Father, we think of you.
Mother, we find the pathway to your door.

Mum and Dad,
Why did you abandon me?

Why did you abandon me?

DEATH

The Fertilizer:
   Who's that...?
   Кто это?..

The Machine:
   Come to mummy. Do you feel better now...?
   Иди к маме. Тебе уже лучше, правда?

The Fertilizer:
> I'm so sorry...
> *Прости меня...*

The Machine:
> There really is no need to apologize.
> *Тебе не за что извиняться.*

The Fertilizer:
> I'm so very tired.
> *Я так устал...*

The Machine:
> You can sleep soon.
> *Ты скоро заснёшь.*

The Fertilizer:
> What did I do?
> *А что я сделал?*

The Machine:
> Learn and remember. Forgive and forget. Imagine.
> *Учись и запоминай. Прости и забудь. И еще, представь себе...*

The Fertilizer:
> Imagine. Imagine if we could begin our little life all over again.
> *Представить себе? Что было бы, если бы мы могли начать нашу маленькую жизнь сначала,*
> Imagine if it was all nothing more than some Electronic game.
> *что было бы, если бы это была просто компьютерная игра,*
> Imagine if I knew then what I know now.
> *что было бы, если бы я знал тогда то, что знаю сейчас...*

The Machine:
> So, what did you learn?
> *Так что же ты сейчас знаешь?*

The Fertilizer:
> I can't quite remember, but I'll try and be better next time.
> *Точно не помню, но в следующий раз я постараюсь быть лучше...*

The Machine:
> That's all anyone can hope for. Don't be afraid, you're safe now.
> *Это и есть наша единственная надежда. Ну, а сейчас бояться уже нечего, ты - в безопасности.*

The Fertilizer:
> One question...
> *Один только вопрос...*

The Machine:
> One answer then. What's the question?
> *Нт? Ладно, один ответ. Ну, что?*

The Fertilizer:
> Well.. There's a strange sensation on the cheek.
> *Я чувствую что-то странное на щеке.*
> It has not felt such a thing before.
> *Такого чувства раньше не было.*
> It is damp, and warm, and salty. Please tell me what it is...
> *Что-то влажное, теплое и солоноватое. Пожалуйста, скажи мне, что это?*

The Machine:
>Ah. That is what human beings used to call
>A tear.
>*А-а, это то, что люди когда-то называли*
>*слезой.*

TRANSFIGURATION

The Programmer:
>Deus Ex Machina.
>*Deus Ex Machina.*
>
>And if you are dismayed, be cheerful now.
>*Si tu t'étonnes, réjouis-toi maintenant*
>Our revels all are ended.
>*Notre fête est finie.*
>These, our avatars, are all spirits,
>*Tous ces avatars ne sont que des esprits*
>And are melted into air.
>*Rien que de l'air.*
>Thin air.
>*De l'air*
>
>And like the baseless fabric of this vision,
>*Et, comme le tissus sans trame de cette vision*
>The cloud-capped towers, the gorgeous palaces,
>*Les tours ennuagées et les palais somptueux*
>The solemn temples, the giant Screen itself,
>*Les temples solennels et même l'écran géant*
>All of which we inherit shall dissolve.
>*Tout ce dont nous avons hérité va disparaître*
>
>And, like an insubstantial pageant faded,
>*Et comme un cortège évanescent*
>Leave not one megabyte behind.
>*ne laisser présent aucun mégaoctet.*

> We are such stuff as dreams are made on.
> *Nous sommes ce dont les rêves sont faits.*
> And our little life is rounded with a sleep.
> *Et notre petite vie est entouré par le sommeil.*

We all know the ending of life is an undignified affair for most humans. A good death or a heroic death is a rarity. The best we can hope for is a peaceful and painless death. If we're very lucky, we can also hope for a dignified end to our little life. In my experience, those deaths that are ushered along with increased doses of morphine delivered via a computer-controlled pump seem to offer the easiest ending. The closing sequences of *Deus Ex Machina 2* are hallucinations of course. An imaginary ride on an imaginary roller-coaster in an imaginary wheelchair with imaginary wings. And all those memories, wrongly remembered.

These final sequences of *Deus Ex Machina 2* are inevitable. In which case, they are stuffed with sentimental hokum and not a few clichés. In fact there are only two moments in the entire game when the machinations deliberately take over the flow. One moment is in the Infancy sequence, when the authoritarian, sneering voice of the Defect Police orders you to jump without question. The order is barked, "Wait for it. Wait for it. JUMP!" And your avatar jumps on command. There is nothing you can do about it, because orders is orders, and there is not one of us who has not been bullied and acquiesced. The other moment is at the transition from senility to incapacity, when we fall to our knees and give up the struggle.

I can best express this in terms of all the Irish Setter dogs I have ever had the privilege to count as companions. Dogs do not live as long as human beings, but compress their lives into a fraction of our own. And so, I have had too many opportunities to witness that moment when what once was a playful puppy, and then a loyal farter, falters, and then falls. The utter helplessness of the moment, and then the confusion because the dog cannot fathom why it no longer functions.

And then that last eye contact before the light of intelligence glazes over. This is the final moment of transition in the game.

It will happen to me, and if it has not already happened to you, it surely will. But we can only imagine and dream of being able to change our own little life next time round. Unlike in *Deus Ex Machina,* here in the real thing there is no replay option.

I believe that death is the end, and that the desire to exist in an afterlife is understandable but bonkers. I used to envy people with strong religious convictions or spiritual beliefs, because I thought it gave them comfort when facing death. But the more I witness their passing, the more miserable, distressed and afraid they seem than we, the godless. So why did I use a gospel choir for this sequence?

What I don't dispute is that the concept of transfiguration after death has given rise to a lot of bloody marvelous art, some sublime music and the sort of rituals that do more good than harm. The singing of Alidor Nzinga and the Congolese gospel choir of refugees living in London is deeply moving and very beautiful, and I am proud to be a citizen of a nation that offers such people sanctuary, even though I do not share their faith. I wanted unaccompanied singing for this sequence of the game to reflect the fact that as far as I'm concerned when we face death we are alone. A simple arrangement was just fine, heartfelt, without embellishment or overamplification.

I warm to the notion that the way you behave in this life will determine how you return in the next. As such, *Deus Ex Machina* should appeal more to the Dalai Lama than the Pope. Wouldn't it be wonderful if people were rewarded for living a good life by being reborn with the eternal optimism, beauty and good nature of that Irish Setter I keep going on about. Wouldn't it be just if people were punished for deliberately living a bad life by coming back to the ceaseless, smelly toil of the dung beetle, gathering and rolling balls of shit. But alas, death and transfiguration is only the stuff of myth and video games. This game in particular.

You cannot "win" during the course of your long life in *Deus Ex Machina*, you can only go with the flow, embracing the good and avoiding the bad, trying to learn and do better next time round, or deliberately seeking out the bad just to see what happens, or doing nothing at all except let the game play you. Or, of course, a combination of all of these choices. And so, as I set out at the beginning of this little book, *Deus Ex Machina* recombines the same four basic elements as every other good, bad or indifferent video game. It is mostly bunkum, with a bit of chess, dice and ping-pong chucked in for good measure.

Let me define bunkum for you, when applied to video games. Bunkum is related to what illusionists call hocus pocus, or sleight of hand. It is also related to what confidence tricksters refer to as a sting. And it is very closely related to what Alfred Hitchcock popularised as a macguffin in cinema plotlines. In video games, bunkum is essentially a device for taking the player's attention away from the fact that the game is lacking in actual play. And *Deus Ex Machina* is almost totally lacking in actual play.

The most successful protagonists of bunkum I have ever met called themselves the Bollock Brothers, and as such they could never have been accused of misleading the public. The way they made money was to go round a whole load of pubs and clubs and challenge anyone who would listen to guess the number of testicles they possessed between them. Little Bollock Brother would offer odds of five-to-one to anybody who guessed the right number, and they never paid out once as far as I know.

It was the odds themselves that were the bunkum, the flimflam, the hocus pocus, the macguffin, because they implied that players had a one in five chance of guessing right; namely the regulation issue of one pair of balls each totalling four, or three bollocks if one of the Brothers was half a scrotum short, or two if both Brothers only had one ball or one had a pair and the other none, or maybe they only had one between them, or there was the possibility of zero if neither of them had any testicles at all.

Big Bollock Brother seemed quite a shy gentle-giant sort of a chap who never spoke a word unless he had to, but in fact the flimflam could never have worked without him. Little Bollock Brother was the garrulous one who reeled in the punters and laid out the odds. After a bet was laid, the Bollock Brothers would retreat with the punter to the nearest private place, usually a toilet, there to reveal the truth. And when those punters lost, they always did so with extreme good humour, often encouraging their friends to try their luck and enjoy losing too. The bunkum was this, Little Bollock Brother had two testicles, just as most men do. But Big Bollock Brother had four, and his double ration was a very interesting sight indeed.

Anyway, the core message of *Deus Ex Machina* is all in the final sequence of the game, as spoken by Ian Dury in his dialogue with The Machine. It is undeniably simplistic and trite, and if you think it's bollocks then you are very welcome to come up with a better one.

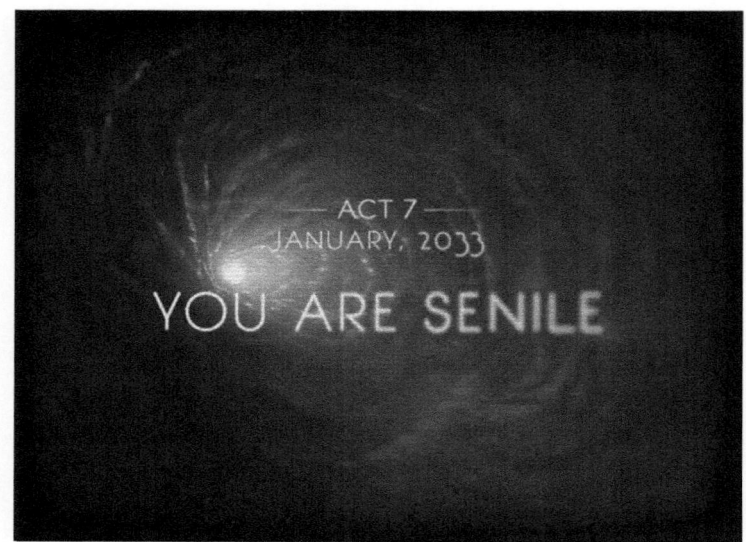

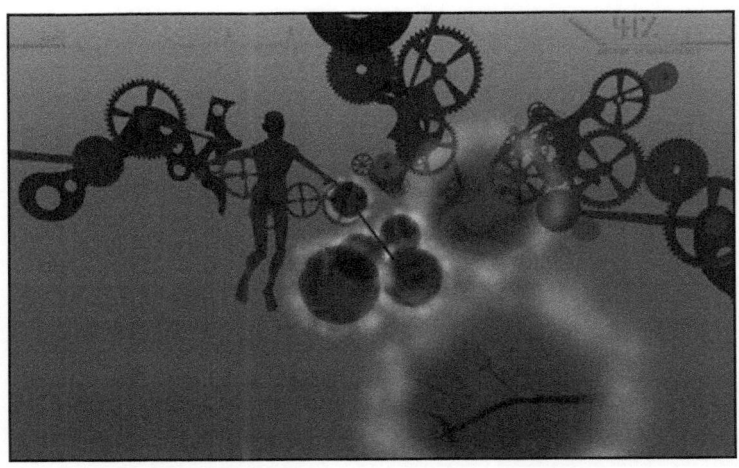

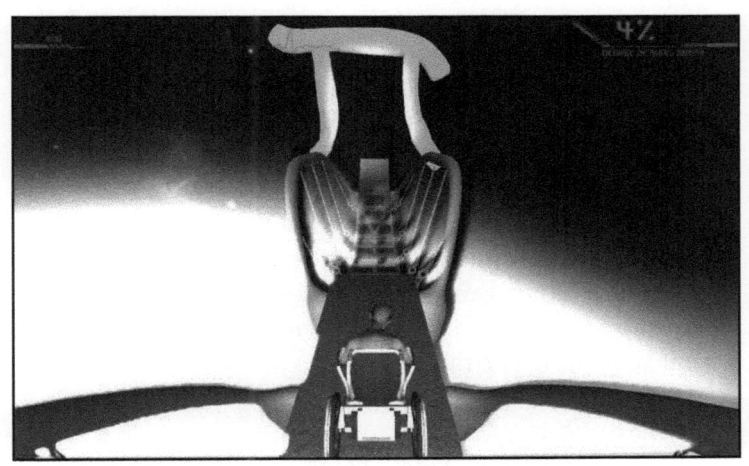

Chapter 16

Update

This was always going to be the penultimate chapter of the book, and although events overtook it all, this chapter is still about trying to bring *Deus Ex Machina 2* to market. It reveals a litany of strategic and financial foul ups, it features my latest brush with mortality, and it lays bare the foibles of an optimist colliding head-on with the Market Revolution. So first of all, allow me to put this Market Revolution in its historical context, starting with when I first got involved with the business of video games, exactly two hundred years after the French Revolution.

The French revolutionary leader Georges Jacques Danton once said, "All revolutions devour their own children", and to prove it another gang of revolutionaries came along and chopped off his head. In the revolution that was video games, it went something like this.

> 1977 to 1981
> Enthusiast creates video game > Enthusiast sells video game to other Enthusiasts.

> 1981 to 1985
> Enthusiast turns into Video Games Entrepreneur > Video Games Entrepreneur either goes bust or goes nuts. Either way, the spark of fun dies.

> 1985 to 2009
> Video Games Entrepreneur gets mangled by parasites including Licensors > Creatives > Designers > Agents > Producers > Bankers > Publishers > Accountants > Merchandisers > Lawyers > Publicists > Distributors

> Wholesalers > Retailers > Advertisers > Reviewers > Pirates.

2009 to present day
Video Games Enthusiast comes up with video game idea > other Enthusiasts sit in judgement to fund it before it's even written.

In other words, the revolution has more or less turned full circle just like the French Revolution, and all thanks to a phenomenon known as crowd-funding. And much more importantly, crowd-funding has turned the whole thing upside down and inside out. Well, there's no fool like an old fool, and here's how this old fool managed to screw it up the launch of *Deus Ex Machina 2* all over again.

I always wanted to involve players of *Deus Ex Machina 2* as much as possible in its development and progress, just like the players of my primitive games broadcast via radio in the 1970s, and just like the PiManiacs who took part in those real-world treasure hunts of the early 1980s. And so, three years before its planned release, I started to invite anyone who fancied joining in to visit a website dedicated to the game. Once they got there, I asked them to freely confess a secret crime they had committed. Their confession then appeared online for all to see, and if they wanted to post a mugshot of themselves for viewing in a section called *The Dissident Files*, so much the better. As usual, all I asked in return was their email address, so I could try and wheedle some money out of them when the time came. I also asked what country they lived in, to figure out some sort of global marketing strategy. And I asked what format they would prefer the game to be released on, for obvious commercial reasons.

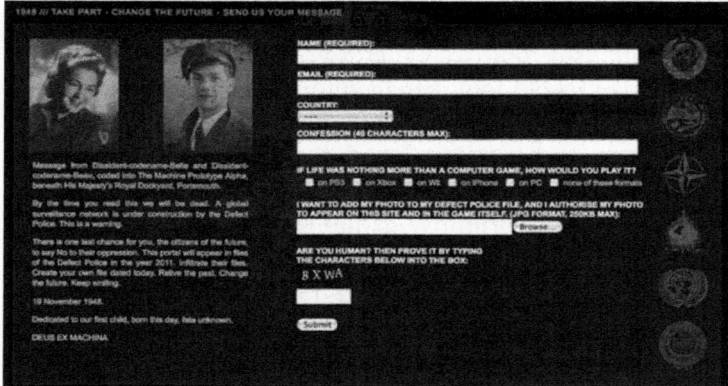
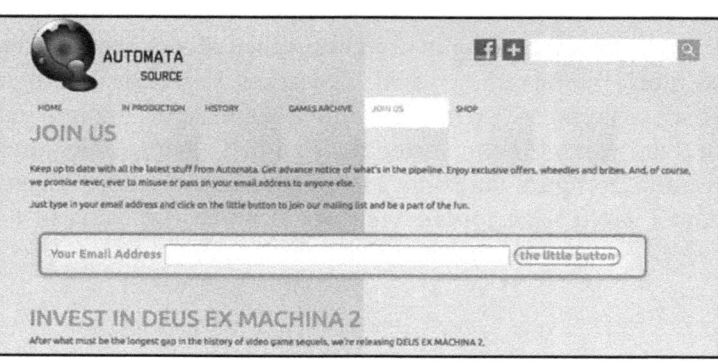

And for some of them, I asked for the rights to use their image in the final sequence of the game, called simply "Thanks". I stole that idea from the end credits of Spielberg's 1993 movie *Schindler's List*, where the faces of holocaust survivors take over the screen and build into a mosaic of triumph-over-adversity, although I thought tumbling picture playing cards would be more effective, a bit like the denouement of *Alice In Wonderland,* that I referenced at the start of the Infancy level of the game. And I also wanted to express my genuine thanks to certain people out there, some of whom had waited thirty years for what was in my head to make it to the screen, and some of whom weren't even born when the original game was launched.

And I admit that I always planned to try and raise some modest funding from people who wanted to see their faces in the game, and would be willing to pay for the privilege, as a consenting two-way reward.

Proto-players started signing up in the summer of 2010, and I was able to begin building a global map of potential sales, nation by nation. The demographics were fascinating. To begin with, and not in the least surprisingly, the vast majority of my dissidents were ex-Spectrum retro players based in the UK, and they said they wanted to play the game on PCs and Apple Macs. From their confessions, many of them were familiar with the original game, and either quoted from the libretto or referred to a particular sequence. If I supposed they were at school or still in their teens when *Deus Ex Machina* was first inflicted on them, then they would have to have hit their late-to-mid-40s by now. And if I accepted they were not posting false names and images, then the split was around four males to every female.

But by the summer of 2012, things were changing fast. More and more younger people joined in and signed up. Some smarties quoted references to Christopher Lee in *Star Wars, Lord Of The Rings, The Hobbit* and even *Dracula*, and others quoted Ian Dury, more so after his music was featured in the opening ceremony of the 2012 London Paralympics. The geographic split for every 10 potential players of a new version of *Deus Ex Machina* was 3 North Americans, 2 Brits, 2 Europeans, 1 ex-colonial transplant of British culture in Australia, New Zealand or South Africa, 1 BRIC representative from the new superpowers of Brazil, Russia, India or China, and 1 other from somewhere else on the planet. And most of them said they were interested in playing the game on mobile platforms, specifically on Android and iOS smart phones and tablet devices.

On the one hand this was a complication, because it meant I'd have to translate the text and lyrics into more languages than I'd anticipated. But it was great news about the mobile formats and my ideal mechanism for playing the game, because chances were that players of the new version would want to use earphones to make the soundtrack play inside their head and gently jiggle with the built-in gyroscopic motion of their handheld devices to control the gameplay. Perfect self-contained paradise.

Disappointingly, the younger little darlings were still overwhelmingly of the male persuasion, and I would have my work cut out to get more players from the distaff side. Similarly, it seemed I would have a major problem attracting the silver surfers of my own age. But as the slow-burn continued, more women joined in the fun and the average age of everyone interested began to climb again.

As it turned out, the outreach campaigns designed themselves, mostly thanks to ready-made networks on Facebook and YouTube. The most obvious bunch to contact was the extraordinarily large number of retro-gaming groups, who cross-fertilised one another like a field of frisky ferrets. They conveniently gathered themselves into special interest game-players, most of which I could tempt with an aspect of *Deus Ex Machina* I hoped would appeal specifically to them, including nostalgia freaks, disabled gamers, anti-warmongers, feminists, silver surfers, transsexuals, the obese, the anorexic, the orphaned and the bald. And with Christopher Lee on board, I was able to extend the hand of fiend-ship to several generations of his fans.

But I was inexperienced in the two extraordinary phenomena which pitched me right back to the future. Those twin-phenomena were downloads and crowd-funding.

In very recent years, players had leapt at the chance to download video games direct from the creators straight on to portable devices, and those same players were also given a chance to get involved with funding the production. And as for all the intermediary parasites, it seemed that at long last they were getting squished. By the time I fully cottoned on to what was happening, I had begun to believe we were right back where we started at the dawn of a new golden age in video games creativity.

In the heyday of Automata, we would think up a game in the morning, and have it finished by closing time at the pub. Seeing as we paid ourselves £25 a week each and worked out of a room above Dorothy's Wool Shop, our overheads were modest. Seeing as how it took less than a week to create the artwork, the soundtrack, the advertising and the time to buy some jiffy bags and a sheet of stamps, I'd say that the total development cost of an average early game was around £150, about $250. We sold loads of our games mail-order with no intermediaries, or direct to our lovely players in the flesh at computer fairs, often at a healthy discount. As our American cousins would say, go figure.

At the end of this book I have included my Top Ten Tips for Successful Video Games Creators, but I never heeded anyone's advice in this business myself, and I don't really expect anyone to heed any advice from me. Furthermore, I hate to dampen the enthusiasm of the new generation of games-makers, and I know that self-delusion can be a great motivator from personal experience. But hey guys, and the vast majority of you are guys, you can't eat pixels, and you can't pay the rent with them. Last year, of all the oodles of commercial video games and gaming apps that made it to market, each one taking weeks and often months to produce, the average revenue generated was less than £200. In my country today, the National Minimum Wage rate for a twenty-year old is around £6 an hour. Go figure.

And when you have gone figured, I invite you to forget the past and embrace the future, because everything has changed once again. And for the better. The financial crash of 2008 not only brought traditional banks into disrepute, it knackered the chances of speculative investment for a generation. And it also gave rise to an online alternative that bypasses traditional financing altogether. It is now possible to discover if a game is liable to be a commercial success before it is even written, by inviting potential players to back a concept themselves via the amazing phenomenon of crowd-funding. And the world leader in crowd-funding is called Kickstarter.

Kickstarter is already a major impact on the future of how video games are brought to market. And not just video games. The same goes for every kind of creative enterprise, including new books and mainstream cinema productions. It does this by getting as many potential players as possible to invest in a title's chances of success at the concept stage. And I'll let you into a secret, raising the money is not even the most important bit. The most important bit is the ability to do a load of market testing in the real world with real players. If there's not enough interest in the game, and it fails to achieve its target funding, then not a penny of any pledged funding gets handed over from the potential player to the potential games creator. This is a very crude form of market-testing, but it's certainly effective, and has already had the ability to kill off a dud game before any more significant time and effort is wasted on it.

On the other hand, loads of recent titles have exceeded their targets and been overfunded by Kickstarter enthusiasts several times over. These committed gaming investors become ambassadors for success, networking with other potential funders and encouraging them to join in the fun and become stakeholders as well. That's usually achieved by good old-fashioned bribery, where the games creator offers funders and stakeholders various incentives. These are mostly low-cost inducements such as free copies of the game, access to unpublished material, tacky merchandise and even a say in how the game is eventually put together. And it goes without saying that potential funders must be satisfied that the people behind the proposed game are credible, have a good track record, a great concept, and as much chess, dice, ping-pong and bunkum as necessary.

And just as modern funding has undergone a revolution, so has the distribution process, all thanks to the ease and speed of digital downloading. But today's games players are being spoon-fed their pleasures on the basis of instant gratification for zero upfront cost. The future of making money from video games is not from selling the damn things, but by giving them away, reeling the player in on the drug-peddler principle.

The drug-peddler gives away free samples at the school gate, safe in the knowledge that once the victims have been hooked they will pay for a continual stream of self-gratification in the future. This is how the 'freemium' model works for video games. You give away the initial fix, and then charge to satisfy the long-term addiction time after time with in-game purchases for additional levels, extra resources, virtual currency, cheats, and so on, as well as transmedia delights in the form of books, music and dopey merchandise.

The Kickstarter fundraising model started in 2009, and when it did I was reminded of that old plastic bucket we had used to collect funds from supporters during the Automata versus Waddingtons court case back in the 1980s. In essence, a few creative people thought up an idea, then held out a virtual collection bucket in the hopes that a lot of consumers would support their idea by pledging money. In exchange, the creative people promised to reward the potential consumers with a load of stuff, which was mostly virtual. It was bunkum on a vast scale, but bunkum that made everyone happy if it was successful. And if it failed to achieve the funding goals then no harm was done, because the pledges were only pledges, and only got cashed in the event of hitting a predetermined goal with successful funding.

Since I started out in video games, I had only ever dealt direct with the players, so the idea of using Kickstarter to continue doing exactly that was nothing new. I had never sold out to banks, advertisers and all the rest, so Kickstarter would allow me to keep this independence. But above all, I saw Kickstarter as a way of getting players to have a voice and vote on how they wanted the game to turn out.

The Kickstarter campaigns for *Deus Ex Machina 2* were never the prime way to fund my project, which I thought was already funded twice over. Once by the entrepreneur and atoning former software pirate Mário Valente, alongside his tame bank and the Quirakafleeg gang in Portugal, and again by the underwriting and reserve funding of my partners in the reincarnation of Automata, at least as far as the mobile versions were concerned. As for the PC and Mac versions, having spent all the available Portuguese money by the May of 2013, it was obvious that no more funds were coming our way, thanks to the disastrous Iberian economic climate and the wobbly Lisbon banks. It was also obvious that this Kickstarter thingy could allow the expansion of the project to include Android and iOS formats for the portable devices that my dissidents had confessed to wanting. And we could also try and cater for ports via our Unity development platform, including simple migrations to the open source Linux platform, as well as mind-bending mutations to Oculus Rift, which would allow players to experience the visuals inside their heads in 3D.

And then I went and screwed everything up. I managed to snatch defeat from the jaws of victory, and I ruined my first ever Kickstarter campaign. At least I couldn't share the blame with Christian Penfold The PiMan this time. I blew it singlehandedly.

Weeks before I launched the *Deus Ex Machina 2* fundraiser on Kickstarter, I had drawn up a carefully costed battle-plan for raising a modest $50,000 to complete the game, enhance it and bring it to market for all the target formats. This seemed perfectly achievable, following hot on the heels of two other Kickstarter campaigns that had just achieved spectacular success with raising funds for retro remakes by other ancient Britons. One was Charles Cecil, who had raised three quarters of a million dollars for a new title based on his 1990s *Broken Sword* series, and the other was Pete Molyneaux, who had raised over half a million quid for a reinvention of his 1980s hit *Populous*. I know and respect both these men, and it seemed like a great time for me to go for a measly fifty thousand dollars.

Then in June 2013 I got asked to appear in a movie about the history of video games. It was called *From Bedrooms To Billions*, and it was being made by a lovely duo called Anthony and Nicola Caulfield. And guess what, it too was being bankrolled by a successful Kickstarter campaign that attracted almost four times their funding goal. I was told my performance was great, that I was a natural in front of the camera, and that I came over like a benign Dumbledore with Tourette's Syndrome. When the prerelease clips went public, mature women sent me fan mail and total strangers wanted to be my Facebook friend. And I rode the egotistic superhighway right up my own anal sphincter. I told myself that if a movie where I simply talked about *Deus Ex Machina* could raise big bucks on Kickstarter, then I could raise even bigger bucks by crowd-funding the real thing.

And so it happened that I abandoned my original modest goal and doubled it. Not content with that, I added a load of delusional stretch goals to include delusional ambitions. When I say I was delusional, I mean pitifully delusional. My delusion manifested itself by inviting backers to raise upwards of a million dollars so we could translate the game into every known language on the planet, make the movie of the game and do a live stadium performance for a global videocast, complete with full orchestra, mass choirs and celebrity performers. Oops.

In spite of my idiocy, things were looking good, mainly thanks to a public relations campaign masterminded by the human dynamo Danielle 'Woody' Woodyatt and her gang at the Lunch PR company. Woody had been responsible for some of the most successful launch campaigns in modern video gaming, including *Resident Evil*, *World Of Warcraft* and *Assassin's Creed,* and she generated a truckload of positive coverage from the traditional and online media for *Deus Ex Machina 2*.

Mel with Anthony and Nichola Caulfield, between shoots of From Bedrooms To Billions

Reboot

Original Kickstarter campaign

We reached my original Kickstarter goal of $50,000 on 4th July 2013, but we failed to hit my deluded overambitious target in grand style. In other words, under the all-or-nothing rules of Kickstarter, not a single penny was raised and the entire project now seemed to be wobbly as far as the public was concerned. It took me a week to completely apologise to my colleagues, while I licked my wounds and absorbed the horror of what I had just done.

My injured heel-bone was still not perfect, so apart from the inability to kick my own arse, the thing that caused me most affront was whenever a Kickstarter funder cancelled their pledge. The first time it happened, I wrote to the renegade to ask what I had done to offend them. How could I make amends? I thought it was really personal. Of course it wasn't really personal, but I was new to crowd-funding. Although I had backed a dozen Kickstarter projects myself, I didn't think that people would casually break their vows for no apparent reason.

For me Kickstarter was like a marriage contract. A public pledge to love, honour, cherish, share, and grit your bleeding teeth, until death do us part. My electronic marriage had failed. But at least there were some electronic children as a result. In fact there were hoards of them, including all the contact details of the Kickstarter backers, along with all their votes and play-testing of the pre-release version of the game. So everything was not quite lost.

The canny Samuel Beckett's take on coping with failure was, "Try again, Fail again. Fail better." So I thought I may as well take his advice, and in less than a fortnight I put together a Reboot campaign on Kickstarter with a funding goal a fraction of the previous megalomaniacal attempt, and with all the loony targets stripped right back to the bone.

Second time round it didn't fail. In fact it did just fine. Not only that, but the minor success of the second campaign followed hot on the heels of the major failure of the first one, and it brought with it some unforeseen benefits. Woody and her gang at Lunch PR generated a new round of publicity success. In a gesture of bountiful generosity, our audio producer Golden Ears announced he was waiving his entire fee to help the cause. Supporters started sending in donations via PayPal. And best of all, most of the original backers were now acting as beta-testers on all the key elements of the unreleased game. We were very close to completing *Deus Ex Machina 2* in spite of everything.

***

Is *Deus Ex Machina* a video game at all? Probably not, but all I did was write it, so I don't think I am the best person to ask. Better to ask video game players and best to play it yourself. But before anyone can play the game, it's necessary for them to get hold of a copy, and despite the fact we had been more than three years into the production, that was the part of the plot that had been left hanging.

Originally, my Portuguese chums were going to handle the distribution of the game, but it had been decided that the reputation of Automata had more clout than an Iberian start-up, and we were best placed to do this from the UK. And so it was that we delayed setting up global distribution via the central hub for downloading gaming software created by independents like us. And the name of this mighty distribution organisation was Steam.

The Steam network was initially developed to deliver games running on Microsoft Windows, and by the time we got our act together it had expanded to include Apple Mac and Linux platforms, as well as both iOS and Android mobile devices. In other words, Steam was perfect for us. On the first day of September 2013, when we finally had a game that had been debugged, play tested, tweaked, polished and generally ponced up, 75% of the world's PC games were being bought via Steam, there were over 65 million Steam accounts covering all our target formats, and at least seven million steaming Steamers active at any given time. All we had to do was submit *Deus Ex Machina 2* to a panel of mature, expert and savvy Steam assessors who would recognise the concept and the quality of our game and release it to an eager public. Unfortunately Steam changed the rules on August 31st and handed over decision-making to a bunch of bananas. Green bananas.

Democracy is a very good thing, except when green bananas are enfranchised. When Steam set up its Greenlight community the idea was to give its gamers voting rights on what gets released. At first sight this struck me as a great way of fast-tracking the best examples of creative video games. But as it turned out, the vast majority of voting Steamers who commented on *Deus Ex Machina 2* had a matching age and IQ level. I'm all for power to the people, but this was power to the banana-brained.

I suppose I should have recognised the warning signals as soon as I submitted the game concept to the Steam Greenlight online gateway. It wasn't that I had to pay them a hundred dollars before I could get abused, it was the fact that their game categories were mind-numbingly banal. In fact it was like being back in the mental straight-jacket of the 1980s, when wholesalers, distributors and retailers could not accommodate anything outside of the norm. But this was much more depressing. Now it was the players who had been processed by the Defect Police.

Steam invited me to tick an appropriate box to categorise *Deus Ex Machina 2*, a product that could not be categorised when video gaming was in its infancy, let alone now. I was offered the choice of Casual, Platformer, Massively Multiplayer, Racing, Horror, Shooter, and similar formulaic pap. I toyed with the idea of ticking all the options, but I thought it best to be honest and accept the fact that no category fitted and the Steaming voters may not be wholly accepting of my game.

Spy764 11 Dec @ 2:28pm
What the fuck was that? Seriously, just

MoreC4Please 8 Dec @ 6:08am
I dunno guys...I'm not gonna suffer any
is crack rocks.

aolas 6 Dec @ 7:42pm
F**** drug trip cool :) brig it now

Dragoman 6 Dec @ 8:25am
T_T huh? what is this? WTF man? 💀

Dr. Waddles 4 Dec @ 2:03pm
WTF!!1 WAT IZ DIS?!?!?!?1

xaneks 3 Dec @ 10:09pm
Dafuq is dis shiz. ACID TRIP YALL!

Fozilc 1 Dec @ 12:32pm
Yup, just what I was looking for.

chaosdirge 27 Nov @ 4:31am
Did I pop a pill... did someone fill my ro
bad trip ...

Coffer 26 Nov @ 8:46am
To the people thinking "what the hell is
art-house game, I.E. Stanly Parable, D

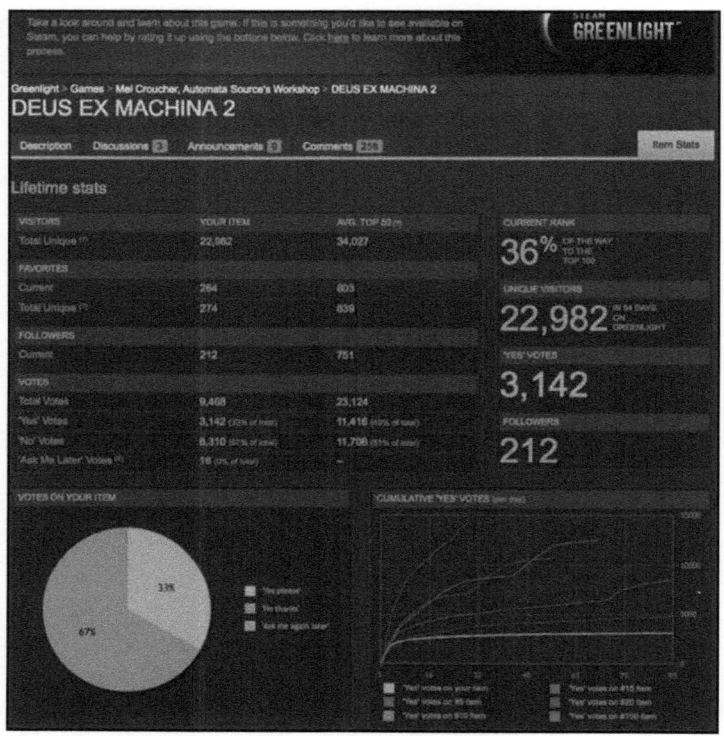

Deus Ex Machina 2 attracted positive reaction from 33% of the Steam Greenlight community. Almost all of it was from mature players who already knew the history of the game or invested a few minutes to absorb the video and the sales pitch. These positive votes were vastly outweighed by a torrent of rabid abuse from all corners of the Earth. Their average level of criticism would have been "what the fuck", if only they had all learned how to use vowels in their communications. And of those who could use vowels, many complained that my game was an attempt to rip off that best-selling video title *Deus Ex*! Maybe that's forgivable, and I hope they all get well soon. But one thing was clear, thanks to the verdict of mainstream players, Steam was not going to distribute *Deus Ex Machina 2* any time soon.

I not only needed to find another way of distributing the game, I needed to categorise it so it could fit on today's virtual shelves. The game has always been what some people call a transmedia entertainment. A rock music album with moving pictures. A movie with an immersive soundtrack album. An interactive video with a book tacked on. A bit of a creative mess. But the real question is, will players treat it like a video game? And the likely answer is yes, probably they will. And that may well be its downfall in purely commercial terms.

Deus Ex Machina always takes exactly one hour to play and it always follows the same linear sequence. So it's not much of a game then, at least it's not much of a game for anyone expecting surprises. But if you were the sort of baby who peed your pants over nursery games that were totally predictable, like *Peep-oh* and *What's The Time Mister Wolf*, then you may not want surprises, because you get your kicks from anticipating the inevitable.

The fact that you are reading these words proves that *Deus Ex Machina* is not simply about the gameplay. I reckon the gameplay, the soundtrack and this book are part and parcel of the whole, and as such *Deus* is what the world now calls transmedia. I don't consider a video game that involves a cereal packet, a comic book, a Tweet or a flashmob to be transmedia, unless it makes a real contribution to the entertainment. In other words if it don't add to the story then it ain't transmedia.

Creating merchandise to cash in on a successful creative title is nothing new. The writings of Charles Dickens in the 19th Century spawned the Pickwick Cigars brand. Unlike lazy product placement in contemporary movies and games, that was a genuine precursor of current transmedia, because Pickwick Cigars did not exist before the Dickens novel, and would never have existed without it for sure.

I have resisted temptations and offers to include third-party branding, product placement or sponsorship in *Deus Ex Machina 2*. The transmedia elements are home-grown. And even though the soundtrack album or this book can be enjoyed, or not enjoyed, on their own merits, I have intended them to add to the whole and not simply be bolted on into a forced-marriage of convenience. In my meetings with Apple High Command about *Deus Ex Machina*, during which they have been embarrassingly supportive, I suspect there is some sort of plot going on to drive me insane with kindness, the movers and shakers at Apple get very excited about selling transmedia direct from the game, and Lord bless them for wanting to make it easy for me to tout my other stuff like this. Unfortunately, *Dues Ex Machina* is not the sort of game where you can buy extra lives or levels, so I've also buggered up that opportunity big time.

When I started writing this book there was a transmedia feeding-frenzy going on in certain creative and commercial circles, but the power of transmedia has never really resided with them. Most brand managers and media-buyers I talk to have an antique grasp of the potential of combined media. They want to view a traditional balance sheet that shows, "This campaign had a marketing budget of X, the number of consumer-leads added to the database was Y, and we generated Z. So the return-on-investment was X/Y=Z". Or was it?

In fact there are no restrictions or rules whatsoever. Some of the worst video games ever made have swallowed huge marketing budgets. Some of the best have cost next to nothing. But not one of them enjoyed success or suffered failure because of cross-over merchandising or transmedia.

I started off this little book saying there are no new conceptual elements in video gaming, and everything is derivative. However, we are still scratching the surface when it comes to how these derivatives are presented and experienced.

Back in 1930, technology advanced to embrace stereo. Further back in 1838, a dubious public was offered 3D stereoscopic technology. And the hallucinogenic alternative-reality experiences of the near-future that are presented to us in wham-bam science-fiction movies are already available for anyone who can afford overpriced screens and audio systems.

For us cheapskates, Augmented Reality is a commonplace app for superimposing the bleeding obvious on a world delivered via overpriced 3D television and binaural stereo. But you can get all of these experiences during a session in my local pub for next to nothing, delivered by beer.

We have been attaching passive delivery systems to ourselves for a long time, in the form of mass-produced lenses, wrist watches, and headphones. But now there is a new generation of gamers and consumers who habitually experience the world through active delivery systems as extensions to their eyes, ears, mouths, limbs and physical locations. We currently call these devices smartphones or Google Glass and experience them as add-ons, but it is probable that the next generation will embed interactive delivery systems into their sensory organs. And good luck to them, as long as they stay out of my local pub.

Thanks to non-stop lobbying from the Automata Players Tribune Matthias Rich, I agreed to produce *Deus Ex Machina* for the Oculus Rift virtual reality headset if ever we got over our current hurdles, and I freely admit I have no idea how it will feel to experience it until I do so myself for the first time. There are probably fewer potential players with access to Oculus Rift today as there were potential players with access to a Sinclair Spectrum when it first came out, so my business sense doesn't seem to have changed much.

All fashion is fickle and no forward-planning can be of any use. We cannot avoid a backlash against crappy transmedia by attempting to control mass appeal. In both social media and transmedia it is the users who have the real power of command, not the developers. I think this holds true for all cultures, even lemming cultures and fundamentalist cultures. I believe that transmedia content will be affected by internal checks and balances triggered by external influences. A backlash cannot be avoided but it can be accommodated, because of natural, self-selecting content. For example, developers tasked with selling revolting high-caffeine drinks may exploit cross-promotions in extreme violence or extreme sports in video games. They do not care at all if they offend the bulk of society, because they are only interested in their target market, which mostly consists of male masturbators. Similarly, developers tasked with selling funeral plans could do worse than tailor their transmedia content to baby-boomers weaned on love, peace and The Grateful Dead.

Experience tells us that the vast majority of consumers are content to be passive. They always will be. The reason why they are idle slobs does not concern me. How to involve the active minority of games players is what concerns me, and the twin mechanisms are as old and as universal as time. The twin mechanisms are greed and fear. They often combine in the form of peer-group pressure, so greed becomes a hunger to experience something that others seem to be enjoying, and fear becomes a desire not to be left out. What changes everything is the fact that this active minority of fellow-travellers can be contacted globally via little screens, and even if they constitute a tiny percentage of the world population, they number tens of millions. Oh brave new world!

Apart from a label as insubstantial as "transmedia", the most appropriate slot for *Deus Ex Machina 2* is probably "art game", which is hardly the most popular or fashionable gaming category for mainstream players. But a successful so-called "art game" like the wonderful *Limbo* is really a traditional platform game with a thin layer of puzzles on top, all dressed up in a somber expressionist art style. In other words, not even art games are really art games, and I don't think *Deus Ex Machina 2* really fits into this category either. It simply is what it is, and mainstream distributors will always find it awkward to embrace.

The most sympathetic distributor I turned to was an outfit called GOG, an acronym for Good Old Games. They specialise in classic games as well as innovative, independent stuff that gives the finger to restrictive digital rights management, and our initial discussions were positive.

The scheduled date for the release of *Deus Ex Machina 2* was November 19th 2013, my sixty-fifth birthday, the day society would officially recognise me as a geriatric and award me my Old Age Pension, the day I could claim to have experienced six of Shakespeare's seven ages of man, and the day this book was to have been launched at the UK National Centre for Craft & Design, where the original game was already on exhibition as part of the "golden age" of the British video game industry.

The morning of my birthday was beautiful. Clear blue winter skies and bright sunshine, tra-la. After I unwrapped practical presents from The Worker Who Married Me, the dog and I trotted off for our seaside walk before breakfast. These early dog walks are my favourite thinking times, and this was a perfect opportunity for planning what had to be done that morning.

I would officially approve the final versions of the game for the PC and Mac, with its new end sequences and enhanced user controls. I would hit the button for the game's release to our backers, supporters and early adopters. I would email GOG digital distribution with a neat little deal they couldn't possibly resist. I would then sign some personalised *Deus* posters hot off the press from the very same printer who had produced the originals thirty years before. Then it would be lunchtime and the birthday celebrations could begin. None of this happened, because half way through walking the dog Death beckoned.

Deus Ex Machina *on exhibition at the National Centre for Craft & Design*

There is an ancient tower built by an ancient king that guards the mouth of the ancient harbour near my home. As the dog sniffed the seaweed and slime below, I was attracted by a small bunch of flowers above and climbed up to read the memorial card. It was to an heroic man named Marco Araujo who a year before had rescued two children from the sea but had then been swept out to sea himself and drowned. As I contemplated the accidents that are life and death and turned to climb back down, I slipped and fell onto the stone slabs below. Maybe the weakness from my failed housebreaking injury of exactly three years before played a part, or maybe it was simply carelessness and stupidity. Either way, the sound of breaking bones was sickening, the pain was indescribable. I found I couldn't move, and the tide was coming in much too fast.

The dog sat to attention just like the fictional Lassie before it runs off to arf the grown-ups that the kid has fallen down the well. But instead of organising a rescue party, he just flinched every time I howled in pain. And this is the point where I declare my thanks to the O2 network coverage, the Apple iPhone and a fully-charged battery. I phoned The Worker Who Married me. She would know what to do. She always did.

As the paramedics pumped me full of morphine, the last sound I remember was a walkie-talkie squawkie about calling out the rescue helicopter. The next sound I remember was a repetitive bar of music going "plinky-plunky, bim-bom", as the angels plucked their harp strings to welcome me through the gates of Heaven. It was only when I was wheeled into the operating theatre that I recognised the musical composition was by Brian Eno. I was not in Heaven at all, but in Hell. It was the welcome jingle for Windows XP, and the soundtrack to my bionic enhancement of 23 metal adornments sticking out of my leg, nine long screws and titanium plates holding my bones together, and a piston-hinge thing last seen in a Victorian toilet cistern and now resident in my hip. I was in big trouble.

During the days and nights that followed, I had plenty of time to query why the hospital staff were logging on to Windows XP several times an hour, to upload or retrieve data, and then logging off again. It turns out to be the only way the system keeps running without falling over. And the audio identity jingle played "Plinky-plunky, bim-bom" to mark every single log-on.

It is time-consuming and clunky, but the medics have no alternative. Over four hundred million copies of Windows XP were flogged globally from October 2001 to June 2008, and I was astounded to discover that 85 per cent of the UK's National Health Service computers still run Windows XP. That's way over half a million machines. The reason I am astounded is because Microsoft support has written off Windows XP for technical back-up, fixes or patches to help keep the system running, and the same goes for security updates against viruses or malicious software. "Plinky-plunky, bim-bom."

I had to get out of there.

The site of the fall (circled)

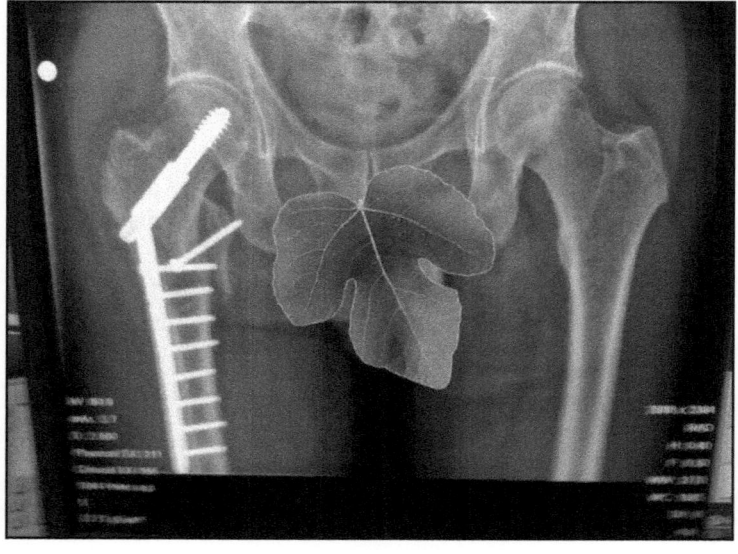

I am Machine X-ray

Rufus the Red Setter

The Worker Who Married Him and Mel before the accident

***

I won't be starting over when it comes to bringing the PC and Mac versions of *Deus Ex Machina* 2 to market. There's plenty to salvage from before my unfortunate accident, and I've had time to rethink the mobile versions too. I've always loved those dark expressionist movies from the 1920s, and that's how I want these alternative evolutions of the game to look and feel. But the final chapter of this story can't be written, of course, because the game has yet to be released to the public, making this book part of the game in itself, where the ending can only be determined by you the reader, and you the player.

Maybe I'll write a final chapter when I can walk again. Maybe I won't. But I guess this is where I came in, still plugging away, still trying to flog my music in the guise of game soundtracks, and still trying to force-feed my writing to an audience more interested in instant gratification than mere words. Retro games are back in fashion, so for me retro is the new tomorrow. It's a bit like all those clapped-out old rock bands going off on a final pension tour. Like them, it seems all I had to do was fail to die and hang around long enough to be rediscovered as a dinosaur. Albeit a dinosaur with a fan base. Not that I'm ungrateful, merely a bit bemused to find myself as a little footnote in books about the history of video games, and a bit amused to find my stuff is being taught on university courses, and a bit confused to discover examples of my work on exhibition behind glass cases in museums and galleries.

For a while, a generation ago, the UK led the world in video game creation and innovation. It may not have been structured or planned, but it really was quite something. I feel the same sense of energy, fearlessness and fun that we enjoyed in the early 1980s, remixing and peddling our four basic elements of chess, dice, ping-pong and bunkum. I believe there are boundless possibilities with home-grown success for video games creators who have the audacity to question the status quo, and who have the will to try their luck without recourse to worn out organisations and banks. Let the good times roll, all over again. Automata is back and I relish new opportunities to be in direct contact with my players again. Not so much Back To The Future, as Future To The Backer.

So, here we are. One Chapter to go, and maybe now you understand why the title of this book is *The Best Game You Never Played In Your Life*.

Keep smiling.

Chapter 17

Thanks

"Hi, I'm Matthias. By day I'm a stone mason, I live in Bath with my wife, daughter and cat. I'm a creature of the arts and technology. I became a full time geek in 1984 by accident when I naively loaded something called *Deus Ex Machina* onto my 48K Spectrum. It changed my brain chemistry forever and permanently raised the bar on my expectations of what a digital game can be. Since then I have been on many adventures, eating gold rings, jumping on mushrooms, exploring tombs and getting my hands dirty in the occasional war. Lessons learnt so far: the most memorable adventures, the ones that really stick with you and talk to your soul are not about conflict and fighting, they are about imagination, and the reminder of the greater truths like personal connections, beauty, art and being."

MATTHIAS RICH
Automata Game-Player's Tribune

"My arrival at Automata in the Spring of 1982 was a surprise, mostly to me. After being interviewed by Mel Croucher and Christian Penfold, I knew this wasn't going to be an ordinary job. They never kept books, and had all their receipts in a tea chest. Sorting out the accounts was part of the job. I liked these young men and soon settled into a world I knew nothing about. We became very busy and moved to a bigger office with a shop outlet as well as a growing mail-order company. Very soon I was packing, wrapping and shuffling under the weight of the parcels to the local Post Office. All my work was carried out on an IBM typewriter. I mean everything, letters, receipts, publicity, storyboards, and those endless labels. I willingly shared my space with Rory the red setter.

As business increased, Mel bought a machine to duplicate cassettes and let me loose on it. Big mistake! We attended Microfairs, usually in the Ally Pally. Christian was always The PiMan in a much-too-tight pink suit. That was when Lady Claire Sinclive was born. Me! Our 'fans' would queue at the doors for hours before the fairs opened and rush to our stand.

Automata games were fun and we always made the charts. No killing games for us! Our comic strip on the back page of Popular Computing Weekly, mimicked daily life at Automata and what was happening in the news at the time. It was outrageous, and I would like to place it on record that The PiMan was not the father of my child. Controversy was no stranger to the men at Automata. When Waddingtons tried to sue us for copyright they hadn't bargained for Mel Croucher. Mel and Christian were not the most fashion-conscious of young men, in fact they were scruffy, but on the morning of the court case scruffy Mel turned up in a dapper white suit, defended us and won the day. He was clever with words. Waddington's didn't stand a chance.

We had our own magazine in which I had a Lady Claire's Agony Aunt page for our PiManiacs, among all the comic strips, cartoons, games, and the vital mail-order forms. I was getting my own fan mail from all over the world, and I also had marriage proposals, which of course were all turned down, reluctantly.

Mel had always been ahead of his time and to prove it, *Deus Ex Machina* was born. I had every faith in the success of this game as the first computer movie. It was slow to start but then we were getting huge orders. Mel had given Andrew Stagg his chance to shine as a programmer, a great opportunity for this young man. The Automata experience was one of the most influential times of my life both as Lady Claire Sinclive and as Carol Ann. Magical, fun, hard work and almost unreal. I hope *Deus Ex Machina 2* will succeed, if the world is ready now."

CAROL ANNE WRIGHT
alias Lady Claire Sinclive

"I worked for Automata for two years before I saw the writing on the wall, when Mel stopped enjoying it and it went tits up. I left to be a freelance programmer in 1985. They call that 'going indie' now. I was young back then, only seventeen, and that couple of years was a fantastic time and taught me loads as I was growing up. Mel Croucher and Christian Penfold were the only bosses I ever had, and I left just before Mel quit. *Deus Ex Machina* was my greatest ever achievement then, and probably still is to this day. But who knows what we could have done if the sales had matched all that industry hype and the awards we got. The levels of publicity and rave reviews should have led to a great future, so what happened was bitterly disappointing, and ultimately led to me leaving the industry for over a decade. It's only in recent years that the truth has come out about the outrageous piracy of our software that went on around the globe. It would have kept Mel at Automata and me in business, and ultimately changed my life if all those players had bought legitimate copies!"

ANDY STAGG
original coder, Deus Ex Machina.

"Without Mel, Automata was obviously smaller. We certainly never went bankrupt - we never had any money in the first place. We wanted to show the bastards there was a great deal more to home computer technology than had ever been achieved before. Basically we won awards all the time we kept our mouths shut, then one day I told it like it was and the industry wouldn't touch us with a barge pole. Anyway, old Uncle Mel Groucho buggered off to do other things, I'm still not sure what, something to do with writing and music I think. I used to look after his dog sometimes, at least the dog was pleased to see me, or maybe it was the sausages."

CHRISTIAN PENFOLD
The Pi-Man

"Back in 1985 I remember my grandfather getting a brand new green and black screen, breezeblock-sized 'laptop'. He worked in telecomms at the time and I always remember him having new fancy gadgets around the place. He never seemed to mind me and my sister getting sticky finger marks all over his new goodies though, and so it was my grandfather who first let me loose on a computer. Playing *Digger* on his laptop that year is perhaps one of my earliest memories. I remember an incident having my juice cup taken away from me for using the keyboard as a table while I tried to get to grips with this frustrating game, so perhaps this is my earliest instance of Game Rage too. I have worked with Mel on websites for some amazing clients, top musicians, best-seller authors and more than twenty movies. As for *Deus Ex Machina*, are you kidding. I was four years old."

RICK FOYLE
website creator and graphic artist, Deus Ex Machina 2

"Mel Croucher was a disruptive young man when he came to my computing classes in the 1960s. I remember him because he was on the first course I ever taught. He had bad skin and scruffy juvenile whiskers and he was full of himself. What I would call a clever-dick. About twenty years later, I saw him on a TV documentary, talking self-opinionated rubbish about computers taking over the world. If he claims he was a pioneer of video games in this country, then I suppose something I taught him sank in. He contacted me for this via Facebook, and I am not at all sure why I responded. Probably just to call him a disruptive clever-dick. I know my students used to call me suggestive names. But let me tell you, I could twist them round my little finger. They were typical males, and like most young men I suspect Croucher will never grow up."

FRANCES MINKEY
alias Miss Crunt

"Hello. I'm the One That Got Away. I grew up in the golden era of video games, the 1980s, when I got hooked on the wonderful world of computers at an early age. I had the honour of working with Automata in the early days, where I wrote on a couple of Pi-Man games, and I have been making games ever since. From bedroom to indie and even Triple-A titles. OK, Double-A at a push. My career highlights include the cult Spectrum game 'Rex' and the award winning Gameboy 'R-Type', but I don't like to brag about it. Alright then, I brag about it all the bloody time. Apart from my love of video games, my life-long ambition is to get a proper job one day, so I can retire from it! To this day I still blame Mel Croucher for my four decades in the games industry, and I'm pretty sure Automata still owes me nearly a pound in royalties."

JAS AUSTIN
Games Creator

"April 1985 was an exciting time. I was a spotty 15 year-old, with spiky hair. In my little world, it was a time of electronica, synthesised music, videogame hardware from Atari, Intellivision and CBS, Spectrum computers, tape cassette recorders with dirty heads and C60 tapes with start-end times scribbled on card, like secret codes. I was working as a Saturday boy in a local computer shop in my hometown of Norwich, and I lusted over the latest software and hardware releases. It wasn't a particularly glamorous shop, the ceilings were low and it smelled of stale sweat and cigarette smoke, but it was geek heaven to me. Back in those days, computer games came on cassette and the packaging was uniform in either single or double sized packs. This made merchandising the games on the shelves easy because it was one of two heights.

Then along came a game that put a spanner in the works and made displaying it 'challenging'. That game was called *Deus Ex Machina* and selling it to the public wasn't the easiest thing in the world. I'm not sure how we got our copies of the game, because it was only sold direct via magazine adverts. Maybe our boss was dealing with some nefarious characters at the trade shows. I remember looking at the box for *Deus Ex Machina* and thinking 'Ooh wow! Dr. Who is in it.' But when I loaded up the game I was left scratching my hairsprayed head, wondering what I was supposed to do. For this naive teen, who was more used to *Chuckie Egg* than fertilizing one on my black and white portable telly, it was an experience. Then I went back to playing *Jet Set Willy*."

MARTIN SNELLING
Community Manager Sega, Marketing Manager Climax Studios

"I vividly remember the summer of 1985. Playing *Deus Ex Machina* late into the night, lights out except for the CRT tv glow and using headphones for the full stereo experience. And I didn't want to wake up my parents, of course. I was already a fan of concept albums, and I replayed the game, again and again, not to get a better score each time, but to repeat the music and the haunting experience. I can still quote word for word the whole soundtrack, even to this day.

I was a 15 year old kid with too much free time on his hands playing any ZX Spectrum games I could pirate. And, sure enough, *Deus Ex Machina* was one of those. One of the pirate software houses that I worked for, cracking speedloads and whatnot, had actually bought the original. I got the opportunity to enjoy the whole package, even if just for the small period of time it took me to make a master copy of both data and audio cassettes and send them for duplication.

Throughout the rest of the 80s, the 90s and the early 00s, as I used every new game platform, I always wondered why didn't anyone remake *Deus*, and take advantage of the graphics and sound capabilities that had become available. And every time thinking, 'if someone doesn't do it, I will. Someday...'.

And that day really came. I was amazed that Mel Croucher actually replied to one of my emails, I met him, one of my teenage idols, on a cold morning in London. When we signed the contract and Mel trusted me with a huge amount of memorabilia and the audio master reels, I couldn't believe that we would actually be remaking the game. I spent one full week in a state of disbelief wondering if I was actually awake. And now, waiting for the launch date of his reimagination of the game, I still feel that sense of wonder, playing the game into the late night hours. Playing *Deus Ex Machina* is one of the most powerful memories of my teenage years. Being involved in the remake will surely be one of the best memories of my life."

MÁRIO VALENTE
Reformed Pirate, Keeper Of The Faith

"I knew that Deus Ex Machina was going to be the start of a completely new type of video game, so I jumped at the chance of programming the C64 and MSX versions. It was obvious to me this was a major event, probably one of the most important computer games ever written, and that its influence would be immense. Working on *Deus* affected my own games writing, which lead to *Rock Star Ate My Hamster* and *Slightly Magic*. I probably spent eight months of my life programming the two versions of *Deus*, which I'm very proud to have done. Nobody could work on *Deus* without glimpsing the future of computer games. Everyone knew that nothing was ever going to be the same again. Except of course that everything was the same, for ever and ever. We all knew *Deus* was ahead of its time, but I seriously never thought it would be 30 years before it'd return.

I can't think of any other medium which has so tragically turned its back on such rampant creativity. And by turning its back on *Deus*, another hundred games which would have been sparked by the game's success themselves never got written. And the lack of each one of those hundred games led in turn to the lack of another hundred games, until mediocrity was the norm. Actually until mediocrity was the very best that anyone could do, compared to *Deus Ex Machina*. Maybe we had to wait for the internet, and the rise of the Indie developer. Maybe we had to wait for Kickstarter, and the death of old structures and limits. Maybe the time has finally come. Maybe tomorrow is finally here."

COLIN JONES
author and games creator

***

If I had to do it all over again, I'd do it all over you. If I could come round to your house and personally enact the game, perform the soundtrack, and read you this book aloud as I tuck you in and bid you goodnight, believe me I would. And we'd be arrested by the Defect Police before curfew. My sincere thanks to every one of you who helped me bring all the elements of this together.

MEL CROUCHER
January 2014

Roll of Honour

DEUS EX MACHINA
THE BEST GAME YOU NEVER PLAYED IN YOUR LIFE
SUPPORTERS, BACKERS & CREATIVE TEAM

Michael Addabbo
Petter Ahbeck
Ali Al-Romaithi
Joaquim de Almeida
Pedro Almado
Eugene Alper
Josef Andersson
Paul Andrews
Pedro Angelo
John Yani Arrasjid
Ross Ashley
Christopher Ashmore
Jonas Atterbring
Jas Austin
Simon Austin
Jeong Saeon Auh
Ron Baalke
Donna Bailey
Steve Baines
Jonathan Baker
Michael Baker
Jani Balazs
Sandra Baptista-Marreiro
Mark Bardell
Mike Barnes
Colette Barr
Fierman Baarspul
Andrew Bartie
Felipe Augusto Batista
Jacob Bean

Robert Beever
Ryan Bellward
Thomas Elkjaer Bentsen
Brad Bergman
Brian Bertine
Jasen Betts
Antony Birkin
Kristian A Bjorkelo
Truls Bjorvik
Cody Black
Chris Blackwell
Igor Bobrovskii
Phil Bond
Meindert Bontekoe
M Bordet
Claudio Bottaccini
Gary Bracey
Gareth Brading
Frank Braungardt
Magnus Brautaset
Ruben André Breiseth
Trevor Briscoe
Paul Broadhurst
Shari Bromley
Matthew Brong
Stephen Brown
Bob Bruce
Richard Burton
Nolan Bushnell
Brett Butler

Michael Caddick
Colin Campbell
Graham Campbell
Alonso Carbajal
Steve Caplin
Mary Carewe
Chaz Carlson
Olavo Carvalho
Simon Carr
Thomas Carr
Alex Carrington-Moule
Bill Cassidy
Anthony Caulfield
Nicola Caulfield
Charles Cecil
Peter Chadbourne
Clem Chambers
Paul Chaplin
David Chapman
Jacques Chapon
Fred Charles
Chien-Kang Chen
Jason Chipper
Amaury de Cizancourt
Barn Cleave
Link Cloud
Per Klitgaard
Andrew Clucas
Andrei Cojocaru
Stephen Colbert
Tim Cole
Jonathan Cook
Agustin Cordes
Aaron Corff
Alasdair Coutts
Brendan Coyle

Rob Crow
Crouch End Festival Chorus
Miss Crunt
Adrian Cummings
David Curral
Marius Dagestad
Michelle Das
Ray Davis
Stephen Dawley
Kalan C Dawson
Paul Desmond
Marc Tarres Deulofeu
Terry Devine-King
Bill Devonshire
Tristan Donovan
Daniel Dornhardt
Matthew Downs
Nicola Drew
Baxter Dury
Walter Dyar
Shaun Dyer
Birgit Schreyer Duarte
Rene Dufour-Contreras
Petter Duvander
Igor Dvorkin
Natalie Earwaker
Rick Eastman
Peter Eastwood
B Alan Eisen
Ian Ellery
Kay Elspas
Gary Elvin
Chris Evans
Robin Evans
Quentin Fagan
Ben Ferguson

Guild Fetridge
Oliver Feucht
Adam Fielon
Taylor Flagg
Sulene Fleming
Darren Fogarty
Petter S Fossum
Ricky Foyle
David Francis
Tobias Franke
Sydney Fraser
Robert V Frazier
Horst Freyer
Rupert Fuller
Jose G
Tim Garland
Rafe Gaskell
Zachery Gaskins
Tobias Gasser
Oliver Geddes
Chris Gibbons
Ethan Glasser-Camp
Barry Gledden
Tjark Gloe
Peter Glover
Tom Goeckel
Stephen Goss
Kevin Grasso
Henry Greer
Mark Gregory
Isabelle Grell
Kristian Hallstrand
Harlequin
Michael Hartmann
Matthew Harold
Cody Harris
Hannu Hautalampi
David Hayward
Andrew Hewson
Markus Hietanen
James Hinks
Mathilde Hjort
Jakub Hlozek
Ben Hockley
Gareth Hodges
Christoph Sicarius Hofmann
Gunnar Hogberg
Geoffrey Hogg
Rich Hollins
Andrew Hosking
Jonah Hottendorf
Adam Houston
Richard Hovenden
Andrew Huang
Badr Hubais
Malcolm Huggett
Daniel L Hughes
Jeffrey Hulford
Sharon Hunter-Fennell
Thomas Hurst
Toyozo Ida
Juan Cardona Iguina
Gavrilo Ilijev
Nick Ingham
Martin Insterberg
William Irving
Raveem Ismail
Jamil Ismaili
Peter Jacob
Rosalie Anne Laura Jackson
Chris James
Dave James

Michal Jarosz
David Jatzke
Karl Jeffery
Gregory D Johnson
Lars Erik Johnsrod
D I Jolly
Sebastien Jomphe
Colin Jones
Rachel Jones
Peter Jones
Thom Jorgensen
Peter Jovanovic
Max Juchheim
Stelios Kalogreades
Michael Keith
Dan Kellaway
Scott Kellaway
David Kelsall
Zsolt Kémeri
Idris Kennedy
Michael Kennedy
Lars Kerkmann
Riaz Khan
Ellie Kidd
Richard Kimmings
Lim Hoe Kit
Paul Klaene
Kurt Johann Klemm
Inge Klepsvik
Jesper Fyhr Knudsen
Jan Erik Kordahl
Maarten Koster
Andrzej Kozakowski
Bruno Krippahl
Karolyne Kunyak
Patrick Kurts

Jouni Lahtinen
Lamat
Joe Covenant Lamb
Warren Lapworth
Oleg Larikov
Raymond Lau
Joseph Lawson
Christopher Lee
Steven Lee
Gary Leicester
Casey Lent
Callum Lever
Timo Liimatta
Johnny Lithium
Manuel Loeffler
Stuart Lofthouse
Jay Loring
Tiago Loureiro
David Lucardie
Mark Lukens
Steven Lund
Steve Lycett
Lucas Nascimento Machado
Colin Mackleworth
Chris Madin
John Maier
Francesco Marcolla
Marino Martial
David Matney
Steve Maxsom
Sabrina Mazza
Alex McIntyre
Ben McClure
Geraldine McDaid
Andrew McDermott
McGee

Ross McGrath
Bob McPhail
Jon Meers
Shane Mengaziol
Kyle Messineo
Andreas Meyer
Anja Mikolajek
Thierry Milard
Lee Milby
Justin Miller
Nigel Milnes
Jeremy Milsom
Marie Mint
Ole Mogensen
Eva Montgomery
Bernard Moran
Corrado Morgana
Alexander Morozov
Bryony Morris
Paul Morrison
Markus Mosbech
Kjell Atle Mosbron
Paul Mottram
Phil Murgatroyd
Douglas Murray
Thomas E Murphy
Drew Nazarian
Mark Neesam
Kevin Neve
Thomas Nickl
Muhammad Norazri
Graeme Norgate
James Nowlan
Alidor Nzinga
Andrew Ogier
Vasco Oliviera

Anthony Olver
David O'Brien
Conor O'Neill
Markus Orasch
Robert W Orris
Pamela Palmer
Daniel Parson
Matthew Pass
Matt Peacock
Mark Pearce
Jason Peddler
Christian Penfold
Antonio Perestrelo
Rodrigo Perez-Mendoza
Maria Vall Personat
Janus Sommer Petersen
Thomas Petto
Richard Pix Pickles
Malgorzata Pietsch
Emiel Piket
John Piper
Duncan Pittock
George Poles
Daniel Policarpo
Christine Poundford
Adrian Powici
Neil Pratt
Chris Preece
Keith Preston
Angelo Del Prete
Neil T Pritchard
Alan Purdom
Mark Quinnell
Angus Rae
Bernard Rebours
Malcolm Reid

Matthias Rich
Sean Ritzo
Joseph Robinson
Henrique Rocha
Joseph Rodgers
Liviu Romascanu
Alexander Rose
Caleb J Rose
Paul Rosenberg
Royal Philharmonic Orchestra
Ben Royle
Iain Russell
Giacomo Russo
Birgit Sabin
Pedro Santos
Richard Sargent
Christi Scarborough
Kathrin Schellmann
Christian Schlecht
Sven Schmalfuss
Gunther Schmidl
Thomas Schwarz
Simon Scott
John Scriven
Adam Sebestyen
Frank Senyszak
Dan Shea
Michael Sherby
Alexander Shvarts
Gavin Sibbald
Matthew Sibbald
Matt Singer
SJ
Rhea Smith
Jason Smyth

Daniel Snellgrove
Martin Snelling
Jonathan South
Michael Spoerri
Andrew Stagg
Starker
Daniel Llorin Stauffer
Patrick Stender
Richard Stern
Simon B Stirling
Mike Stobbie
Paul Stone
Van Strevett
Jim Studer
Andy Sturgess
Mikhail Sudakov
Patrick Sugden
Paul Sumner
Louise Sutherland
Michael Suelmann
Jaroslav Svelch
Anders Svensson
Carl Swaby
Jeffrey Sweeney
Stefan Szczelkun
Jorge Tanimoto
Mark Taormino
Colin Tate
Joao Teixeira
Kevin Thomsen
Steven Threadgold
Jessica Tibber
Pedro Alexandre Timoteo
Karl Todd
Fred Tortonesi
Caroline Tremble

Diego Truyen
Panagiota Tsimpalidi
Alex Turnpenny
Graham Tyson
Adrian Urquhart
Jouni Uuksulainen
Mário Valente
Antonio Valjean
Albert Valls
Jaimie Vandenbergh
Richard Vanner
Jan Van Dosselaer
Chris Van Graas
Steve Van Maanen
Jaron Viëtor
Daniel N Viggiani
Jesper Vikstrom
Thomas Vitr
David Walford
Jake Warren
Spirit Warrior
Andrew Watson
Garod Weresheep
Sam West
Stefan Westerlund
Paul Whelan
Pete White
Dan Whitehead
Chyna Whyne
Adam Whyte
Chris Wicksteed
Steven Wilkinson
Oliver Williamson
John Wilson
Debbie Wiseman
Andy Wood
Dave Woods
Danielle Woodyatt
Levi Workington
Carol Ann Wright
Stanley Yamane
John Yeates
Xu Ying
Alexander Young
Brett D Zeigler
Sami Zolbster

Mel Croucher's Top-10 Tips For Successful Video Games

1. The easiest way to end up with a small fortune from video games is to start out with a large fortune.

2. Never innovate. Let others break new ground and avoid their mistakes like the plague.

3. Of the four components that constitute every video game, ignore the chess, the dice and the ping-pong. Go for the bunkum.

4. There is no college or university course that can teach you how to create a successful video game. You've either got it, or you ain't.

5. Identify your ideal players in terms of age, sex, proclivity, and favoured format. Then stir their emotions every way you can.

6. Use crowd-funding data to find your potential players, and allow them to do your game testing and quality control for free.

7. Ask what potential players think about every aspect of your game and go with the majority verdict. If none of them like it, kill it.

8. Get your distribution in place way before you finish the game. Like now.

9. Try to avoid serious injury, especially on your birthday or on launch day.

10. Go to www.DeusExMachina2.com and click on the SHOP. My Secret Tip for how to make a buck from a video game failure will then be revealed, if you click on a magic PayPal button. Thank you.

www.ingramcontent.com/pod-product-compliance
Ingram Content Group UK Ltd.
Pitfield, Milton Keynes, MK11 3LW, UK
UKHW042320220126
10245UKWH00051B/86